NO PLACE TO
CALL HOME

*Inside the Real Lives of
Gypsies and Travellers*

Katharine Quarmby

ONEWORLD

A Oneworld Book

First published by Oneworld Publications 2013

ISBN 978-1-85168-949-1
eBook ISBN 978-1-78074-106-2

Printed and bound in Great Britain by Page Bros Ltd
Cover design by Rawshock

Oneworld Publications
10 Bloomsbury Street, London, WC1B 3SR
United Kingdom

NO PLACE TO
CALL HOME

Also by Katharine Quarmby

Scapegoat: Why We Are Failing Disabled People

CONTENTS

PROLOGUE

I drove out to Dale Farm on the morning of Wednesday, 19 October 2011, with a sick feeling in my stomach. This, at last, was eviction day for some eighty or so Irish Traveller families, after ten long years of wrangling. There were to be no more phoney wars.

The McCarthys, the Sheridans, the Flynns, the O'Briens and the Slatterys, among others, some of whom I'd first met more than five years earlier, were going to leave their beloved home, Dale Farm, with its scruffy dogs and bumpy tracks, its immaculate gated pitches and tidy caravans and chalets. Back in 2006, there had been little to no press interest in the site, and I had to persuade my editor at *The Economist* that this was a story worth covering. She gave me 850 words.

Now, I had to park at a garden centre a long walk down the lane because there was no room nearer to the site. The world media were there – from Japan, the US, Canada and mainland Europe. I noticed that the air smelt foul. Three helicopters hovered overhead as a plume of smoke drifted upwards from a burning caravan. A few masked protestors shouted obscenities at the police. Many of the Travellers were close to tears, although a few remained defiant. Eviction day was underway.

Mary Ann McCarthy had left the site a few weeks earlier. Grattan Puxon was holed up inside the embattled encampment and wasn't answering his phone. Finally, two legal observers smuggled me in.

I walked round to the back, where the police and bailiffs had breached the defences at 7 a.m. I almost immediately ran into

Michelle and Nora Sheridan, who were both near tears. Nora told me: 'I saw someone being tasered: he fizzed, I tell you,' as she tried to stop her three boys from going near the police lines. Michelle added: 'Yes, some of them were throwing stones but it was inhumane. I was running away with a child in my arms. I was terrified.' Tom, her youngest, who was just eighteen months old, was crying in her arms. Nearby I saw Candy Sheridan, the vice-chairwoman of the Gypsy Council, negotiating with the Bronze Commander to get an ambulance on to the site to evacuate two sick residents.

I looked around at this site that I had visited so many times over the past years. The caravan was still burning, and activists scurried around with little rhyme or reason. A community was being dismantled, real people were losing the only home they'd ever had, yet the scene was unreal, like seeing agit-prop theatre in the round. Dale Farm was a paradox – an iconic symbol of the struggle of nomadic people to find a place to call home – yet in so many ways completely different from life for most Romani Gypsy and Traveller families in the UK. What, in the end, did the battle of Dale Farm signify, and how did it connect to the wider story of the nomads in our midst, and the settled community's relationship with them? What was this fight really about?

Katharine Quarmby

INTRODUCTION

This book is about some of the last nomadic communities in the UK – called by many names, but generically known to most people as 'Gypsies', a contested word that includes, in fact, many separate communities. They include the English and Scotch Romanies, the Welsh Kale Romanies, the Irish Travellers, the British Showpeople and (New) Travellers, as well as their own offshoots, including the Horsedrawns and the Boaters. What unites all of them is their struggle to survive, make homes and hold fast to cultures that often bring them into conflict with the so-called settled community.

I knew, from the moment that I was commissioned to write a book about Britain's nomadic peoples in the wake of the eviction from Dale Farm, that I had to go much further afield to set that particular location in its rightful context as merely one part of a long and bitter struggle for Traveller sites in this country. Dale Farm was and remains highly significant, but I wanted to visit other trouble spots and interview other nomads – English and Scottish Romani Gypsies and Travellers, and even some of the newly arrived Roma, whose voices also should be heard.

This book, therefore, has its roots in Dale Farm, the first Traveller community I ever visited and of its inhabitants. But it is also the story of another site, Meriden, occupied, like Dale Farm, without planning permission, by Romani Gypsies with roots in Scotland, Wales and England. I also travelled to Glasgow, to interview Slovakian Roma, who had arrived rapidly over a few years, and agencies working with them, and travelled to both the Stow and the Appleby horse fairs to visit Gypsies and

Travellers in trading and holiday mode. I went to Darlington in the North-East to visit the much respected *sherar rom*, elder Billy Welch, who organises Appleby Fair and has big dreams about getting out the Gypsy and Traveller vote, and to the North-West to talk to the devastated family of Johnny Delaney, a teenager from an Irish Traveller background who was kicked to death for being 'a Gypsy' ten years ago. I travelled down to Bristol to talk to veteran New Traveller Tony Thomson about life on the road in the 1980s, and being caught up the vicious policies of the Conservative government at that time. I also journeyed into East Anglia, where New Travellers, Irish Travellers and English Gypsies have made homes, and north of London, to Luton, to meet some of the destitute Romanian Roma who have created a vibrant community in the heart of England with the help of an inspirational Church of England priest named Martin Burrell. I was also invited to a convention in North Yorkshire by the Gypsy evangelical church, Light and Life, which is growing at an exponential rate and whose influence on nomadic cultures in the UK cannot be underestimated.

I could have travelled more – to Rathkeale, where English–Irish Travellers go for weddings, funerals and to have the graves of their 'dear dead' blessed once a year, or to Central and Eastern Europe, where most of the world's Roma population (and the smaller population of Sinti and other nomadic groups) live. But I chose to concentrate on the experience of Gypsies, Roma and Travellers living in the UK – to go deep, rather than wide. But it was striking that many of those I interviewed would phone me from abroad, or from hundreds of miles away from their actual home, completely comfortable having travelled miles to find work – as long as they were with family – or were earning money to keep their family.

I've also looked at the resurgent creative life of Britain's nomads – in poetry, the visual arts, drama and music. I regret not having either the budget or the time to reflect as deeply as I would have liked to on other nomadic British communities – circus and Showpeople as well as the Welsh Kale Gypsies. But their unique experiences deserve books and attention to themselves, rather than a superficial mention in this one. Of course, any book about Gypsies, Roma and Travellers cannot possibly express the depth and width of the cultures; I just hope that I have given a glimpse into a world that is not as secretive as people claim, but which is understandably private and focused on keeping close family ties alive under enormous stress.

At the heart of this book is the story of families from both Romani Gypsy and Traveller backgrounds caught up in the bitter conflicts at the Dale Farm and Meriden settlements. These families have come to public prominence over the last decade and, over the last six years, all of them have been kind enough to share some of their history with me, for which I am deeply grateful. Between them they have experienced forced eviction, racist crimes, multiple health problems, obstacles in obtaining education and, of course, life on the road, not only in Britain but abroad too. Despite all this, the families I have met have long and proud histories; they are steeped in the traditions and culture of their peoples, which they are rightly anxious and proud to preserve.

I met the Sheridans and the McCarthys in 2006, when I first visited Dale Farm. Mary Ann McCarthy was clearly the matriarch of the Irish Traveller site and, like many journalists, I was taken to see her that April. Her gentle welcome set the tone for my many encounters over the years, and I was sad to see her forced to fight for her home. I met Nora and Michelle Sheridan, who have risen to prominence among the Dale Farm community during the fight over the site clearance, on that same visit. They, like many other families, have been hospitable to me in uncountable ways, sharing their hopes and their worries about what the future holds for British nomads. I met the Townsleys and Burtons at Meriden in 2011. The Townsleys are an old Scottish Gypsy family, mentioned as far back as the time of Bonnie Prince Charlie, and after much travelling around the UK, and even as far away as Canada, put down tentative roots in the Midlands. The well-known English (and Welsh) Gypsy Burton family have traced their line back as far as 1482. The Townsleys and the Burtons are neighbours and close friends.

But these individual stories are only half of the picture. When I set out to write this book, I wanted it to move between the settled community and the nomads with whom we share this island – to give an account of the conflict that has risen between these two ways of life, and other, happier times when we have lived alongside each other in some harmony. I come from a diverse family myself – my family by birth is partly Iranian and partly English; my family by adoption, partly Serbian, Spanish and English. My Iranian birth father sailed the high seas in the Iranian Navy before being jailed after the Iranian Revolution – my birth mother was a white English girl in a seaport. My father comes from a Yorkshire farming family that can trace its roots back hundreds of years. My mother's family is a hotch-potch of Spanish socialists, artists and Bosnian Serb nationalists, some of whom were jailed for their beliefs. She came to England after the Second World War, not able to speak a word of English. I live in the British settled community but I cherish the fact that, like many, I have roots in more than one community, both here and abroad. I wanted *No Place to Call Home* to speak from that middle point of view.

It has been difficult to encompass both viewpoints, however, because speaking to one side has sometimes meant the other side has sheered away from contact. This was particularly true at Meriden, where contact with the Romani families there meant that those on the other side of the fence, the residents from the settled community, felt that they would not get a fair hearing. My experience encapsulates the problem that we face: neither side feels as though it is being treated fairly. How we get over that – how we play fair with each other – is our challenge, and our necessary goal. Pitting local settled people against nomadic people (who are also often local too) benefits nobody. Both sides in this conflict have inherited a legacy of bitterness, contempt and even, in some cases, hatred between each other. But we do not have to be bound and constrained by that common past. We need to find a way to talk to each other and to move beyond our historical differences.

After all, these divisions are artificial. Since the first Roma, Irish and Scotch Travellers arrived on Britain's shores, perhaps as long ago as a thousand years, these groups have intermarried with settled people. That practice continues today – ethnic Roma from Central and Eastern Europe are now marrying into English Gypsy and Irish Traveller families, as well as into the settled community. It is estimated that as many as thirty per cent of people in the county of Kent may have Romani blood, and similar estimates hold true in other areas, particularly in the North-East, East Anglia and around London. For all the wish to hold fast to a proud, sometimes separatist culture, DNA testing of some of the oldest Romani Gypsy families appears poised to find that these lines are heavily European, though they may well carry Asian phenotypes in keeping with their origin stories.[1]

As someone who is myself half Iranian and half English, I find these sorts of discoveries exhilarating rather than worrying. Not everyone feels the same about ethnic diversity, but the truth is that no pure bloodlines divide the settled community from British nomads. We all belong to these shores and may as well learn to live together, or at least alongside each other, better than we do at the moment. Indeed, most of the English and Scotch Gypsies, as well as the Irish Travellers who were born here, are more British, ethnically and culturally, than many of us in the settled community. Visiting the horse fairs where Gypsies and Travellers trade together is a glimpse into two sometimes separate cultures, but it is also a glimpse back into Old England. Once-cherished skills like riding bareback, skinning rabbits, handing down songs in the oral tradition, making pegs, cooking outdoors over campfires and trading horses, for example, are part of our ancient common culture, not skills that set Gypsies and Travellers apart from everyone else.

Despite all the grimness of the Dale Farm eviction, despite the racism that so many nomads confront, despite the contaminated conditions in which so many are forced to live because of the paucity of sites, I am hopeful. I am hopeful that things will change for the better, for all of us. This isn't wistful optimism, however. Right back in 2006, on my first visit to Dale Farm, I was struck by the resilience, optimism and kindness of so many of the Travellers I met. More than six years on I can see change and revival at every level. The Pentecostal Life and Light church is *for* the Gypsy people, led by the community and increasingly self-confident about its identity. Like the black Baptist churches in 1960s America, it is giving Gypsies and Travellers the tools they need to speak out – to serve as witnesses to their condition and as actors to change it. Perhaps a leader in the mould of Martin Luther King Jnr will come from this root. The strong edicts against drunkenness, domestic violence and drugs have something of the early Methodists in them too, with their emphasis on self-reliance and pride. Many Irish Travellers maintain a strong Catholic faith – I don't think I have ever met as many devout people as I have in getting to know Gypsy and Traveller families over the past few years.

The increasing importance that the communities themselves place on education, particularly among women and children, is heartening. Seeing Gypsy and Irish Traveller women – Candy Sheridan, Maggie Smith-Bendell, Siobhan Spencer and Janie Codona, to name but a few – speaking out about their communities and politics is truly exhilarating. The growing number of self-confident Gypsy and Traveller artists working in the visual arts, poetry, drama and music, and making international connections, has something to teach us all on this insular little island. The push by elders like Billy Welch, and influential men and women in the Irish Traveller community, including Candy Sheridan, Alexander Thomson, Pat Rooney and others to get out the Gypsy and Traveller vote, could give the communities the electoral pressure they so clearly need to push through proper accommodation and respect for their communities.

Lastly, in this book, I have used the words 'Romani', 'Romany', 'Romanies' and 'Gypsy' somewhat interchangeably. Some people from that particular community use one to describe themselves, some another. Indeed, artists, activists, academics and community members continue to debate which word they prefer to this day. A number of internationally renowned artists have now 'reclaimed' the word 'Gypsy', as they say it describes an international identity better than the words 'Rom' or 'Roma'. This is not for me to judge. I have, in all cases, tried to use the words that the person used to describe themselves in each case. Any insult is inadvertent and should these choices offend anyone, I apologise.

1
'CHANCE OF A LIFETIME'

He was waiting outside Wickford station for me, an unassuming, quietly spoken man, wearing a black felt fedora, which was his trademark. The fine April morning suited Essex, particularly this part of the Essex countryside, where the garden centres and the houses start to run out until you turn a corner on a dusty, hole-pocked road and find yourself in view of a Traveller site.

The man in the fedora was Grattan Puxon, who had been campaigning for Traveller sites for over forty years before this trip in 2006 to visit Dale Farm. From the outside, it had all the trappings of a place under siege – the heavy gate made of scaffolding poles barred the way in, though a banner inscribed 'Save Dale Farm' fluttered invitingly. Dale Farm, billed by the authorities and the media as the largest encampment of Gypsies and Travellers in Britain, sprawled over several acres and was home to about a thousand people. Some of the pitches had barbed wire running along their perimeters.

Grattan turned right onto the grandly named Camellia Drive and came to a cream-coloured chalet set in an immaculate pitch, which was decked out with flowers in pots, a low red-brick wall and statues of lions proudly sitting on the gateposts – a chalet belonging to Mary Ann McCarthy.

Mary Ann, a softly spoken grandmother of seven with dark, carefully set hair, welcomed us into her spotless chalet. Grattan and I sat down on her cream three-piece suite, covered in plastic to protect the fabric, and were offered cups of strong tea. In the kitchen, one of Mary Ann's daughters was hard at work scrubbing out every single cupboard. Most people from the 'settled community' have heard that Traveller sites and homes are dirty places – a pernicious myth. The chalet was tidy and clearly cherished, with alcoves built to show off statues of Jesus and the Virgin Mary, alongside Mary Ann's Crown Derby china and lovingly dusted wax flowers and fruit.

In 2004, she had taken the fateful decision to move to Dale Farm. She was a widow and she needed to find a way to support herself. 'It was government guidance; they told us that Gypsies and Travellers should provide for themselves, so we did that,' she explained. 'We bought the scrap yard: one half of it was already passed for planning permission and our relations were living there.' Her five daughters and son-in-law lived on the site, and she had grandchildren dashing in and out of her chalet before and after school. She was learning how to read for the first time. She and her grandchildren would pore over the easy readers they would bring back from school, learning together.

'Dale Farm is the chance of a lifetime. We can get education, start to use computers and all. We won't have the time to get education if we get moved from post to pillar again,' Mary Ann told us. 'We want to live like human beings, not like rats.' Dale Farm was the epitome of a settled, matronly, Traveller's life and her chalet was the perfect home – 'We get smothered living in a house; we feel like we have been put in jail.'[1] But her wish to be left alone to live with her family in a close-knit community was not to be.

Mary Ann's neighbours, sisters Nora and Michelle Sheridan, jointly cared for their elderly parents, John and Mary Flynn, who had moved onto the site partly because of health problems. They didn't want to be on the road again, with police constantly pounding at their caravan door. It was a hard decision to make for a family used to travelling. 'The Sheridans have always got together in big groups, particularly in seaside towns. I remember them turning up at Great Yarmouth one year with around five hundred trailers, and another big get-together in Rhyl in Wales ... Dale Farm was a big compromise, to settle down,' remembered Grattan.[2]

Nora and Michelle also wanted to give their young children an education. Like Mary Ann, they felt that schooling was a vital part of their children's hopes to establish a stable way of life. Neither of the Sheridan sisters had gone to school much, and they had both struggled with literacy. A few months before, the local primary school had duly accepted some forty-five Traveller children, but their attendance had thus far been somewhat erratic – and troubled. When they arrived in the schoolroom, all of the non-Traveller children, some three-quarters of the entire intake, had been almost immediately withdrawn from the school. Essex County Council had pledged to keep the school open, though the district council leader questioned this decision: 'If only a few children turn up each day, shouldn't our resources be spent elsewhere?'

Mary Ann's son-in-law Richard Sheridan had spoken out on behalf of the many very young and very old and very sick people who lived at the site, finding comfort in a place where each family could have its own well-kept patch of land. They found that comfort in the sense of community. 'When Dale Farm was destroyed, they destroyed a community, a village,' as Candy Sheridan, a member of the Gypsy Council, loosely related to Nora and Michelle Sheridan on her father's side, would later put it.

But it was a village with just three or four extended Traveller families, living on pitches without planning permission. It was, right from the start, contested land.

Whatever the families wanted, the legal machinations to evict them were gathering pace. Basildon District Council, which was responsible for the site, had voted the year before to evict the people who were living at Dale Farm illegally, at an estimated cost of £1.9 million. Malcolm Buckley, who led the Conservative council at the time, argued that Basildon provided more pitches than most local authorities do. Limited planning permission had been granted to a small number of English Gypsies in the 1990s on a site adjoining Dale Farm. Basildon just could not handle more people moving onto Dale Farm.

Around the year 2000, Irish Travellers started to move to Dale Farm. Two Irish Travellers, Patrick Egan and John Sheridan, and a third man, Thomas Anderson, had bought the land at Dale Farm. They acquired it from Ray Bocking, a scrap-yard owner who had recently been bankrupted for breaching green-belt provisions enforced by Basildon Council in 1994.

There was already a cottage on the site, and Patrick Egan moved into it. He named it 'Dale Farm House', and he and the other owners set out to divide the remaining land into pitches. They charged up to £20,000 for each pitch – for many of their fellow Irish Traveller families an entire life's worth of savings. Nonetheless, news spread quickly, and family after family, many loosely related – Egans, Flynns, McCarthys, O'Briens and Sheridans – moved in.

The council and several people living nearby noticed that the number of caravans was increasing sharply. One horrified local resident was Len Gridley. His parents had bought themselves a retirement home, a spacious bungalow called Windy Ridge, in the green belt in 1984. Windy Ridge backed onto Dale Farm. The year they moved in, a handful of English Gypsies from the Saunders and Beany families, had occupied a field in Oak Lane. Len's family were at first perturbed, as were other residents in the local village of Crays Hill, but the Gypsy families integrated relatively well, with their children mixing in easily at the local primary school. But by 2003, the rateable value of Windy Ridge had been cut in half – due, Len said[3], to the nature and great number of families occupying Dale Farm.

It wasn't just Windy Ridge that was down in value; others had seen property prices fall by twenty per cent, according to Len, and it was all due to the Irish Traveller encampment. 'Say if an elderly couple want to sell up, a young couple wants to come in, they ask, "Where's the local school?" They go there and find out what the history of the school is – the sale falls through. I mean, who wants to move into a village where you haven't got a school, you haven't got the pubs, because these people have ruined it all?'

Len saw clear distinctions between the peaceable English Gypsy families, who kept themselves to themselves, and the Irish 'clans', as he called them, who had arrived more recently. Like many other Essex folk, he had known English Gypsies for years. 'I was brought up with the English Gypsies, they came every year to the bottom field. And I can tell you, when they left every season, that field was left cleaner than they come; they took the attitude we are coming back next year so they don't leave a mess,' he said. 'My sister even married an English Gypsy, and they are still together.

'It's all these immigrants, these Irish are immigrants, they have come over here and abused the system,' explained Len about his views at that time. 'And if they need alternative sites, they should be limited to ten or twelve caravans. You have to limit the size of the sites and scatter them. It was so big, they took the attitude "in numbers we can have mob rule, intimidate people"; they didn't get away with it with me, because I fought back.' Len was sure that others had been intimidated, however. 'That's why people won't speak out against them,' he said.

The settlement had completely changed the Essex way of life, in Len's view. 'The noise, at night-time, you get the tooting and everything else. You couldn't shut the door and pull the curtains shut and say they weren't there. When the English [Gypsies] were there, they had a rule: they were living in a community and didn't want anybody to complain. There was no rubbish in the road … It was when the Irish came that the English left; they didn't want to be tarred with the same brush.'

It was true that the English Gypsies who were living at Dale Farm mostly sold up and moved on not long after the Irish Travellers arrived. But it's not clear whether this was in response to the influx of Travellers or the shooting in October 2002 of an English Gypsy, Billy Williams, in what some claim was a land dispute and others say was an issue of mental health.[4]

As the number of families grew, Len became more and more obsessed – by his own admission sometimes donning camouflage gear and watching the Travellers from the back of his garden. 'I saw smuggling there – cigarettes being smuggled in, sofas, three-piece suites,' he said.

This allegation might well also have had some truth in it, or at least a fair amount of attention to the proceedings of the local courts and newspapers. The affable Richie Sheridan, one of the many Sheridans who had moved to Dale Farm, had been convicted two years earlier for cigarette smuggling.[5] He had allegedly brought the contraband cigarettes into the country in three-piece living room suites that had been manufactured in Poland. In June 2006, just two months after my first visit to Dale Farm with Grattan, Richie pleaded guilty to conspiracy to fraudulently evade excise duty and was sentenced to twelve months in prison.

The stereotypes were settling in along with the residents. Villagers complained of other anti-social behaviour at and around the site: rubbish strewing the road, drunkenness, risky driving. David McPherson-Davis, a local parish councillor, well remembers those early stand-offs. 'Around 2002 the Irish Travellers started to arrive, and the English Gypsies moved off. We saw the site being bought and divided into chunks – 2002 to 2003 was the worst time for our community. There was a definite trend of Irish Travellers trying to dominate our village; there was sheer confrontation in the shops, and in cars trying to drive us off the road. That was mostly the young men, and it was shocking and appalling.'

Len's parents were upset by the situation. They couldn't sell Windy Ridge and move to the Canary Islands, as they had long dreamed of doing. Len spoke with bitterness about how the Irish Travellers had changed their lives. After a number of threats – from both sides – Len was issued with a panic alarm, which he still carries with him at all times. He says his mental health has suffered and he has had to seek psychiatric care.

He felt that the village itself was being shattered. 'There's no village community now, no one talks to each other now,' he said with despair. 'We tried to get a residents' association together, but other than a couple of families in this village, I no longer have the time of day with many of them.'

•

Some of the Travellers had sought out Dale Farm after being evicted from other sites, including one notorious eviction nearby in Borehamwood.[6] In November 2002, after the Conservatives took control of the council and Malcolm Buckley became leader, he and the council decided to take decisive action. They, too, would evict the Travellers.

They were stymied. John Prescott, then Deputy Prime Minister, gave the Travellers two years' leave to stay. Once a ship's steward, Prescott had often been the Labour Party's voice on matters of the working class. 'The Travellers had moved on there at Dale Farm and ignored the planning requirements,' Prescott recalled in a rare interview.[7] 'I didn't support them living there without planning permission, but the main consideration for me was to give their children the right to go to school, and provide them with time to deal with the problem. I told them, "Come the end of the two years, you will have to go. Accept that you will comply with planning."'

By 2004 or thereabouts, with this limited leave to remain in place, the community had reached an uneasy truce. For the most part, the Irish Traveller men were away working much of the time, and the women were settling down and sending their children to school. Many were hurt by the persistent hostility they faced, both in the village and in the local media, but they were committed to making something out of Dale Farm. They organised a regular litter pick-up in the lane, clearing the rubbish by hand, even though some of the younger residents throw things out of car windows as they make their way to the site. They wanted to stay put – for the first time in their lives, they had found somewhere that they could call home.

Prescott's limited permission to remain ran out on 13 May 2005. It was then that court action to clear the site began in earnest.

The next month, on 8 June, the council called a public meeting to decide whether to force the Travellers to leave the site in compliance with green-belt law. Three hundred people crowded into Basildon's Townsgate Theatre. They included the actor Corin Redgrave, who was running for Parliament on the Peace & Progress party ticket. Redgrave delivered a passionate speech in support of the Travellers, who he called 'the most deprived community in the country'. As he made his case, he collapsed. He had suffered a heart attack and nearly died. The meeting was cancelled and the decision to evict was temporarily postponed.[8]

Not long afterwards, the council passed an order requiring the Travellers to move on. But Basildon officials and local politicians knew there was a fight ahead. The residents at Dale Farm applied for judicial review, pushing off the council's ability to set a firm date for clearing the site. 'We have made a reasonable provision. Any alternative site in the district is unacceptable, the site is unsuitable for anyone to live on, and there is a potential issue around contamination,' Malcolm Buckley explained at the time. 'We don't think we should be penalised for our generosity'.

Some in the larger Basildon community felt that generosity was exactly what was needed, most notably a number of parishioners from the Catholic Church of Our Lady of Good Counsel in the nearby parish of Wickford. One was former social worker Ann Kobayashi. 'I became involved first because … the priest asked me to go up there; I had never been to Dale Farm then,' she recalled. She was surprised to find the numerous families on the site. They had been all but invisible to her. 'He asked me to help with a benefits matter, as I had a background in social services. I had never imagined the site was there. Even though I was part of Wickford, I didn't know it was there.'

During her benefits visits, Ann met Grattan. Soon after, she too became involved in the bigger campaign to save Dale Farm. At that stage, Grattan was playing everything strictly by the book. 'It started off as "don't concede, we want to preserve this".' As it became more likely that the green-belt argument would win the day, there had to be a back-up plan. They needed to have somewhere to go; they couldn't assume they would be able to stay. 'Grattan for years was pursuing the legal route, and then the council homelessness route, in order to demonstrate willingness and in a sense put pressure on the council to provide culturally appropriate alternatives if Dale Farm had to be conceded,' Ann said. Grattan wasn't a committed activist – he was a confirmed advocate. 'Every week he visited, filled in forms, did legal aid stuff, gave advice, all the other stuff that comes up, that carries on in any group that has literacy difficulties – they have umpteen bits of paper they can't manage.'

Sean Risdale, then the policy officer for the East of England at the Commission for Racial Equality, was first sent out to Dale Farm around this time. 'I became aware very quickly that Travellers were probably more discriminated against than any other grouping in society,' he said.[9] At the time, the office of the Deputy Prime Minister estimated that there were sixteen thousand Traveller caravans across Britain, with only seventy-four per cent of them located on authorised sites. Thirteen per cent camped illegally on other people's property. The rest – another thirteen per cent – were on sites like Dale Farm, where the travellers own the land but do not have planning permission to live on it.[10] Risdale knew that twenty-five per cent of the 300,000-strong Traveller community lived or regularly passed through the nation's eastern counties. 'My immediate reaction was, "What is all the fuss about?" This was a well-ordered set of domestic plots in the middle of a sprawling ex-scrap yard, not a beauty spot violated by unruly incomers ... a warm, friendly place to visit, with a very strong sense of community cohesion.'

The judicial review of the council's eviction order had been expected to come as early as May 2006. The Commission for Racial Equality, then a staunch ally, had intervened in the proceedings to make sure the court took into account the district's legal obligation to promote good race relations. Risdale was also aware that Prescott's office had reckoned that another four thousand pitches would need to be found to accommodate Travellers who did not have permission to live on their land. These four thousand pitches had yet to be found.

At the same time, politicians closer to the ground were being lobbied intensively by the residents of Basildon district, who were urging immediate action – that is, immediate eviction. They needed to lay out a line of arguments to help ensure that the Commission for Racial Equality's intrusion would not put a halt to their community improvement plan. John Baron, the local MP, was under special pressure from constituents, who were increasingly irked by the lack of progress. Shortly after the temporary leave had expired, in July 2005, Baron had raised the issue in the Commons. 'In 2003 in essence the government gave the Travellers two years to find alternative sites, during which time no enforcement action could be taken by the council. Yet, during this time, the site quadrupled in size,' he said. For the record, he had 'no problem' with 'law-abiding Travellers' but 'no one can accuse us of discriminating against Travellers or of being intolerant or racist. All that we ask is that everyone obeys the same set of rules, especially if they wish to live in the community. Clearly, that has not happened at the illegal Crays Hill site.'[11]

Separately, Malcolm Buckley called in a firm of bailiffs, Constant and Company, that specialise in removing Travellers, to see if they would take on the job. 'We have solid expertise going back around five, six years; we go all over the country using common law methods to evict,' the company's managing director, Bryan LeCoche, said proudly. 'The Crays Hill situation, that's more of a one-off action … I've got nothing against Travellers, they are our stock in trade, but what is the contribution made by Travellers to this country?' he asked. This eviction would go ahead, just like any other. But, rather prophetically, he knew that the aftermath would be different this time – even if the logistics were much the same, the sort of job that wouldn't 'faze' his employees. 'We have built up a reputation to deal with this very sensitive issue; we are not rent-a-mobs … It is usually fairly cordial – we do respect the fact that these are their homes which are taken into safe storage.'[12]

On the way to Dale Farm, Grattan had taken a detour to Hovefields, which was then under more immediate threat of eviction, to look into charges that Constant and Company's bailiffs could be violent – which LeCoche refuted. The five families living at the smaller site expected to be evicted at any time. One of the mothers, her pale face drawn with stress, had been evicted several times before. 'I was looking at fifty or so police and bailiffs in bullet-proof vests, and I asked them not to block us in, but they did. That was Constant and Co.,' she said.

If the council managed to get their way, the Irish Travellers who had put down roots at Dale Farm would be on the road again before too long – yet another generation of unwanted nomads.

2
NEIGHBOURS AND NOMADS

In a gentle, lilting voice, Mary Ann McCarthy shared the story of her life before Dale Farm. She was born in Dublin, and her family travelled all over Ireland in a horse-drawn wagon while she was growing up. As the economic situation in the Republic worsened in the 1950s, attitudes towards Travellers became more hostile, and her father took the decision to make a bigger move. 'My father sold his caravan, two horses and a car and we came over on the boat to England, and we went to Birmingham. We had no place to live and my father bought a bus for us to live in.' Life changed overnight – no more cooking outside. 'We were in this car park in Birmingham so we couldn't light a fire.' Life in the Midlands proved hard, with constant evictions.

Mary Ann's family, like many, took the evictions in their stride and kept on travelling. 'At first it was fine, but it got worse and worse, and more and more difficult to travel.' At eighteen she met a man at a fair and got married. Her newlywed life was no honeymoon. 'I would try and sell from door to door, he would look for tarmac or scrap, and that's one thing you can say about Travellers, if one thing fails, they turn their hand to something else. We worked hard our whole life.' They got a caravan for their first home – Mary Ann's first experience of living in a trailer. 'I never really lived in a trailer until I got married, that's when I moved into a trailer with a motor and then it was the travelling life for me. It was more convenient [than a horse-drawn wagon], especially when you had children. You could go places faster, it was a better way of life.' There was also safety in numbers. 'We always liked to travel together, families did, because you always felt kind of safe if you were at the side of the road; sometimes you would get a lot of hassle, people pegging stones on top of you, you always felt more secure.'[1] A couple of decades later, nearly a thousand people were gathered with her at Dale Farm.

Catholicism had always been important to Mary Ann: 'When I was travelling, I'd never miss Mass of a Sunday ... I always found the priests very nice, the ones I have met.' At Dale Farm, she joined her neighbours in attending the 'settled' church in the nearby village of Wickford, arriving at Mass in big groups. This stoked resentment among some of the residents of Basildon, who felt their community was being overwhelmed.

'Some local people have achieved success by moving out to these un-made-up roads, living a semi-rural life ... They've bought a little bit of countryside – they may have been denied building and planning, makes their lives hell – and suddenly this foreign group comes along; they are Travellers, they are Irish, and they are Catholic and I don't think you can underestimate the latent anti-Catholicism here,' former social worker Ann Kobayashi recalled. 'They couldn't have lined up three worse tics: Travellers, Catholics, Irish – gee ... And the impact of having a hundred or more people joining a parish is considerable.'

The local priest, Father John Glynn, was very welcoming of the newcomers in his parish, 'I'll be up there at the site if they evict the Travellers,' he said. 'And my poster will say, "This is ethnic cleansing. I'm ashamed to say I'm British."'

The dislike, contempt, even hatred for Mary Ann and her fellow Irish Travellers have deep historical roots. As early as the 1500s, the English were busying themselves with attempts to change the law in order to send Irish and Scotch Travellers back to their country of origin. Irish Travellers of this period were often called 'vagabonds' or 'rogues' – from the Latin *rogare,* to beg. They were said to possess dubious morals and dirty habits. Not much had changed in the five hundred years that followed, judging by the events in Basildon.

The Travellers were not, of course, the only vagabonds in Elizabethan England. There were roaming theatrical troupes, of course, but they were mostly considered benevolent, with a patron or 'master' taking responsibility for them. It was the other nomadic peoples – the Gypsies – who were subject to the terror of vagrancy acts. And they came under attack shortly after they arrived on the country's shores.

They were mostly called Egypcians then, because they were thought to come from Egypt rather than India, according to the historian Angus Fraser and the celebrated Romani scholar Ian Hancock. Until this time many Gypsies in England, as elsewhere in Europe, had been granted 'counterfaicte passeports' by state or church dignitaries. These identity papers asked local authorities to allow them to pass through their territory unhindered. For the most part, the system had been tolerated, though one record of banishment from a then-independent Scotland, dated 1505, stating that a Gypsy had been transported to Denmark at the order of James IV, has been found.[2]

Regardless, Gypsies arriving in Britain were visibly outsiders. One account, dated 1528 and cited by Hancock in his book *The Pariah Syndrome*, claimed that there were some ten thousand Gypsies in the British Isles at that time.[3] Two later commentators, William Harrison and Samuel Rid, bookended the height of the 'invasion' between 1586 and 1612.[4]

The earliest, scattered mentions of the Egypcians were positive. The High Treasurer of Scotland, at the behest of King Henry VII, paid ten French crowns to some Gypsies, 'possibly for some sort of entertainment', according to Fraser. 'Alternatively, it may have been a charitable payment to Gypsies in their capacity as pilgrims.'[5] *A Dyalog of Syr Thomas More, Knyght* recounts how one of the witnesses at an inquest had been an Egypcian woman 'who had been lodging in Lambeth, but had gone overseas a month before, and who could tell marvellous things by looking into one's hand'.[6]

Such sympathy and awe was not uncommon, but it could turn to hostility or indifference overnight. In 1530, the first anti-Gypsy act – the Egypcians Act – was passed. Though it named the Gypsies as the titular foe of society, the law targeted all those who wandered from place to place, making themselves vagrants. As Leanne Weber and Benjamin Bowling point out, 'Visible minorities have been particularly vulnerable to exclusion beyond national borders at moments of collective identity-building, for example during the emergence of a secularised Tudor state. Gypsies, whose travelling bands were initially welcomed by villagers as a source of exotic entertainment and trade, were later targeted by a series of harsh measures … Irish vagabonds, often travelling in extended family groups and thought to be of dubious morals and dirty habits, were ordered home after punishment under the Vagrancy Act of 1572.'[7] The Egypcians Act gave the Crown power to remove the Gypsies from England – by any violent means necessary.

The full list of punishments included in the act were depressingly similar to those which had been meted out by the states from which the Gypsies had fled – banishment, beatings, brandings, slavery, execution. The act stated that 'hensforth no such Persone be suffred to come within this the Kynge's Realme'. Any Gypsy attempting to enter England had his property summarily confiscated and was ordered to leave within two weeks.

Gypsies were soon being effectively enslaved in Britain. In 1547, Edward VI instituted a law which required that Gypsies were 'branded with a V on their breast, and then enslaved for two years. Such slaves could be legally chained and given only the worst food; they could be driven to work by whips. If no master could be found, they were to be made slaves of the borough or hundred or employed in road work or other public service … if the criminals ran away or were caught, they were to be branded with an S and made slaves for life.'

Similarly, Scottish Gypsies were put to death '… on the mere ground of being Egypcians … The cruelty exercised upon them was quite in keeping with that of reducing to slavery the individuals', according to a chronicle discovered by Ian Hancock. He noted that, employed as coal-bearers and salters in the eighteenth century, Scottish Gypsies were effectively, in the words of an eighteenth-century commentator, 'in a state of slavery or bondage ... for life, transferable with the collieries or salt works'.

This living prison was non-negotiable. The oft-repeated mantra at Dale Farm – 'We've got nowhere else to go' – was even truer a century or more ago, with Gypsies being forced from one country to another in the search for both economic security and a peaceful existence. In continental Europe, the Romani people were being enslaved in Spain and Russia. In what is now Romania, their conditions were terrible. They were not allowed to speak their language. The Roma people were divided into field slaves and house slaves, depending on the whims of their new masters, and female house slaves were given to visitors for entertainment; they were often brutally treated. 'Punishments for the slaves included flogging, the *falague* (shredding the soles of the feet with a whip), cutting off the lips, burning with lye, being thrown naked into the snow, hanging over smoking fires and wearing a three-cornered spiked iron collar called a *cangue*.'[8]

These inhumanities lasted for more than three centuries, until well into the nineteenth century. Slowly, beginning in the 1830s, parts of Romania put an end to some of the slave practices, until slavery was abolished completely in 1864, when an estimated 600,000 Roma were set free. But 'following their liberation nothing was done to educate or reorient the freed slaves and bring them into society; instead it was their former owners who were paid by the government for their loss', in Hancock's telling.[9]

Gypsies were routinely deported to serve as slaves in other states. As early as May 1540, a number of Gypsies were shipped to Norway from Boston, in Lincolnshire; between 1530 and 1554 another fourteen deportations are recorded. In 1549, the young King Edward gave commands for local magistrates to search through Sussex for Gypsies and other vagabonds, so that they could be expelled from the county.

Vagrancy was the great fear of the sixteenth century, and Gypsies who arrived at this point were in the eye of the storm.

Irish Travellers were in some ways even worse off, as aliens. Dr Robbie McVeigh, now an independent researcher in Scotland, argues that this is the time when anti-nomadism developed as a valued pillar of the denizens of so-called Middle England, and it remains in force today. 'If modernism was about ordering and controlling, then the nation-state became the key mechanism for securing order and control. And no one threatened the emerging hegemony more than the nomad, whose mode of existence was the very antithesis of modernity.'[10]

Some Travellers were deported in a purge in 1540, but a full-hearted campaign began with the Act for the Punishment of Vagabonds, which came into force in 1572.[11,12] Under the law, vagabonds were branded as 'outrageous enemies to the common weal', and those who were convicted of this 'trade of life' would 'be grievously whipped and burnt through the gristle of the right ear with a hot iron'. If 'some honest person' took pity and agreed to become the vagabond's master for at least one year, the punishment might be set aside. In his book *Masterless Men*, the historian A.L. Beier argues that 'rather than sheer numbers, it was the fact that [they] were alien groups that caused resentment'.[13] Mary Ann might nod her head at that.

Even in the early accounts, stereotypes and prejudices were sticking to the Gypsies and the Travellers, sometimes lumping the two groups together. They were, in the memorable phrase turned by the sociologist Stanley Cohen, transforming into 'folk devils' who seemed sent as a plague on the ordinary folk during a time of 'moral panic'.[14] In 1571, for instance, it was revealed that the Duke of Norfolk had been lured into the Ridolfi plot to assassinate Elizabeth and put Mary, Queen of Scots on a Catholic English throne. Extremist Protestants in the Netherlands had rebelled against their Spanish rulers, putting nineteen Catholic priests to the gallows; later that year, thousands of Protestants were murdered by Catholics in Paris. Over the next fifteen years, war would break out between Spain and England – and Mary,

Queen of Scots would be executed. These were times of dramatic political and economic change. Outsiders were suspect, Catholic ones especially so. Scapegoats were needed to manage social turbulence, just as they are in the present day.

Thefts were quickly and routinely blamed on wandering people, as they are all too often today. Gypsies' 'dark skins made them seem ugly and reprehensible; their long hair and ear-rings and outlandish attire were offensive to many', as Angus Fraser notes. Already, there were tales circulating about the fortune-teller who wooed customers into a gauzy glimpse of their future while 'an attendant child' stood by 'as cut-purse'. Fraser points to a play attributed to the German *meistersinger* Hans Sachs which 'leaves Gypsy reputations in shreds' by 'associating them with theft, lock-picking, purse-cutting, horse stealing, casting of spells and general witchcraft and trickery'.[15] Even when they 'offered legitimate services to the settled population, they were at risk from the ill will attracted by transient traders who violated local monopolies, or from the abhorrence that occupations such as pedlar or tinker or entertainer aroused among those in power'.[16]

The high point of hostility came between 1550 and 1640. Shortly after the 1554 Egypcians Act was adopted, it was used to expel Gypsies from Dorset. They ended up in Gloucestershire, where they were scourged. In 1569 the Privy Council asked all county officers to hunt down the Gypsies in their area. In 1577 several Gypsies were hanged in Aylesbury. In 1596 196 gypsies were rounded up in Yorkshire, and those of full age – 106 men and women – were sentenced to be hanged; only nine met that awful fate. In 1624 eight men were put to death in Scotland for being Egypcians – six of them from one family, the Faas. In 1636 the Privy Council once again put pressure on local officers, ordering 'the provost and bailies of Haddington to despatch another band of Gypsies – the men by hanging, and women without children by drowning, while women who did have children were to be whipped and burnt on the cheek'.[17] In 1650 thirteen people were sentenced to hang at Bury by Judge Hale. It would be the last known time anyone was hanged for being a Gypsy. [18] After that, deportation to America and the Caribbean became the favoured punishment, according to Ian Hancock.

Over the eight years before that last hanging, during the English Civil War, Oliver Cromwell's Irish campaign had deprived many Catholic landlords of their lands. Some say that the oldest lines of Irish Travellers are descendants of these landless nobles, who were forced to take to travelling as a means of earning their living when the Puritan Moses came to power. Under Cromwell's rule, it had become a hanging offence not only to be born a Gypsy, but to associate with them.

Nonetheless, some Gypsies and Travellers managed to survive and even prosper. They were useful traders who could bring to the settled, and often isolated, rural population a range of rare goods that would otherwise be unknown to them. They made a living by travelling and hawking (selling small home-made goods) or tinkering (repairing pots, pans and kettles), useful, skilled services in an agrarian society with low mobility. In his history of Gypsies and Travellers, David Mayall lists chair-bottoming, rat-catching, basket-making, wire-working, fiddling and mending bellows as typical Gypsy and Traveller 'professions' – similar to the dealing and smithing that Romanies had taken up in Europe.[19] Gypsies were also enlisted for seasonal employment on farms, harvesting fruit and vegetables, and later hopping in the Kentish fields. Their 'adaptiveness', many academics and activists believed, had been key to their identity and their survival then – and remained so now. This was also true in mainland Europe. According to Donald Kenrick and Grattan Puxon, authors of the masterful book *Gypsies Under the Swastika*: 'However low their position, they occupied a place in their community.'

Could the same be said at Dale Farm?[20]

It seems almost impossible that an illegal caravan pitch might trace its origins back to the fights between Catholics and Protestants that raged five hundred years ago. But during the Tudor period, another change was afoot: the enclosure of land. Wool was becoming a valuable commodity, and it was making English lords rich. The more common land that could be enclosed for their own private sheep grazing, the richer the lords got.

As enclosures tightened the grip on the rural landscape, itinerants, once seen as useful if not essential to the rural economy, became increasingly suspect. 'Itinerancy served merely as a cloak for a deviant range of predatory, parasitic and criminal activities', in the words of David Mayall. If a Gypsy were to make a rural living, in the traditional way, they were 'backward and primitive' – a malevolent force holding back the new 'civilised, industrial society'. When the movement to enclose the land started in earnest in 1820s England and Ireland, the Gypsies and Travellers who had managed to find a small foothold for themselves were in trouble once again.

The scene on the ground was grim. The writer William Cobbett, grandson of an agricultural labourer, travelled on foot and on horseback, patiently chronicling the effects of the enclosures on what had been an agrarian South of England, between 1821 and 1826. While he only mentions Gypsies once in his masterpiece, *Rural Rides*, they were caught in the trap of all poor working men who had been disadvantaged by the new enclosure laws. (Nomadic folk were also at the mercy of the turnpike acts, the latest of which had been passed in 1822.) 'At Cheriton I found a grand camp of *Gipsys* just upon the move towards Alresford … I pulled up my horse, and said, "Can you tell my fortune, my dear?" She answered in the negative, giving me a look at the same time that seemed to say it was *too late.*'[21] As he continued on his way, he came upon 'a few miserable tumble-down houses' – the fate of labourers at the mercy of landowners who, he said, were '"deluded" by their own greediness'.

Before the enclosures, Gypsies could settle where they wanted, and then move on. The nineteenth-century poet John Clare memorialised this lost way of life in his poem 'Langley Bush', which forms part of his *Enclosure Elegies*:

Both swains and gipseys seem to love thy name
Thy spots a favourite wi the smutty crew
And soon thou must depend on gipsey fame
Thy mulldering trunk is nearly rotten thro.

As the land available to Gypsies and Travellers disappeared, rural magistrates started to take a harsh line. Magistrates in Sussex issued a notice in 1799 lamenting the 'great number of Gipsies and other Vagrants of other descriptions infesting this County; were pleased to order that if any Gypsies or other Vagrants of whatever description should be found therein after the 25th day of March next, they will be punished as the Law directs'. After the Napoleonic War of 1817, the Norfolk Magistrates passed a resolution whose wording echoed the infamous Vagrancy Act of the sixteenth century: 'all persons pretending to be Gipsies, or wandering in the habit of form of Egypcians, are by law deemed to be rogues and vagabonds, and are punishable by imprisonment or whipping'.[22] In some places Gypsies were sent to prison without being charged under the Vagrancy Act. In one famous case, from 1864, the Reverend Uriah Tonkin of Hale, Cornwall, committed seven Gypsies to twenty-one days of hard labour, justifying the penalty in a letter for the Home Secretary, Sir George Grey. Tonkin said the Gypsies had no visible means of support, as required by the Vagrancy Act, and wrote that his punishment was intended to serve 'the safety of the county'. The House of Commons supported him – though five of those sentenced were children, some as young as eight. Local residents were outraged, with the press reporting that the verdict was meant to 'smite the poor'.[23]

While the enclosures were introduced in subsequent laws over the course of the nineteenth century, the historian David Mayall estimates that in just two years, from 1871 to 1873, the commons were reduced from 8 million to 2.6 million acres.[24] With so little land at their disposal, Gypsies and Travellers became ever more visible – and more subject to hostile scrutiny.

Mayall speculates that the local constabulary were often unwilling to arrest those known to them as friends, so Gypsies and

Travellers were an easy group to blame for disruptions to the enclosure laws. 'Not being of the community, there was no protective bond of reciprocity of friendship, custom and goodwill' for these already long-persecuted peoples. 'It suited the magistrates who wanted a conviction and the local population who sought to divert blame and attention to seek the offender in the Gypsy camps, irrespective of the true location of guilt.'[25]

Sometimes villagers and nearby folk took direct action, as they did protesting against Dale Farm and Meriden (albeit more peaceably of late) generations later. 'In 1799, near Bath, a violent affray took place between the Gypsies and a farmer assisted by his neighbours, resulting in the successful eviction of the nomads,' Mayall notes. It wasn't an isolated incident. Nearly a century later, in 1874, 'a vigilante group visited a Gypsy camp near Sale, near Manchester, pulled down the tents and attacked the Gypsies, inflicting serious injuries'.[26]

The Gypsies could not turn to the police for help, however, because the police had already decided that they were the criminal element.

With rural communities becoming more and more aggressive and with work becoming more scarce, Gypsies and Travellers looked for land on the margins of cities. As Weber and Bowling argue, 'Industrialisation created new waves of demand for mobile labour', including itinerant populations. Moving to urban areas did not, however, release them from scrutiny. Cities, especially London, had applied the tenets of the Industrial Revolution to their governance. In the modern, Victorian age, 'institutions such as the "new police" emerged to produce order at town and county level and allay fears about mobility'. And in 1856, the new police's jurisdiction had been expanded to cover the boroughs around London, 'justified primarily by the need to suppress vagrancy'.[27]

The development of the modern police force, academic John L. McMullan argues further, was clearly linked to the policing of vagrants. The key thinkers of the period from 1750 to

1840 – men such as John Fielding, Patrick Colquhoun and Edwin Chadwick – were fixated on the role of vagrants in disturbing the social order. Many of the people caught in their nets were Travellers and Gypsies.[28]

Fielding, who oversaw the policing of London in the 1760s and 1770s, wanted a unified constabulary system. He feared the growth of labouring classes freed from the feudal bonds of the past. He also believed, crucially, that 'The basic means of securing the peace of society was by a general renovation of morals: strict censorship for public activities, tougher regulation for the drink trade, moneylenders and pawnbrokers and a closer inspection and supervision of itinerants, vagrants, ballad singers and paupers.' His tactic was to create lists of specific, suspected groups, including vagrants, itinerants and singers, who would be closely supervised.[29]

When Patrick Colquhoun, a former Glasgow merchant and then a sitting London magistrate, surveyed London in 1797, he felt it was a 'magnet for predatory crime, vagrancy and social disorder'. He built on Fielding's call for stricter law and order. The poor were idle and villainous, in Colquhoun's view. In his 'Treatise on Police', he argued that London was too large, too anonymous, to be controlled by an old-fashioned methodology. He divided the nation's population into seven broad social classes, the lowest and seventh class of which were 'paupers and their families, vagrants, gipsies, rogues, vagabonds and idle and disorderly persons supported by criminal delinquency'.[30]

Edwin Chadwick, for his part, instituted a Royal Commission in 1836 to examine rural policing. He was an advocate for reform, singling out vagrancy as an issue to address, especially when foreign migrants such as the Irish were involved. He pointed to the cheapness of their lodging houses, which catered to nomads. He said that thieves, prostitutes and vagrants 'seem to belong to one great criminal profession and constantly migrate from one large town ... to another', resorting frequently to 'road-side public-houses' for protective shelter.[31] Chadwick proclaimed that such 'flash houses' provided a network of communication among thieves. Without them, 'many would be forced into honest productive labour'.

Luckily for Gypsies and Irish Travellers, Chadwick's General Police Bill of 1854 was a failure. But though none of these three thinkers succeeded in forging the modern police force that they dreamed of, they cemented the stereotype of the nomad who is profoundly, dangerously unsettling to settled society. As Gypsies and Travellers clustered their wagons on the periphery of the big cities in their search for land and work, the ire of the police was focused on the vagrant poor.

It was around this time that England's fascination with its resident nomads split into two. On the one hand their very presence was problematic – here were the archetypal 'dirty thieving Gypsies', the scavenging brigand, in Royce Turner's words.[32] On the other hand they were transformed into invisible rural sprites, romanticised by a series of Victorian writers. This sentimentalisation was encouraged by the Norfolk author George Borrow, who did much to popularise the idea of a mystical people living off the land, with an all-seeing eye that could offer one's destiny or curse one's fate. (The 'racialisation' of Gypsies started much earlier, however, with the writings of Heinrich Grellman, who traced the Gypsies' roots back to India in 1783, and whose work was translated into English in 1807.)[33] These airy depictions of the 'true Gypsy' partly fed a keen sense of disappointment when Gypsies and Travellers failed to live up to the hype, however.

As Ian Hancock wrote: 'George Borrow's writings have stimulated the creative muse for innumerable writers about Gypsies for more than a century and a half.'[34] Borrow is best known as the author of *Lavengro* and *Romany Rye*, travelogues in which he claimed to have come to know many English Romani Gypsies. *Lavengro* appeared in 1851, and *Romany Rye* was published six years later – just as Britain was reaching the height of power, fuelled by the smokestacks of the country's factories turning the raw materials of the Empire into consumer goods. The Industrial Revolution, still in its early years, had already posseted pollution, stench and poverty on the masses. 'Readers' imaginations

did not need to be transported to Borneo or Zulu-land or Nepal'
for escape, Hancock has said, 'when this dark and mysterious
eastern population occupied their very doorstep'.[35] The idealised
Gypsies of the imagination 'lived apart from all this and above
it, noble savages untouched by civilisation, representatives of a
vanishing rural era who had refused to relinquish it for the sake
of progress'. Those who did not were 'not real Gypsies but mump-
ers, diddicais, pikeys, people with little or no Romani ancestry
who got the "True Romanies" a bad name'.[36]

Both the romanticisation and the persecution intensified,
gathering pace, during the nineteenth century. Mr Rochester,
disguised as a Gypsy fortune-teller in *Jane Eyre*, terrifies – and
entices – the women of Thornfield. J.M. Barrie's *The Little Minister*
culminates in a fevered bodice-trembler. Even as late as the 1920s,
the Gypsy mystique was being trotted out to titillating effect in
D.H. Lawrence's novella *The Virgin and the Gypsy*. As historian
George Behlmer has said, the Gypsies' 'literary friends generated
"a very craze of the Gypsy" that had no European equivalent'.
This led to the establishment of the Gypsy Lore Society in 1888.[37]

Despite the craze, during the nineteenth century many laws
were used to prosecute Gypsies and other nomadic people – the
Poor Law, the Vagrancy Act, the Hawkers Act, the Highways Act,
and the Health, Housing and Education Act. As the Agricultural
Depression took hold, and economic security became harder to
obtain for everyone, Gypsies were a useful scapegoat. Fortune-
telling, camping, begging, and taking sticks without permission
were now considered to be crimes, not just suspicious or supersti-
tious. Non-Christian practices around birth, marriage and death,
such as burning belongings owned by the dead, were also viewed
with scepticism. Gypsies were grouped with the urban working
classes in their want for Victorian moral guidance.

In his book *London Labour and London Poor*, the journalist
Henry Mayhew, a future editor of the influential *Punch* magazine,
offered one of the most graphic and belligerent descriptions of
what he termed the 'Wandering Tribes in General', who were
set apart from the civilised classes by both their moral and their

physical differences. Mankind, he argued, had always consisted of 'two distinct and broadly marked races, viz, the wanderers and the settlers – the vagabond and the citizen … The nomad is then distinguished from the civilised man by his repugnance to regular and continuous labour – by his want of providence in laying up a store for the future – by his inability to perceive consequences ever so slightly removed from immediate apprehension – by his passion for stupefying herbs and roots and, when possible, for intoxicating fermented liquors – by his extraordinary powers of enduring privation – by his comparative insensibility to pain – by an immoderate love of gaming, frequently risking his own personal liberty upon a single cast – by his love of libidinous dances – by the pleasure he experiences in witnessing the suffering of sentient creatures – by his delight in warfare and all perilous sports – by his desire for vengeance – by the looseness of his notion as to property – by the absence of chastity among his women – and his disregard of female honour – and, lastly by his vague sense of religion – his rude idea of a creator and utter absence of all appreciation of the mercy of the Divine Spirit.'[38]

Mayhew's sketches of street folk – pickpockets, beggars, prostitutes, sailors, and so on – were all drawn on this view of the nomadic underclass. But he also grafted social theories and policies into his reportage. He saw himself as a 'traveller in the undiscovered country of the poor', trying to rescue lost tribes. As one contemporary reviewer of the volumes wrote: 'He has travelled through the unknown regions of our metropolis and returned with full reports concerning the strange tribes of men which he may be said to have discovered. For, until his researches had taken place, who knew of the nomad races which daily carries on its predatory operations in our streets and nightly disappears in quarters wholly unvisited by the portly citizens of the East as by perfumed whiskerandos of the West End?'[39]

Gypsies and the Irish poor could not escape the attention of writers and would be do-gooders once they entered urban areas. Itinerancy had been respectable once, but it was now watched with extreme vigilance, as the historian Raphael Samuel has said.

'The wandering tribes (like other nomadic peoples) followed well-established circuits and journeyed according to a definite plan ... Their comings and goings were closely bound up with the social economy of the town ... the wandering tribes were often the subject of hostile legislation, whether to bring their lodging houses under inspection and control, to bar them from using city wastes, or to harass them from pursuing their callings on the city streets. Their children, after 1870, were subject to the eager ministrations of the School Board Visitors; the camping sites of those who lived in moveable dwellings fell one by one to the speculative builder or the railinged enclosures of the public parks. But it was economic change, in the later Victorian years, that really undermined them – the growth of more regular employment, especially for the unskilled, and the decline of the 'reserve army of labour ... the displacement of travelling labours by regular farm servants ... the extension of shops to branches of trade which previously had been in the hands of itinerant packmen and dealers'.[40]

Tatty old tents made of old skirts started to appear across the marshes at Plumstead. In West London, a Gypsy camp was set up by Latimer Road, in an area awaiting the heaving rows of terraced houses that were being mapped across Victorian London; another was established near to the market gardens in West Kensington; still another, smaller encampment was squatted at the bottom of the old Hermitage Road, among the dull dust-heaps that were driven down from the more happily named Green Lanes. Closer to the river, in Battersea, two long lines of wagons had made camp. One writer of the time wrote of the 'curious air of domesticity ... women, most of them stamped with their tribal characteristics, sit on the steps of the wagons, some at needlework, others merely gossiping. Other housewives are engaged on the family wash'.[41]

The family of the celebrated Romani academic Ian Hancock lived in what was called the 'metropolitan Gypsyries'. Like other Gypsy children of the late-Victorian era, Hancock's father was forcibly removed from his parents by the authorities. In 1879, two thousand Gypsies descended upon the London Gypsyries.

'The ugliest place we know in the neighbourhood of London, most dismal and forlorn, is ... Shepherd's Bush and Notting Hill', the *Illustrated London News* reported. 'There it is that the gipsy encampment may be found, squatting within an hour's walk of the Royal palaces and the luxurious town mansions of our nobility and opulent classes ... It is a curious spectacle in that situation, and might suggest a few serious reflections upon social contrasts at the centre and capital of the mighty British nation, which takes upon itself the correction of every savage tribe in South and West Africa and Central Asia.'[42]

The Battersea Gypsies, for their part, stayed put for much of the year. As another Victorian writer and sometime philanthropist, Charles Booth, found when he enquired, 'These people, living in their vans, come and go, travelling in the country part of every year ... They move about a great deal within the London area as well as outside, but are usually anchored fast all winter, and throughout the summer one or another usually occupies the pitch.'[43] As the weather warmed, however, Gypsies and Travellers were known to move around. September hop-picking was the 'jamboree of the wandering tribes'. Mayhew called it the 'grand rendez-vous for the vagrancy of England and Ireland'.[44]

The Irish poor, Mayhew wrote, had a 'positive mania' for hopping, and for many other poor families it was the only holiday they got each year, albeit a working one. Was it perhaps here that some of England's Irish poor saw English Gypsies and wondered whether their nomadic life was a better one than staying put in the foul London rookeries? Indeed, St Giles in central London, which was pretty much closed in the summer, soon filled up again in the winter. York Irish and West Ham Irish, for their part, kept at potato-lifting till later in the year, returning as late as November.[45]

The 'Poor Irish', as they were often known, came in for a double dose of suspicion – being foreign as well as nomadic. Although there had always been Irish migration to Britain, the first great wave came during the famine of 1840, when both 'Irish tinkers' and poor Irish migrant workers were moving from island to island, including members of the extended McCarthy family. The two groups seemed to merge and flex their identities as they looked for seasonal work. Were the Irish Travellers a distinctive people, or were they just another clan hoping to find a job? For their part, the Irish Travellers 'regarded themselves as a distinctive minority group', according to Jim MacLaughlin. 'As Gammon-speakers [i.e., speaking the Traveller language] and as a group with well-established genealogical linkages and a whole range of distinctive cultural practices, they perceived themselves as a people set apart.'[46]

In England, eager philanthropists and Christian do-gooders such as George Smith of Coalville decried 'the Gypsy problem'. A self-educated man who rose to manage a brick yard, Smith made it his mission to improve the conditions for the children working in brick yards. Next, he turned his attention to canal-boat dwellers, then to English Gypsies, who, he said, had been elevated in the public mind by the rose-tinted depictions put forward by 'daisybank sentimental backwood gipsy writers'.[47] Smith had another view. He laid into the Gypsies with vigour. They were 'an unfortunate race of beings': 'A motley crowd of half-naked savages, carrion eaters, dressed in rags, tatters, and shreds, usually called men, women, and children, some running, walking, loitering, traipsing, shouting, gaping, and staring; the women with children on their backs, and in their arms; old men and women tottering along "leaning upon their staffs"; hordes of children following in the rear; hulking men with lurcher dogs at their heels, sauntering along in idleness, spotting out their prey; donkeys loaded with sacks, mules with tents and sticks, and their vans and waggons carrying ill-gotten gain and plunder.'[48]

Smith's campaign – which he called a 'crusade' to 'save' the Gypsies – took many forms. He visited Gypsy encampments – and claimed he was loved by many in the community. That seems improbable, given the rest of his work. He lectured up and down England, wrote pamphlets and lobbied MPs for laws to control the Gypsy lifestyle. He asked Parliament to introduce mechanisms similar to the rules he had successfully instituted for canal-boat dwellers with the Canal Boats Act of 1877 and 1884. For English Gypsies, this would involve a number of restrictions: compulsory planning permits for all dwellings; compulsory attendance at school for children; and separation of male and female sleeping quarters. There would also be 'encouragements', verging once again on the draconian, for Gypsies to settle and forsake their nomadic way of life.

Smith's Moveable Dwellings Bill was introduced in 1885, but it was blocked by MPs. It was considered too expensive, for one, but it was also being resisted in the first organised campaign of opposition by nomadic people. They had gathered together in the United Kingdom Showmen and the Van-Dwellers' Protection Association, and sought backing from a libertarian grouping within Parliament, the Liberty and Property Defence League. The former group was not made up of Gypsies – they even disassociated themselves from such people – but its spirited defence of nomadism, motivated by some degree of self-interest, helped to kill the bill.

'Coalville' Smith died a disappointed man in 1895.[49] He had failed to make his life's work a reality in England. But in many ways he triumphed north of the border, where far stricter legislation was being introduced, inspired by his campaigning.

Written records from as early as 1491 indicate that 'Spaniards' danced before the Scottish King on the streets of Edinburgh, according to Donald Kenrick and Colin Clark. 'These "Spaniards" may or may not have been Romanies – the evidence is somewhat inconclusive. However, in 1505 a small group of Romani Gypsies certainly arrived. James IV granted them an audience.'[50] They add that some sources suggest that Scottish Travellers are able to trace their roots even further back, as far as the twelfth century, when a group of 'Tinklers' was identified and given some protection under the law. Over the subsequent centuries, Clark and Kenrick believe that the two groups – the indigenous Travellers and the Romanies – intermarried.

It is thought that two main events added to the numbers of nomadic people in Scotland – the Jacobite rebellion and the Highland Clearances. Many Scottish Gypsy families, including the Townsleys, who later took up camp at Meriden in the English Midlands, fought on the side of Bonnie Prince Charlie at the Battle of Culloden. After the Jacobites were defeated there in 1746, the Gypsies ended up on the road.[51] Then, in the eighteenth and nineteenth centuries, Scottish lairds evicted thousands of their former servants and labourers, often with great brutality, so that they could introduce sheep and deer farming. Many Traveller families were evicted from the Highlands and Islands at this time.[52] This complex history is reflected in the 'Cant', the Traveller language, which draws on Romani, Scots and Gaelic words.

In 1865 the government introduced the Trespass Act, which controlled the movement of Scottish Travellers and gave the police extensive powers to move them on. Thirty years later the Secretary of State for Scotland, Sir George Trevelyan, set up a committee 'to call attention to habitual offenders, vagrants, beggars and inebriates in Scotland'.[53] The policy towards Gypsies and tinkers (as they were called) was discussed in section two of the report, relating to vagrants and beggars. It was urged that children be forcibly separated from their parents, who were described by some of the witness testimony as excessively criminal and prone to drunkenness. Gypsies and Travellers were accused of neglecting their children and spreading infectious diseases. 'Coalville' Smith's work was showered with particular accolade.

Some witnesses were more positive, with one praising the Townsley family (also called the Townies) for their hard work as basket-makers. Another said that their open-air life was a healthy one. The chief constable of Perthshire, for example, in whose patch the Townsleys and other families often stopped, stoutly denied the link with criminality and also said that they rarely annoyed other citizens.[54] He added that they were in the main 'quiet and orderly ... affectionate and fond of their children'.[55] The chairman of the Perthshire Committee on Vagrancy reported that Gypsies were not a large problem. 'They are more easily managed than

worthless strollers who call themselves working people ... My
gamekeepers would rather manage the tinkers than any of the
loafing communities of the village.'[56]

But these reasonable voices, advocating support for the Gypsies
and relief of their poverty, rather than a clamp-down, did not win
out. Instead, the Rev. John McCullum, a Free Church Minister
for Loch Tay, was heard out. His proposal was to gather all the
children into a central institution in order to 'extinguish the class
as distinct from the rest of the community'.[57]

In 1895 the Scottish government introduced the Gypsies, Irish
Travellers and Pavees [another term for Irish Travellers] in the Tent
Act, aimed at cracking down on itinerants. The law decreed that
a landowner could have no more than two tents on his land at
any time; if there were more, the owner could be fined. Mostly
motivated by the Church of Scotland, the government next proposed to corral Gypsies in reservations. Gypsy children would be
forced into state education. In 1908, the policy had escalated to
the enactment of legislation granting the government the power
to remove children from their families. Boys were sent to work
on the warships and trained in the art of soldiering, while girls
were raised in service. A reservation in Dunkeld, where the children would be educated together – 'a school for tinkers' is how
Scottish Traveller Jess Smith has described it – would be set up.

Many children were wrested away from their parents – some
in heart-breaking circumstances. One such, Sandy Reid, was
taken from a tent in a Fife wood with his sister Maggie, from
his Traveller parents in 1959. He was fostered and placed into a
number of children's homes, and said he was sexually abused in
one of them. His mother hunted for her children for the rest of
her life. She died at the age of forty-one, without being reunited
with them. The Scottish government has never apologised for this
policy, which continued until the 1960s.[58]

In England too, the idea of a reservation was pursued tenaciously. Encampments in the New Forest, where Gypsy families
had lived for generations, were used as a testing ground for the
policy. From the 1920s through to the 1960s, English Gypsies were

rounded up and forced into compounds within the forest. This was nothing like a nomadic family choosing to stop for the week or the month, though the authorities tried to make it seem so because of the historic use of the land by the communities. Unfortunately it suited powerful people, some of them politicians, to do so. In a report to a House of Commons Select Committee, Lord Arthur Cecil was asked about grievances against the Gypsies. He replied, testily: 'They are a great nuisance to everybody ... I am specially troubled by gypsies myself. I have two instances which I cannot turn them away from within one hundred yards of my house.'[59,60]

The hatred of the Roma people, intense enough in the UK, was magnified in mainland Europe. It was impossible to watch the treatment of the Roma on the continent without fear for what fate they might face should they ever be forced to leave the country. Those who arrived in Britain from Europe as refugees – for example, in 1904 the 'German Gypsies' and then in 1911 and 1913 the 'Gypsy Coppersmiths' – were treated with hostility and suspicion. The identity of English, Welsh and Scottish Gypsies, especially, was shaped by the Holocaust, or, as it is known by the Roma people themselves, the *Porrajmos*, or the Devouring (a phrase coined by the Romani scholar Ian Hancock).

Manfri Frederick Wood, an English Gypsy who fought in the Fifth Airborne Division (and who later became the first treasurer of the Gypsy Council), claimed to have been one of the first Allied soldiers to enter Belsen concentration camp after liberation. 'When I saw the surviving Romanies, with young children among them, I was shaken. Then I went over to the ovens, and found on one of the steel stretchers the half-charred body of a girl, and I understood in one awful minute what had been going on there,' he recalled. Charles Smith, an English Romani Gypsy and one-time chair of the Gypsy Council, later visited Auschwitz with a small delegation of Gypsies. 'We stood there, a group of English Gypsies from England, there in the gas chambers. I felt sort of honoured to be there – all of us survivors of a Gypsy Holocaust that had been going on for a thousand years continuously ... Auschwitz being just a peak period in Gypsy genocide.'[61]

That sense of a collective, centuries-long experience of persecution remains strong today. The emotional scars also run deep, perhaps partly because this part of the Holocaust has never received the same amount of attention as the extermination of Jewish people. Yet Roma and Sinti (the second largest nomadic group) people were also judged to be racially inferior by the German authorities. They too were interned, subjected to forced labour. Many were murdered.

Historians estimate that the Germans and their allies killed around twenty-five per cent of all European Roma.[62] Of the slightly less than one million Roma believed to have been living in Europe before the war, at least 220,000, and possibly as many as 500,000, are estimated to have been killed.[63] According to the US Holocaust Museum, German military and SS-police units allegedly shot at least 30,000 Roma in the Baltic states and elsewhere in the occupied Soviet Union; *Einsatzgruppen* and other mobile killing units were targeting Roma at the same time that they were killing Jews and Communists. In occupied Serbia, German authorities are known to have killed male Roma in shooting operations during 1941 and early 1942. Women were murdered, along with children, in mobile gas vans in 1942.

In France, between 3,000 and 6,000 Roma are thought to have been interned and some were shipped to German concentration camps. Romanian military and police officials deported another 26,000 Roma to Transnistria, a section of south-western Ukraine placed under Romanian administration for just two years, 1941 and 1942. Thousands of those imprisoned starved or died from disease. The Ustashe, a separatist organisation that had taken charge in the power vacuum in Croatia, exhibited particularly chilling efficiency in its campaign to eradicate the Roma. Almost all of the Roma population of Croatia, around 25,000, were murdered, most at the concentration camp of Jasenovac.

Many Roma were also incarcerated by the SS at Bergen-Belsen, Sachsenhausen, Buchenwald, Dachau, Natzweiler-Struthof,

Mauthausen and Ravensbrück. In December 1942, Himmler ordered the deportation of Roma from the so-called Greater German Reich.[64] Most went to Auschwitz-Birkenau, where the camp authorities housed them in a special compound that was called the 'Gypsy family camp'. Altogether, 23,000 Roma were deported to Auschwitz. Conditions in the Roma compound (poor sanitation, starvation levels of rations, for example), encouraged the swift spread of deadly diseases – typhus, smallpox and dysentery among them. Epidemics severely reduced the camp population. At least 19,000 of the 23,000 nomadic people sent to Auschwitz died there.

Perhaps the cruellest part of the Roma experience, however, was the appalling series of medical experiments carried out by the infamous SS Captain Dr Josef Mengele and others on many young Roma children. He had received authorisation to choose human subjects for experiments from among the prisoners. Mengele chose twins and children of restricted growth, many of them drawn from the Roma population imprisoned at the camp, as his subjects.[65] Around 3,500 adult and adolescent Roma were prisoners in other German camps, and medical researchers included some Roma for studies that exposed them to typhus and mustard gas, or gave them salt water as their only source of liquid. The Roma were also used in sterilisation experiments.[66]

After the Second World War, discrimination against Roma continued throughout Central and Eastern Europe, beginning with the great reckoning of the horrors of the concentration camps. 'Nobody was called to testify on behalf of the Romani victims at the Nuremberg Trials,' Hancock noted, 'and no war crimes reparations have ever been paid to Romanies as a people.' There were a few mentions of the atrocities carried out against Romanies at Nuremberg, but as Grattan Puxon and Donald Kenrick point out, only six references, making up some seven sentences, in the eleven volumes of the trial transcript.[67] For decades, the Federal Republic of Germany determined that all measures taken against Roma before 1943 were legitimate official measures against persons committing criminal acts, not the result of policies driven by racial prejudice. Only in 1979 did the government change tack, by which time many of those eligible for compensation had died. Even today, neo-Nazi activity in many parts of Central and Eastern Europe is targeted on Romanies, according to Hancock.[68]

In the aftermath of the *Porrajmos,* the shattered community turned further inwards. 'While in the camps, the Gypsies had been unable to keep up their customs – the *Romainia* – concerning the preparation of food and the washing of clothes. They solved the psychological problems by not speaking about the time in the camps ... Few were interested anyway. In the many books written describing the Nazi period and the persecution of the Jews, Gypsies usually appear as a footnote or small section,' said historians Donald Kenrick and Gillian Taylor.[69] In the early post-war years, news trickled out that the Nazi regime had secretly collected lists of Gypsies to target and intern if they invaded Britain. The UK government had built camps for Gypsies fighting or working at home for the war effort; these were swiftly dismantled once the war was over.[70] Many British Gypsies and Irish Travellers who had served during the Second World War were left with a firm sense of determination: never again.

As Charles Smith wrote to conclude his visit to Auschwitz: 'The thing that haunts me most was a photograph of a little girl age about ten or eleven years, hair cropped, wearing her striped cloth, looking straight into the camera, her eyes filled with tears ... a picture of her will always be in my mind. I will remember. I will be vigilant. As a Gypsy I owe that to my ancestors.'[71]

3
NEVER AGAIN

The suffering of the Roma people crystallised a determination: that it would never happen again. Although around a quarter of Europe's Roma population had been murdered, survivors came together again and regrouped, particularly in France and in the UK. Out of the ashes of the Holocaust came Gypsy, Roma and Traveller activism and a trio of key allies comprised of a young journalist, Grattan Puxon, and two academics, Thomas Acton and Donald Kenrick, none of whom were Gypsies themselves.[1]

Of the three, Grattan Puxon was the best known. In October 2011, he had stood beside the actress Vanessa Redgrave as she took up her dead brother Corin's plea to the Basildon Council to rethink its stance on eviction. He had become a de facto celebrity. But his involvement in Gypsy and Traveller politics has its roots in 1960s Ireland, almost fifty years earlier. As Grattan's fellow activist, Thomas Acton, had written around that time, the stereotype of the 'tinker' had by no means been consistently negative in the UK. Instead, he was often seen as 'a happy-go-lucky fellow, descended from archaic kingdoms, speaking half-a-dozen secret languages'.[2] But attitudes had hardened after the Second World War, and worsened yet further during and after the Troubles, on both sides of the Irish Sea.

Three main events, along with quieter political shifts, had spurred many Irish families to move to Britain. The first wave, of course, came with the Great Famine of the 1840s, with more following as civil war broke out in the 1920s, after Ireland formally seceded from the UK and became the Free State (becoming the

Irish Republic in 1948). A steady stream of families emigrated to England and Scotland, trying to gain more security in their lives, as the global depression set in. The advent of the Second World War put everything on hold. But during the post-war reconstruction of England, the prospects for Irish Travellers seemed to improve; there was even a minor employment boom among Irish labourers in England – a far cry from conditions at home, where a state of economic distress had sunk in.

In Ireland the itinerant population were seen, the academic Jim MacLaughlin argues, as 'cultural curiosities in a changing and increasingly materialistic, homogenous and "settled" society'.[3] Irish Travellers were linked in the public mind with petty criminality and poverty – they embarrassed a nation readying itself for a new global identity. They were a threat to everyone's livelihood. The Irish Folklore Commission Survey on Travelling People, which was conducted in 1952, recorded numerous complaints about the group. 'Questionnaire after questionnaire repeats farmers' complaints of Travellers loosing their horses into fields (including fields under cultivation) at night, leaving gates open, and damaging fences'.[4] They were a menace to the social order. Many settled people described Travellers as infestations – 'breeding like rabbits'.[5]

Mary Ann McCarthy and her family left Ireland in the 1950s, fleeing this persecution of the travelling way of life and seeking employment on the 'mainland'. Her father was a musician, as were his brothers. But like other Traveller men, they were willing to turn their hands to anything, including labouring, to keep their families together.

The Sheridans also left Ireland around this time – Mary Ann's neighbours, Michelle and Nora, were in fact born in the UK, and spent their early years travelling around the North of England and Wales while their parents sold antique Welsh dressers around the Midlands. 'I have been all over Scotland, all over North Wales, all over Birmingham, Leeds, Bradford, all over London,' Nora recalled. 'In my life, there's not a part of Britain I've not been in. I was all over when I was growing up and we could move on ten mile, hundred mile, you had to move at least once a week. There were no stopping places, you would just pull into a field, a piece of ground.' For Nora, as for many other second-generation Irish Britons, this is home to her, rather than the country on the other side of the Irish Sea. 'I was born and reared in England. It would be like a foreign country, going to Ireland for me.'[6]

Candy Sheridan, a distant cousin who rose to prominence at Dale Farm during the fight over the site clearance, also spent her formative years in the UK. 'Both my parents are Irish Travellers, who arrived in the UK in 1958. Three of my brothers were born on the Westway site, and I was born in Bristol. We lived up and down the M4, but I was lucky to attend schools, I attended twenty-two by the age of ten.'[7] Then, as now, most Travellers lived modestly.

They left Ireland just in time. Only a few years later, in 1963, a report by the Commission on Itinerancy concluded that the travelling way of life needed to be destroyed in the country. The government's aim was assimilation. Until the Travellers ceased to exist as a distinct group, they would remain a troubled community. In a particularly chilling and resonant moment, the Parliamentary Secretary to the Minister for Justice, Charles Haughey, said, 'There can be no final solution to the problems created by itinerants until they are absorbed into the general community.'[8] At the urging of the commission, the government adopted one of the report's recommendations: that Travellers should be moved into housing.[9] They cited the need to protect Traveller children from dangerous campsites on busy roads, and to get more of them into school – paternalistically minded policies that had been gaining support since the 1950s. As one parliamentary deputy put it: 'If you cannot make citizens out of [the Travellers], put them into homes. It would be better than [having] them going around rearing their children without education and giving them no chances.'[10]

Even worse, though, the Travellers' claim to a separate ethnic and cultural identity was firmly denied. 'Itinerants (or Travellers as they prefer themselves to be called) do not constitute a single homogenous group, tribe or community within the nation, although the settled population are inclined to regard them as such. Neither do they constitute a separate ethnic group,' the commission reported.[11] The solution was to absorb them as a population. 'The colonised had become colonisers,' in the phrase of Sinead Ni Shuinear.[12]

'Their association with poverty, petty criminality and hardship made it difficult to accommodate "tinkers" within the dominant institutions of post-independence Ireland,' MacLaughlin notes. 'Their traditional halting sites disappeared under a barrage of road "improvements". The very occupations that once linked them to settled society were increasingly redundant ... Travellers, like the long-term urban unemployed, also became more visible and increasingly dependent upon the welfare state in this new modernising Ireland.'[13] Nearly overnight, Irish Travellers were officially transformed into social lepers. They were 'pathologically unfit for Irish citizenship'.[14]

Despite the open prejudice, discrimination and assimilation campaign, the numbers of Irish Travellers kept increasing. Many members of the community married young, and most wanted to have large families. Birth rates were outpacing anything the government could do. In 1963 the commission had reported that there were just under 6,500 Irish Travellers in the Republic; by 1977 the Irish Economic and Social Research Institute recorded 1,396 Travellers in the Dublin area alone.[15] In the intervening years, Travellers had become more, rather than less, visible, not only because of their growing numbers, but because they were drifting towards the cities. It was there – in Dublin, especially – that they could make money.

After the Second World War, more and more Irish farms were being mechanised, requiring the services of fewer itinerant and seasonal labourers. Myxomatosis had decimated the rabbit population, a common source of free food among Travellers. 'Within a fifteen-year period the major trades and services tinkers performed had become obsolete,' according to the American anthropologist George Gmelch, who did his first fieldwork among Travellers.[16] There were other advantages to city life, Gmelch noted – work in scrap-metal dealing, going on the dole – as well as less visibility as Travellers at a time when hostilities were increasing. 'Travellers found it easier to gain admittance to pubs and cinemas in urban areas where, providing they were not too unkempt, they had a degree of anonymity. In many small towns and villages, on the other hand, Travellers were not served in public places.'[17]

Grattan arrived in Ireland in 1960 and was soon joined by his partner, the singer and Montessori teacher Venice Manley. Grattan had trained as a journalist on a local newspaper in Essex, but as his national service loomed, he decided to flee to the Republic. This was mainly to avoid being sent to Cyprus, where the British Army was involved in suppressing activists who wanted to free the country from colonial rule. 'I don't believe the state should call you up to go into a war of their choosing. I would have had to go to Cyprus and I had lived in Greece for fourteen years; I wasn't prepared to face off with schoolgirls throwing stones, the EOKA movement. Instead I went to Ireland,' he said.

It wasn't long before Grattan, who was stringing for a number of English newspapers, met some Travellers. He had been commissioned to write an article about a Traveller, and got to know the family. He bought a traditional barrel-topped wagon from the man he'd interviewed, and parked it on council land while renovating a house he had recently bought. In his own lightly fictionalised account of his time in Ireland, *Freeborn Traveller*, which he published in 2007, he wrote of these early encounters in the third person. 'Almost everything about the Travellers appealed to him. They had affected him as nothing had before. Of all possible lives, this was the kind of life he wanted to lead. He itched to consort further with these footless, landless folk. He wanted not only to write about it but share their open-air life.'[18] Within months he had come to know many Travellers living in and around Dublin, helping one, Kevin Keenan, by negotiating to save his family from eviction.

In the wake of the commission's disquieting report, Grattan and others had set up the Itinerants Action Campaign. The summer after the report's release, he was one of the leaders, with John Macdonald and Kevin Keenan, of a march from Ballyfermot, a western suburb on the ring road around Dublin, to City Hall. The Travellers took 'carts and horses and banners saying "No more Eviction" and "Education for our Children"'. The protest was 'not well received; the first Travellers' school, for which they built a hut at Ballyfermot [and where Venice taught with much skill] was burnt down ... by council workmen, on 6 January 1964.'[19] Yet the group carried on, picketing government offices and enlisting support from students and liberals, including church activists, most notably the Quaker Joseph Bewley. Some members of the Catholic Church and two American Baptists also joined them.

Grattan and a few Travellers, led by 'Pops' Johnny Connors, set up an illegal camp, Cherry Orchard, near Dublin, from Easter 1964 till 1965. Around fifty families soon called it home. Grattan had adopted a Gandhi-like approach of non-violent resistance to evictions, and went about teaching the Travellers tactics such as sitting down in front of bulldozer wheels to prevent forcible removal from sites. 'This confrontational and anti-assimilationist resistance was a direct response by radicalised Travellers to the perceived paternalism of the Commission on Itinerancy and its allied Christian organisation,' according to the writer Mary Burke.[20] Grattan was interviewed for a news documentary to air on RTÉ. 'There was an appalling gap between me and them,' he said, trying to explain why he had got involved. 'I should try and describe to them what their rights were ... point out the injustice they were suffering.'[21] But not everyone appreciated his help, and the encampment families started to split over whether the goal of Cherry Orchard should be to make a community or to make a political point.

As the site gained notoriety, more media arrived. The photographer Alen MacWeeney visited the site. To an outsider's eyes, 'Cherry Orchard was a big, rough field. Bushes ran along the sides of what were really three adjoining fields ... facing the pebble-dashed wall of Cherry Orchard fever hospital. Children played in muck and rubble ... horses were tethered with ragged ropes and pups yelped at the piebald horses,' he said.[22] A school was set up on the anniversary of the burning of the one at Ballyfermot, but that did little to paper over the fact that living conditions were terrible. Among the families squatting there was Nan Joyce, an Irish Traveller woman, who had five daughters. In her autobiography, she recalled how 'awful' it was to be at Cherry Orchard. 'The travellers had little huts built with old bits of wood – it was like something you'd see in foreign countries, the way the poor people have to live in shanty towns ... There was no water or toilets. When it rained you'd think the bulldozers had been digging. The rats were in hundreds.'[23]

Eventually, the Travellers left the camp. But they and their supporters had learned much about the values of resistance – and of publicity.

Prominent English figures, including the MP Norman Dodds, the philosopher Bertrand Russell and the Committee of 100, had noticed the campaign and the Irish government's attempts to evict the families from Cherry Orchard. And they had protested too. But in creating a coalition to bring about change, Grattan had also courted dangerous friends. As he disclosed in his book, *Freeborn Traveller*, he had been forced, practically at gunpoint, to hide explosives for a wing of the IRA in the back garden of his house. The experience was unsettling, even many years later.

A splinter group of the emergent IRA had got involved in the Traveller movement, he recalled. 'They had a front organisation called the Civil Liberties League and the Justice for Itinerants and they stood with us at some evictions. But they weren't prepared to use non-violent resistance, they wouldn't sit on the ground with us.'[24] Grattan's memory is substantiated by the historian Aoife Bhreathnach, among others: 'Sinn Féin were attracted to Puxon's radical politics and participated in a protest march to Lansdowne Road ... Those allies were not necessarily advantageous, as Special Branch officers subsequently kept Puxon and other prominent figures under surveillance.'[25] In February 1964 Grattan was arrested on a charge of possessing explosives. 'Some extremist Republican bodies had been amongst the supporters of the Travellers' movement, and demanded reciprocal help,' fellow activist Thomas Acton explained, and 'when Grattan Puxon refused to support some of their activities, they probably informed the police of [the] explosives.'[26]

Looking back on that time, Grattan was reflective. 'It is very possible I was set up; it was a very complex situation. Indeed, I was approached by official IRA intelligence. They wanted me to take part in a court-martial of those involved ... a lot of people were arrested and put into the Curragh' – the infamous military prison in County Kildare used to house many suspected IRA members. Suspicion was running high, most especially among the Irish authorities. The only people who were 'allowed out', he said, 'were those who swore allegiance to the state and on no account did anybody get a job with the government.' This put Grattan in a difficult position – if no one was allowed to roam freely by the government, how had anyone been able to come to him? The IRA could only imagine one reason. 'Now that person who came to my wagon with the explosives, Rob, was in the forestry division,' Grattan remembered. 'He was suspect for that reason, and the IRA reckoned that he was an informer. They had a grudge against this particular group because there had been a raid, taken arms up against the official IRA, before the Provisional IRA. I said no.'

Although he was released on bail, the charge hung over Grattan for the next sixteen months. 'I was given a choice after my arrest', he said – and the choice was not heartening. 'Because my own lawyers were also connected with the IRA, I could either be taken up to Belfast in a fast car or stand trial.' He decided to put his fate in the hands of the Irish courts. 'After sixteen months I had a two-minute trial.' The government dropped the charges.

Many of the Cherry Orchard families moved on to a field near Ballyfermot that had previously served as a dump for spent car batteries. 'The whole ground was contaminated with the batteries, but we didn't know that', Nan Joyce said. 'We never thought about lead poisoning.' Nan's daughter Julie got sick and had to be taken to the doctor, and then to hospital. She, and all of Nan's other children, were diagnosed with lead poisoning. They recovered, but Julie was left suffering from seizures.[27]

After he was cleared of the charges, Grattan returned to England. It was 1966. Not long afterwards, a number of Travellers involved in the agitations of the 1960s followed him, among them Johnny Connors, who moved to the Midlands. But blowback following the report by the Commission on Itinerancy was not the only reason they were leaving Ireland.

Some were effectively refugees, fleeing the fallout from the Troubles in Northern Ireland. As Catholics, Travellers were sometimes targeted by Protestant vigilante groups. By the 2001 census, Travellers accounted for only 0.1% (1,710 people) of the Northern Irish population, but a larger 0.4% of the population in the six border counties – within close reach of the Republic, including, presumably, relatives and trading opportunities there (around 1,727 people in the 2006 Census).[28] Belfast – like Dublin starting in the 1950s and 1960s – hosted the largest Traveller population in the North.

An Irish academic, Robbie McVeigh, has carried out an in-depth project for the Donegal Travellers Project, part of the Ethnic Peace project, in which he held focus group work with a sample number from the Traveller community from each of the six border counties to explore the impact of the Troubles on the community. 'The most striking aspect of the question of the relationship of Travellers to the Troubles is just how little is recorded on the subject. Most research and activist literature suggests that Travellers were completely untouched by the political conflict,' McVeigh writes. 'Travellers are not mentioned in any audit of the Troubles ... But the absence of any written history does not imply that Travellers were uninvolved in or unaffected by the Troubles.'[29]

For the project, McVeigh interviewed 150 Travellers, activists and workers at local organisations about their experiences in Northern Ireland between the late 1960s and 2000. Some Travellers said that they didn't get involved with the Troubles and were largely unaffected – but others told a different story.

Travellers had been helpful to their fellow Catholics in the settled community when Catholics were expelled from the Ardoyne area of Belfast in 1969. They offered the service of caravans and lorries, helping to move people to new homes. But the relationship didn't always work in the favour of Travellers. Some were targeted and punished for alleged 'anti-social behaviour', even by Catholics. Others were asked to move on because a site was somewhere the IRA didn't want police to look.

More often, though, McVeigh found, there was 'a much closer connection to ideologies of Irishness and Republicanism'.[30] Travellers became automatically suspect to loyalists and the police, sometimes merely because of their Catholicism. In some cases, it has been claimed that the authorities tried to fabricate evidence against Irish Travellers. For instance, during the Morris Tribunal investigations in 2006, it came to light that seven Travellers had allegedly been arrested on 23 May 1998 after detectives planted a weapon on a site to ensure that a search could be carried out. 'If it be the case that members of the An Gardaa Síochána were prepared to go to the length of securing a firearm recovered in the course of other operations and planting it on innocent individuals so that they could be arrested ... the implications are shocking,' the Morris Tribunal report said.[31]

In interviews, people shared brutal examples of police harassment directed at Travellers, including a fake execution and the death of at least one man in police barracks in Belfast. McVeigh heard reports of routine 'ethnic cleansing' of Travellers from different parts of the North. A number recalled being targeted by the 'B' Special Constabulary, a 'special' police force created because of the declared state of emergency. As the Troubles worsened, it became more difficult for Travellers to get across the border, and there was a greater risk of getting caught in crossfire. Paramilitary loyalist organisations targeted Travellers on occasion, fire-bombing caravans. Sites along the Shankhill Road in west Belfast and the nearby Bog Meadows were attacked. 'In loyalist areas – where

Travellers had camped for generations – Travellers were expelled,' McVeigh said in an interview.[32]

Where once there had been tolerance, some Protestants exhibited raw enmity. In the late 1980s, the Ulster Unionist Frank Millar, formerly Deputy Lord Mayor of Belfast, openly called for Travellers to be incinerated.[33] Even years after the Good Friday Agreement paved the way to an end to the Troubles, members of a Traveller family, the McDonaghs, were fire-bombed out of their house in south Belfast.[34] The attack came in February 2005 – just a few months before the last weapons in the hands of paramilitary groups were decommissioned. It is not surprising that no Traveller has ever been connected to loyalist paramilitary groups.

A number of Irish Travellers were fervent supporters of the Republican cause, however.[35] In 1981, Travellers staged a demonstration in support of the hunger strikes in Dublin. One interviewee recalled that there was 'great sympathy for the hunger strikers. Any marches going, Travellers were on it'.[36] But McVeigh's sense was that some were intimidated into getting involved, especially in paramilitary matters. One interviewee said, 'If they didn't do a job, their van would be burnt ... I think a lot of Travellers was afeared of the IRA, and they done what they were told to do by the IRA.'[37] Another Traveller support worker had heard Travellers say they had to drive IRA explosives under duress, including to addresses in Newry, on the border.

Some Travellers found refuge from the Troubles in the Irish Republic. But even when they agreed to settle in houses in Ireland, things weren't straightforward. Settled people did not want them there. During the late 1960s, Traveller sites around Galway were attacked by people brandishing shotguns. Those who were happy to move into traditional shelter were not always welcomed. According to Mary Burke, 'A notorious case occurred in Galway city in 1970 involving a Mrs Furey, a Traveller mother of six whose name had been on the corporation housing list for over ten years and who was at that time squatting with her children in a condemned dwelling. A three-hundred-strong group of residents of the corporation (public) housing estate in which

Mrs Furey had been allocated a home vehemently objected to her presence and threatened bloodshed if she arrived.'[38]

No wonder, then, that some, in desperation, moved to England. Irish Travellers at this time were truly caught between the devil and the deep blue sea.

Evictions in England had been growing in frequency for several years. In 1960, the government had passed the Caravan Sites and Control of Development Act, which stated that no occupier of land 'shall cause or permit the land to be used as a caravan site unless he is the holder of a site licence. It also enables a district council to make an order prohibiting the stationing of caravans on common land, or a town or village green.' This effectively prevented Travellers from using the vast majority of their traditional stopping places. Plus, anyone associated with the Troubles was deemed to be a problem – especially after British troops were deployed in Northern Ireland on 14 August 1969.

Shortly after Grattan came back to the UK, he got a trailer and drove it to Stanhouse in Kent. 'I put the trailer on there and it wasn't even noticed for six months,' he said. He then went about his work: establishing a Gypsy Council. 'I got a room booked in a pub called the Bull at St Mary Cray, and I paid my ten pounds deposit, said it was a human rights meeting, and the landlord came to my wagon and said, "We want to give you your money back, we hear it is Gypsies." I said, "No way." Written on the front of the pub was a sign, "No Gypsies".' But that would not stop Grattan.

About fifty people attended that first meeting in December 1966. They included Dominic Reeve, a prominent writer on Gypsy matters, and representatives of the Comité Internationale de Rom, the Romani organisation of Paris, who had become allies during Grattan's time in Ireland. They had been planning an international congress of Gypsies and Travellers, and Grattan, impatient, had decided to start it himself.

The first Gypsy Council manifesto was issued to the press and read thus: 'TRAVELLERS OF THE WORLD UNITE: We live in a world in which many hands are turned against us, the Travelling people ... We are not a small minority, as many think, but a proud people 12 MILLION strong, scattered in every country.'[39] The document put forward three key demands: sites; equal rights to housing, work and education; and equal standing through respect between travelling and settled people – demands that have not been met, in any major way, nearly fifty years later. Though they were unified in these basic demands, right from the start there were tensions between 'hawks' and 'doves' on the council. There were also disagreements between the Irish Travellers and the English Gypsies; about whether or not the movement should be international or national; about whether activism or education and lobbying should be the main strategy for change; about the role of religion in the new movement.[40]

The Irish Travellers who came to England around this time were entering the eye of the storm. Travellers were arriving in increasing numbers, and there were great numbers of scrap-metal-dealing and construction jobs to be had, as English councils cleared slums and renewed urban centres when the economy began to flourish after the stagnant 1950s. 'They faced the usual problems of any mass immigrants; they had to enter into economic competition with often resentful local Travellers and *gaujos*[41], but with an inferior local knowledge of the country and fewer business contacts,' said Thomas Acton. 'They therefore had to use the abrasive methods of price-cutting and quality variation commonly used by businessmen trying to enter a new market, which led inevitably to charges of what would be called in the City "unethical" practices, especially in the "tarmacking" and "scrap collection" businesses.'[42] The competition for these sorts of traditional travelling work became all the more fierce because in the early days most of the Irish Travellers settled in the Midlands.

The area was known for its long history of racist sentiments – in 1964 Peter Griffiths had won in the general election for Smethwick campaigning under the memorably vicious phrase, 'If you want a nigger for a neighbour, vote Labour.' But it wasn't just black and Asian migrants who faced difficulties. Anti-Gypsy feelings ran high – and there was open warfare against the Irish immigrants. By the mid-sixties, local authorities were taking increasingly harsh measures against Irish Travellers squatting on city land, which affected local Gypsies too.

Councillors in the area were prone to claim that all of the Gypsies were 'tinkers' – meaning vagrants and beggars – and should be sent back to Ireland. In 1963, in the Sparkbrook area of Birmingham, local residents persuaded the General Purposes Committee of Birmingham City Council, led by Alderman Harry Watton (known as the 'Little Caesar of Birmingham'), to remove Irish Travellers from fourteen properties on Grantham Road. Their living conditions and behaviour came under intense scrutiny.[43] The Travellers were viewed by local politicians as having no place in the city despite their long history in Birmingham. Watton opined: 'I think you are endeavouring to defend something that is historically outdated: the tinker and the wanderer. There may be places for them in some parts of the world, but there isn't in an industrialised urban community.'[44]

One Birmingham councillor told the *Guardian*: 'The tinker is a throwback to the past and has no place in the life of a modern city, where people come to live in a settled, orderly and mutually helpful society. We intend to make conditions so intolerable, so uncomfortable and so unprofitable for these human scrap vultures that they won't stop here.'[45] The authority's attitude, echoed in the local newspapers, dehumanised the Travellers, presenting them as parasites who had invaded the local community. One headline described them as 'human scrap vultures' swarming in for 'slum drive pickings'.[46] Harry Watton, formerly the leader of the Labour group in Birmingham, interviewed by the folk singer Ewan MacColl in 1964 for the radio ballad, 'The Travelling People', talked in particularly strong terms: 'How far does it come in your mind before you say, "I have done everything I possibly can and I will help the broad mass of these people, but there are some I can do nothing with whatever." Then doesn't the time arise in one's mind when one has to say, "Alright, one has to exterminate the impossibles."'[47]

In the summer of 1967 Birmingham attempted systematically to cleanse the city of Travellers, using a strategy of multiple evictions that would keep Travellers and Gypsies on the move. They were shifted on, time and again. Joseph Jones (known as Joe), now the chairman of the Gypsy Council, remembers being forced to drive around and around the ring roads of Birmingham. 'They used to keep us in convoy, they kept us driving until someone broke away, they kept us driving round the ring road, they would allow us to stop every few hours to feed the children, but apart from that we were continuously on the road.'[48] This was vividly represented on the local TV news, when one reporter was sent out to interview Irish Travellers and English Gypsies who had been forced to park in a lay-by. The children were playing just metres away from a busy thoroughfare. But they had nowhere else to go – and they had been evicted from another pitch just days before. One Traveller told the camera, 'We just keep moving,' adding ironically, 'It's a great life.' Another was more straightforward: 'We get treated like animals.'[49]

Joseph Jones was among those who were constantly shifted about. 'When we were pulling round Birmingham, you was lucky if you got two days. One day I came back and there was a JCB [loader] digging a trench round an empty plot. We'd been out calling all day and lorries pulled up, and I said to the fella, "How did they got towed away?" ... They took us up west Bromwich Albion and down that lane and the front windows of my trailer were broken, the trailer was dented, no compensation – that's the way they were, they were brutal.' The council's fear tactics were captured in 'The Terror Time' by singer-songwriters Ewan MacColl and Peggy Seeger:

> When you need the warmth of your own human kind
> You move near a town
> But the sight of you is offending
> For the police they soon are sending
> And you're on the road again.[50]

Those who did stop on the council-provided sites had few facilities, Joseph Jones remembered. 'We only had a standpipe. You had to dig your own toilet and you paid rent for a standpipe, and in the winter it would freeze up. We would put the cars round it to warm it. That was the council accommodation in those days.'

Sometimes, the conditions were too much to bear. 'We got fed up. So when they came we'd put the children in the front bucket [of the loader] and dare the driver to move. Made a lot of difference when we fought back. We got proper accommodation,' Jones said.

They did not always need to be sent back by force. When Nan Joyce and her family came to England. 'Things were going very bad for us; it seemed everywhere we moved we'd be waiting for something better but something worse always happened. So we packed up whatever we had and went to England … It was really awful in England because the travellers were being hunted and hunted.'[51] After a couple of years the family felt they had no choice but to move back to Ireland, into the heart of the Troubles.

According to Oxford anthropologist Judith Okely, 'Worcester County Council reported that "Irish tinkers" in their area bore "little resemblance to the tinker of Irish legend who seems to have been something of a character and as such regarded with affection". In practice, the Irish label was conveniently attached to any Travellers coming up against the authorities.[52] The Tinkers became synonymous with every unpopular or stigmatised aspect of any gypsy groups: scrap work, travelling, urban proximity, law breaking, elusiveness and independent lifestyle.'[53] There was a desperate need for official sites to dispel the tension.

Thankfully, help for homeless Gypsies and Travellers was at hand – and this time, from powerful sources.

Eric Lubbock had won the Orpington by-election for the Liberal Democrats in 1962, with a swing of over twenty-two per cent over the Conservatives. Previously, he had been a local councillor for the area, which was both urban and rural. 'I represented the village of Downe, and the constituency was a transit point for Gypsies going down into Kent for agricultural occupations, mainly hopping. So I was aware of the Gypsies and Travellers from that point of view, and the planning problems that arose because they wanted somewhere to stop.'[54] When Lubbock got to Parliament after the election, he found an ally in Norman Dodds, who, Lubbock said, 'was about the only person in that Parliament who was involved in pursuing Gypsy rights'. Dodds died in 1965, leaving the issue in Lubbock's hands. 'He handed on the baton to me as it were, when he died. There was no one after Norman died who was actively pursuing the rights of Gypsies and Travellers.' In 1968, Lubbock got the opportunity to introduce a Private Members' Bill and he decided to put forward the Caravan Sites Bill.

The bill contained two main proposals: a restriction on evicting caravans from caravan sites and the establishment of authorised sites by local councils for the use of Gypsies and other nomads. 'So that even at that time we were thinking in terms of accommodation of both permanent sites and transit sites so people could move around the country.' Lubbock recalled that the fact that he was on good terms with Dick Crossman, the Minister of Housing and Local Government, and Arthur Skeffington, the Parliamentary Secretary, was key – 'because they ensured that the bill, even though it was only sixth on the ballot [unless a bill is first or second it normally has no chance of becoming law], was given extra time'. With such support the bill passed on 26 July.

It wasn't a complete victory. The act had a clause allowing the government to decide when to activate it, and the ministers stalled for two years. Because of the time lag, hostile councils, particularly in the Midlands, took the opportunity to push out local Gypsy and Traveller camps, as they would then have no obligation to provide authorised sites for them. The worst would be in and around Birmingham.

Grattan Puxon could not believe how events played out. He stood with Gypsies and Irish Travellers at eviction after eviction. He put his life and his caravan on the line time after time. 'Instead of building the urgently needed caravan parks, councils launched another pogrom to rid themselves of Gypsies ... In Staffordshire that October, one of the biggest police operations in the county's history had been mounted to evict families at Brownhills. A boy of six lost an eye and a hand in an explosion during the first attempt. Detonators had been cast onto a camp fire "by persons unknown". At George Street in Walsall three children were burned to death during a caravan fire, which never would have happened had the corporation not towed the trailer onto a busy street.'

Enoch Powell, who sat in the Commons as a Conservative MP for Birmingham, stoked the fires. He disliked all immigration, and was well known for it, but he was happy enough to target Gypsies and Travellers specifically as well. On 20 April 1968, he delivered his infamous 'Rivers of Blood' speech to his constituency association, advancing repatriation of immigrants as the only way to keep Britain peaceful. Local politicians in the Midlands capitalised on Powell's ideas, drawing on them to build opposition to Gypsy and Traveller sites. On 24 June 1970, Staffordshire County Council called a conference on the matter. Councillors representing Walsall called for 'tinkers' to be deported, although they allowed for 'traditional Gypsies' to have a site in the district as long as it was 'under strict control'.

Anti-Traveller residents in the surrounding communities were represented through 'action committees'. These were described in the Municipal and Public Services Journal: 'It is here in Walsall, a town with the dubious claim to fame among the Gypsies of being "the worst borough in the Midlands for Gypsies" that the redoubtable Joe Lunt runs his anti-tinker action group.' In the publication, Lunt himself was quoted as saying: 'The influx of Irish tinkers is the main trouble ... They are dirty and slovenly. But why should any of them, Irish or otherwise, be permitted to camp where they like, pay no rent or rates, and the local ratepayers have to pay for clearing up the mess they leave behind?'[55] Substitute 'council-tax payer' for 'ratepayer' and the language and sentiment of these early action committees – downplayed, these days, to take account of modern sensitivity around charges of racism – might be heard at council meetings on the subject of Meriden or Dale Farm today.

A large-scale eviction had gone forward in Balsall Heath in 1968. In an effort to stop further action, a group of activists formed the West Midlands Gypsy Liaison Group in September 1969. They hoped to increase understanding among the settled, house-dwelling population of the Gypsy and Traveller lifestyle. Soon they were working with the Gypsy Council in conflicts with local-authority security officers, local residents' action groups and the National Front, which had now joined the opposition to unauthorised camping sites in Walsall. Importantly, the group recognised that the treatment of Gypsies was closely linked, especially in the West Midlands, with the treatment of other minorities.[56]

That said, some settled residents were prepared to welcome Gypsies and Travellers, including on local TV 'vox pop' interviews conducted in 1970. One woman said, 'They are human, why shouldn't they have somewhere to live?' Others chimed in: 'It doesn't bother me in the least, I wouldn't mind living next to them at all,' and, 'If they keep the place clean and respectable, that would be fine.' Sure, some sites had been wrecked, but the Gypsies and Travellers should be 'given a chance'. Almost all residents in the interviews agreed that nomads should be given somewhere to live, citing the fact that other communities had taken in Gypsies and Travellers.[57]

Still, Powell honoured his promise to Joe Lunt to resist all so-called aliens, including Gypsies and Travellers. On 11 December 1970, he penned an incendiary article for *The Times*. Gypsies and Travellers should be dealt with 'through the laws of nationality and immigration', he wrote, and the Caravan Sites Act should be repealed. 'No Gypsies' signs began to appear outside pubs, and during the local elections that year, action groups in the Midlands circulated leaflets that incited racial hatred against Irish Travellers.[58]

Eric Lubbock lost his seat in the Commons that year, when his constituency voted Conservative. But he was back in Parliament in 1971, in the House of Lords, having inherited the title Baron Avebury, and he was able to watch with satisfaction when the Caravan Sites Act eventually came into force. 'Local authorities gradually started to comply with the obligation and with great reluctance and as slowly as they could,' he recalled. 'And to carry on with the history there was a clause in the act that allowed the minister for housing and local government to instruct local authorities to provide such numbers of sites as he would specify and that clause was invoked in cases where local authorities were dragging their feet and not providing for a clear need in their area.'

'They didn't start building the sites immediately, there was a lot of … procrastination,' said Lord Avebury. 'But when the minister started to use the power of direction and local authorities saw the way the wind was blowing, to avoid having directions themselves they built sites, and there were several hundred built in the period from 1970 till 1994 … It was not the total solution to the problem, but if it had been allowed to continue it would have made a substantial contribution to the shortfall.'

Despite continuing pockets of resistance, many sites were built. There was a sense that everyone was in this together. 'Psychologically, people in the localities where Gypsy sites were constructed saw [it] as being part of a national enterprise,' he said. 'There was an act of Parliament and the local authorities were pursuing their obligations under that act … People accepted that provision had to be made, the equation between unauthorised sites and the tensions that exist between the Gypsies and Travellers was understood to a national extent … The benefit of the scheme provided by the '68 act was that people clearly saw it as not just operating in one locality but all over the country.'

That buoyed sense of a national obligation to the Gypsies and Travellers would be gone by the 1990s, when the owner of Dale Farm scrap yard looked around for a willing buyer.

Racism towards Irish Travellers remained rife in Ireland, so there was good reason to try to make the most of what little goodwill had come with the Caravan Sites Act. Sections of the Irish media were enthusiastically promulgating stereotypes about Travellers, suggesting that they were a lower caste of society, and often a criminal one. Sinn Féin processions featuring Travellers probably did not help matters. As the Troubles worsened, Irish Catholic Travellers became a popular target. Fianna Fáil lined up against them.

Nan Joyce, whose family had returned to the Republic after a few years in England, began to take a prominent role in resisting the naked racism endured by Travellers. One flashpoint in the struggle came at the Tallaght Bypass. The road had been built near Dublin but had not yet opened, and a group of around a hundred Traveller caravans decided to stop there, because it had hard standing underneath.[59] They had lived there for nearly a year when the county council decided to open the road in 1981 and evicted them. Six families managed to secure an injunction until there could be a full hearing of the case.

Around the same time, a wave of overtly racist activity was plaguing nearby tenants' and residents' associations. Fianna Fáil politicians led a series of marches with the specific objective of physically forcing the Travellers out of Tallaght. Before the first protest, leaflets were distributed advising men to leave women and children at home and to carry camáns, the sticks used in the ancient Gaelic game of hurley. 'When the march came down there was a lot of chanting like the Ku Klux Klan, they were all shouting "Out, out, out,"' Nan recalled.[60] She was, however, also struck by the number of settled people who supported the Travellers' claim for somewhere decent to live. A group quickly formed to respond to the attacks, with Sinn Féin activists, anarchists and others helping the Travellers at Tallaght.[61] Out of this group the Travellers Rights Committee Minceir Misli was formed.

Both Travellers and settled people joined Minceir Misli in order to push back the racist elements in the area. In the 1982 general election Nan ran as a Travellers Rights candidate to oppose a candidate standing on the platform of 'Get the Knackers out of Tallaght'. Though she lost, she secured twice as many first-preference votes in the polling. Then, shortly after the election, Nan was arrested and charged with the theft of jewellery. The media descended on the story – more so than would be usual for an offence of this type. The charges were dropped a few days later when it came out

that the stolen jewellery had been planted on her by the Gardaí –
just as had been done to Grattan Puxon twenty years earlier. The
arrest had a significant effect on Nan. 'People had come to know
me and trust me, and now I felt everything was gone.'[62]

There were some successes in the wake of the Nan Joyce affair.
The Travelling People Review Body was formed in 1983, and the
Housing Act was passed in 1988, which set out a policy of improving caravan sites rather than pushing Travellers into standard
housing. The Housing Act, in particular, signalled a major shift in
attitudes: the authorities were to examine 'the needs of Travellers
who wish to continue a nomadic way of life' and how 'barriers
of mistrust between the settled and Travelling communities can
be broken down and mutual respect for each other's way of life
increased'. Concepts such as absorption and settlement were
rejected in both the Review Body report and the Housing Act,
and the word 'itinerant' was replaced with 'Traveller'.

Yet, several attempts to segregate Travellers continued, as
in the City of Galway Traveller village.[63] And, as Steve Garner,
an expert in racism, points out, while 'racist prejudice against
non-white and non-Christian population segments in Ireland
decreased between the early 1970s and late 1980s … such bias
against Travellers actually increased'.[64]

Hard as life was for the Sheridans and the McCarthys in
England, they didn't want to go back to Ireland, into the eye of
that particular storm.

On the other side of the Irish Sea, the promise to build sites under
the Caravan Sites Act was honoured in the breach. Local authorities found space for Travellers in the worst places they could
find, where nobody else would ever want to live, often between
a sewage farm and a landfill site. In 1977 the author of a government report, Sir John Cripps, the chairman of the Countryside
Commission, found that some forty per cent of all sites were near
industrial areas and rubbish tips. He said: 'No non-Gypsy family
would be expected to live in such places.'[65]

Maggie Smith-Bendell, a Romani Gypsy who has spent many years assisting other members of her community in submitting planning applications, recalls how '[the] sites were built in awkward, often unhygienic places, to suit the *gorgies* [settled people], not the Romanies who were supposed to live on them. Old rubbish tips were grassed over to create sites, old filled-up cemeteries were covered over with tarmac and declared fit for us to live on them. It is so against our culture to sleep and eat and live above the dear dead people, but it was never considered that being forced to stop atop of graves would affect us all. The camps built on top of tips would release methane gas and were soon overrun with vermin. In time we outgrew the camps, which were never planned to take account of our growth'.[66]

Although some two thousand families had been found sites, around five thousand more were still homeless.[67] The policy had met entrenched opposition on the ground. Official government papers released many years later showed that numerous civil servants had privately conceded that the situation was not going to improve, as council after council demanded exemptions from the legislation. The act was deemed to be largely unworkable.[68]

Marilyn Fletcher, a young American volunteer for Save the Children, witnessed some sites being built in the 1970s and 1980s. In St Albans and Bushey, she worked with English Gypsies who had lived by the roadside for years before the county councils were forced to build sites. She remembered how the parents would tell scary stories to their children – 'Very scary stories of haunted roads, murderers, dangerous animals and long-standing feuds. These had been handed down in the families and related to the areas they'd travelled and stopped in,' she said. 'The parents and grandparents were pretty candid about using these stories to ensure that young children didn't stray far from the caravan [or] tent in risky stopping places, including major A-roads like the Watford Bypass, to reduce their worries about racist attacks and fast traffic. I got the impression that this was common amongst Travellers ... and that it worked well.'[69]

She had previously worked with the West Midlands Travellers School, a mobile education service funded by the Van Leer Foundation and based in Walsall, which many considered to be the epicentre of racism towards Irish Travellers. Walsall's new official site had been established at Slacky Lane. The site, she said, was 'a truly dreadful, dismal place, with toxic waste buried under its acres of humps and bumps. The Travellers stopping there were mainly of Irish origin, with just one English Traveller family in pretty much permanent residence. There was no effort on the part of Walsall Council to evict or provide any services to families there, and the children weren't enrolled at any of the local schools. Some of the families were able to access GP and hospital care – mainly pregnant women and young children. But it was as if they were invisible to statutory agencies. The only sympathetic organisation was the local Catholic Church. And there was just one pub that allowed them in. The families stopping there struggled on very low incomes and were for the most part in very poor health – not helped by the toxic environment on the site.'

If this was the state of Gypsies and Travellers lucky enough to be granted a place on an official site, what could a family expect if they were left to their own devices in finding a home? There were not enough legal sites for the nomadic population. If they illegally took up a place on non-toxic green-belt land, they were more than likely to be moved on repeatedly. So some of them took the calculated risk of squatting on land that no one else wanted, hoping that they would not be noticed, or that nobody would care that they were there – as at Dale Farm, the former scrap yard.

Despite the problems, though, Grattan, Thomas Acton and others felt that there had been immense political progress. At the highest levels, both the Irish and British governments had acknowledged that Gypsies and Irish Travellers had a right to live a nomadic lifestyle. They had been delivered a promised land of sorts. But, within twenty years, their dream of a safe place to pull onto was in tatters, due in no small part to the backlash against another growing group of nomads – the so-called New Travellers.

4

NEW TRAVELLERS AND THE EYE OF SAURON

The beginnings of the alternative 'convoy culture' date back to around 1970, when Jimi Hendrix and 700,000 other musicians and fans descended on the Isle of Wight, where the idea of a 'free festival' nomadic lifestyle was born. People began to live in the vehicles they used to travel to the festivals. Wally Hope (Phil Russell), who had a high profile among London squatters, became a central force, helping to establish the Windsor Free Festival and inspiring a similar event at Stonehenge. (Nearly forty years after his death in 1975, one can still hear the call 'Where's Wally?' at festivals.)

The government's understanding of festival culture, outlined in the 1973 Report and Code of Practice from the Department's Advisory Committee on Pop Festivals, was somewhat sketchy. As Alan Dearling, a much-loved chronicler of the festival scene, observed, the official position appeared to be one of wonder: 'It is remarkable that ... hundred of thousands of people, mainly between twelve and thirty, have elected to spend four or five nights at a time under most uncomfortable conditions and sometimes even worse, away from home, tightly packed, listening to music often produced with low quality amplification.' Officials, Dearling demonstrated, were clearly confused, musing: 'Yet at the same time they have found a tremendous feeling of togetherness.'[1]

The reasons why so many so-called 'hippies' became nomads varied. Colin Clark, who comes from a Scottish Traveller background and has also studied travelling groups, has argued that there are in fact three separate generations of New Travellers. The first was linked to the festival circuit, and the related social justice movements of the 1970s, but many of the second- and third-generation Travellers, Clark argues, were people forced onto the road 'seeking refuge from unemployment, hostile government policies and bleak inner-city environments'.[2]

The first generation of course traced its roots to the 1967 'Summer of Love' and the early free festivals, including the first Glastonbury Fayre, which was held the same year that Hendrix electrified the Isle of Wight. There was growing interest in pagan festivals, with people making the pilgrimage to Stonehenge to celebrate the Summer Solstice. A network of fairs in East Anglia, many with long histories, was revived under the name 'Albion Fairs'. These fairs, which mostly involved local people, inspired similar happenings right across Wales and the South-West. The locals were often joined by people with a more radical agenda – the emergent Peace Convoy. Sometimes they got along. Sometimes – particularly in East Anglia at the most-loved first Albion Fairs – some local people resented them.

It was 'a sort of decentred, autonomous counterculture', said George Mackay, an activist and scholar of the period.[3] 'If you were unemployed during those summers you'd follow the Albion trail from fair to fair, in your own truck or bus, if you had one,' he wrote. 'The sense of locality, of landscape, of rural tradition and history was central ... The British countryside, ignored since the Romantics, since Hardy and the Edwardians, was claiming back some territory [and] interrogating the limits of enclosure.' Some of that spirit came alive in the Peace Convoy. As Mackay explained: 'Many Travellers identify a local or national free festival as the pivotal moment, when the possibility of a kind of change, of something different, was glimpsed, when energy, a good time and some sort of community became woven together, within reach ... As well as rejection and exclusion, Travellers emphasise the attraction of the New Age Traveller lifestyle, as in the Romantic pleasure of rural living.'[4]

But people had also discovered, like many ethnic nomads before them, that living on the road offered economic opportunities too, especially in these days when youth unemployment was soaring.[5] Social security changes in 1988, which denied many sixteen- and seventeen-year-olds access to benefits, as well as the introduction of the Poll Tax, drove more people onto the road. In an in-depth survey of ninety-eight New Age Travellers carried out by the Children's Society, two-thirds said they had been forced into travelling by financial difficulties, relationship breakdowns, leaving care or prison, and insecure housing. Almost one-third said that homelessness was the main factor in their decision, while another third had made a positive choice to go travelling.[6] As one sociologist noted, many New Travellers are 'akin to Baumann's vagabonds who are "on the move because they have been pushed from behind – spiritually uprooted from the place that holds no promise"'.[7]

Tony Thomson, now one of the trustees of the charity Families, Friends and Travellers, himself took to the road in 1981. He had just returned from abroad, where he had been travelling. Only later did he learn that his family had a Scottish Traveller background. These were good times as well as bad times, he recalled. 'In 1984 we ended up travelling on a convoy through the West Country and we were on our way to Corfe Castle, and it was like a cavalcade going through Yeovil, we were dancing and putting on a show, we were a kind of travelling show of odd buses, outlandish vehicles and colourful people.'[8]

The atmosphere darkened as more and more people, driven by poverty, flooded onto the roads, particularly after hard drugs became a part of the scene, mainly through a group loosely called the 'Special Brew Crew'. 'Basically what happened was that in the eighties a lot of people came out into the road without a heritage of common sense. They had been disinherited through enclosures and social fragmentation, so were in the main without a culture, but searching for one nonetheless. What was on offer, a nihilistic and selfish anarchism, was at odds with a commons sensibility. The commons won't sustain that, and people won't help them and they won't make the effort to establish relationships that are sustainable and help them through,' Thomson said. 'A lot of them fell by the wayside. Rave wasn't the problem but speed and other chemicals made people into monsters. [The drugs] destroy [nomadic] communities, just as they have done in urban areas … It affected everybody.'

With more drugs being used by some on New Traveller sites, the lifestyle of all nomads came under scrutiny. There were more conflicts between Gypsies and Travellers and the residents in the settled community. Even if very few were part of the drug scene, they were all suddenly tainted with suspicion, Thomson recalled: there was 'litter, dogs, bad relations … These guys would stay on sites as long as they could, get evicted and then [the] site would get "bunded" up' – with big mounds of earth mounded up around it, to make it inaccessible. This, he said, 'was a loss for everybody, because the state tended to impose indiscriminate sanctions'.

Roxy Freeman, a Traveller, recalled the change in atmosphere when a Special Brew Crew convoy came to an area. 'Their way of life was very different to ours. They were loud, anarchistic, alcohol-fuelled people [who] were rebelling against society and had a point to make. They'd travel in massive groups, take over places and refuse to leave without a fight.'[9] The Brew Crew brought the ire of the police, public and media down onto all Travellers. The *Western Daily Press* of 3 May 1993 ran with the headline, "The Return of the Rat Pack" – and they fully intended to compare the Brew Crew families to vermin, not Frank Sinatra.

Clashes between New Travellers and the police also escalated in the 1980s as the anti-Thatcher Peace Convoy – not linked to the hedonistic Brew Crew – grew in numbers. Margaret Thatcher's Conservative government responded in keeping with its strong 'law and order' reputation – they brought down overwhelming force. A crackdown began in earnest in 1984. One of the first and most heavy-handed police operations involved a peaceful New Travellers encampment at Norstell Priory near Wakefield in Yorkshire. The police who were deployed there came fresh from attending the miners' strike. Tony Thomson was caught up in that particular operation: 'Something like two thousand police attacked us with truncheons and drove vehicles into the camp at high speed,' he recalled. Their homes were systematically trashed and their belongings destroyed by the police – but the New Travellers were not deterred.

Another incident occurred at Cannock Chase. 'We were leaving the site and travelling down the M6. The police commandeered lorries, shut down the M6 and drove through the convoy in articulated lorries, trying to break us up,' Thomson recounted.

In February 1985, a well-established Traveller site, the Rainbow Village at Molesworth, on a disused air base in Cambridgeshire, was next evicted – graced by the presence of Secretary of State for Defence Michael Heseltine, kitted out in a flak jacket. The army was called in to remove the Travellers in the largest military operation since the Second World War.

George Mackay argues that the defeat of the miners – the first set of 'enemies within', as Margaret Thatcher described them – demanded yet 'another enemy, an easier one to flex its muscles at'.[10] The extent of the secret war against left-wing groups under Thatcher only really emerged many years later, in 2012, when a memo was released revealing that a secret army intelligence unit had been set up to infiltrate and destabilise these groups, which the Prime Minister considered to be a danger to national security.[11]

The most infamous campaign, however, was still to come. The army called it Operation Daybreak, but it became better known as the 'Battle of the Beanfield', which broke out on Saturday, 1 June 1985.[12] The year before, some fifty thousand people had come to celebrate the Summer Solstice at Stonehenge, a gathering that had been going on for eleven consecutive years. English Heritage took out an injunction in 1985 to prevent people from approaching the sacred stones, which they believed to be an endangered national monument. With the Solstice approaching, around six hundred Travellers in around 140 vehicles set off towards Stonehenge to attend what they thought would be the annual free festival beside the stones. Many of them were veterans of the evictions of the last two years. A few hours into their journey, the convoy was ambushed by more than 1,300 police officers from six counties. Police intelligence had suggested that the Travellers were armed – but this was faulty. After a first wave of violent assaults by the police, in which windscreens were smashed and occupants dragged out screaming onto the road, most of the vehicles broke into a neighbouring field, derailing the police force's plan.

Eyewitness accounts – from two journalists, Travellers themselves and the Earl of Cardigan, who allowed the Travellers to camp on his land – all substantiate a tale of overwhelming police brutality. The Earl of Cardigan said, 'One image will probably stay with me for the rest of my life. I saw a policeman hit a woman on the head with his truncheon. Then I looked down and saw she was pregnant and I thought, "My God, I'm watching police who are running amok."' Nick Davies, a journalist from the *Observer*, was travelling with the convoy; he remembered the attack as a 'chaotic whirl of violence'. As Richard Lowe and William Shaw put it, it was 'a watershed in the history of confrontation between police and Travellers'.[13]

Dozens of Travellers were injured, and all but a handful were arrested. Every one of the vehicles in the convoy was destroyed. Eventually compensation was awarded to twenty-four plaintiffs, although the money they received from the police was completely absorbed by their legal costs.

Despite the failure of Operation Daybreak, a year later the police were involved in yet another confrontation, this time at Stoney Cross. They adopted two even more draconian tactics: taking the Travellers' children into care and impounding vehicles in what Lowe and Shaw call an attempt to 'decommission the lifestyle'.[14] The McCarthys and the Sheridans remembered that, when they later faced down the eviction at Dale Farm. All the Irish Traveller women chose to keep their children close to them – away from school – during the eviction, fearing zealous social workers.

In the aftermath of the Battle of the Beanfield, other nomads felt the crush from the authorities. Roxy Freeman recalled her time in Shropshire shortly after the operation. 'The Battle of the Beanfield ... was only a few years past, and although we were only one family, and not a convoy of Travellers and vehicles like the ones in Wiltshire, we still felt the suspicion that settled people, and the police, held towards us. Travellers, Gypsies – we were all the same to them – meant trouble.'[15] But the New Travellers refused to go away – despite police operations against them, including Operation Nomad, an intelligence drive mounted to build up a database about them and the growing rave scene in the early 1990s. Save the Children estimated that the figures had grown to some fifty thousand by the early 1990s.[16]

Shortly thereafter, the Thatcher government moved to galvanise opposition to the New Travellers. On 5 June 1986, at the Conservative Party conference, the Prime Minister promised that she would 'make things difficult for such things as hippy convoys'. Later that year the government announced the Public Order Bill, which criminalised trespassing and travelling in a convoy. The government claimed the bill was aimed to discourage the lifestyle of New Travellers, not that of Gypsies. The Home Secretary, Douglas Hurd, referred to New Travellers as 'a band of medieval brigands who have no respect for law and order and the rights of others' during debate on the bill in Parliament.[17] Hurd went on to stress: 'No one wants to criminalise the activities of a group of ramblers, and no one wants to harass genuine gipsies.' But the damage was immediate and unarguable – there was no way under the law to distinguish a Gypsy or Traveller convoy from a New Traveller one. And the Conservatives didn't stand down from their assault with the passage of the act.

In the run-up to the next general election, on 11 June 1987, Conservative party candidate after candidate hurled the Gypsy issue into debates in order to win votes. In March, Peter Lilley, MP for St Albans, announced that no more Gypsy sites should be permitted in green belt or residential areas because the public did not want to live 'cheek by jowl' with these apparently undesirable elements. He was careful to exclude the influx of 'Irish *didicois*' from his attacks; these people were different, in his view, and should not be classed as Gypsies. Another MP, Hugh Rossi, claimed that his constituents suffered 'horrendous problems because of an invasion of the area by so-called Gypsies'. Party officials in Bradford were seen handing out stickers for cars bearing the message 'Keep the Gypsies Out – Vote Conservative'. After protests, the stickers were withdrawn.[18]

Backbench Conservative MPs were happy with the provisions of the Public Order Act, but they wanted to go further still. Their constituents, many of them in rural areas, were complaining that Gypsies and other 'itinerants' had 'invaded' their beautiful villages and were making a mess. The orchestration of talking points was conspicuous, as seen in a study by Royce Turner, who analysed parliamentary language about Gypsies and Travellers around that time and then again about ten years later.[19] Turner observed that many MPs used strikingly similar language to describe Gypsies and Travellers – they spoke of them being dirty or defiling places, of invading, of being criminals.

Ann Widdecombe, who was in 1989 a backbench MP, but who later became a Home Office minister, raised the subject twice in just one year. In the second debate, ostensibly about dangerous dogs, she linked Gypsies to anti-social behaviour, accusing local Gypsies of stealing dogs. 'There are also considerable implications concerning the control of dogs and illegal acts connected with them in respect of itinerants', she said.[20] There were quite a number of unauthorised sites in her district, she reported, and then went on the attack: 'We have a rather romantic view of gipsies [sic]. We think of people travelling in a painted caravan, telling fortunes and selling heather. The reality of the people encamped illegally is that they do not use their caravans purely for residential purposes. They are also carrying out a trade, quite often an illegal one, in the area surrounding the encampment. Breaking up of metal, tinkers' business and other such trades are frequently practised. They all cause a great deal of mess, particularly where there are no proper arrangements for disposal of sewage from the

caravans or proper rubbish disposal. There is no proper arrangement for disposal of trade waste, which builds up and is extremely
detrimental to the environment, particularly to a beautiful part
of Kent. Even where they are not directly responsible for assaults
on the population, the behaviour of itinerants is a problem. Dogs
and cats regularly disappear from nearby areas to these encampments.' The junior minister replying referred to the Public Order
Act: 'It was not intended to be used against gipsies, but if gipsies
fall within the circumstances described in Section 39 they can be
dealt with under the act.'[21]

By the time of the 1992 general election, New Travellers were
again high on the political agenda. John Major claimed that combating them would be a priority for his new government. In late
May a free rave and festival was staged at Castlemorton Common
in West Mercia, attracting twenty thousand people. Rather than
arrest the masses on their way to the event, the police decided
to wait until after the partying had annoyed local residents and
damaged the fields. The media coverage depicted a scene that was
out of control. It played straight into the government's hands.

Immediately after the election, the Home Office and the
Department of the Environment issued a press release announcing the intention to reform the 1968 Caravan Sites Act. In fact,
Major mostly wanted to repeal the obligation for local authorities
to provide or maintain Traveller sites. A Conservative party press
release, dated 27 March 1992, stated this goal clearly. 'Whilst
some Travellers behave responsibly and live happily on authorised
sites, far too many do not. The public expect the government to
take decisive action to bring this nuisance to an end. We will,
therefore, review the present legislation.'[22]

Academic Robbie McVeigh has charted the way in which the
media played its part in whipping up a perfect storm against New
Travellers as well as other nomads.[23] Among the worst offenders
he cites are the *Sun,* which in August 1992 exhorted: 'Hippy
Scroungers must get jobs or starve'. The following summer, the

Daily Star wrote of '£1m wasted on scum' and its leader column demanded 'the scum army should be told they can only collect in John O'Groats. After crawling over broken glass'. Michael Colvin MP wrote of Travellers as 'unwashed scroungers'. McVeigh concludes: 'New Travellers have become the subject of an intensifying moral panic in Britain and Ireland. Constructed as a plague or blight, these nomads have come to be regarded as the bane of "decent folk" in the 1990s.'[24] A great moral panic was taking hold. Criminal elements were taking over – and they had to be stopped.

The government duly responded. In 1994 Michael Howard, the Home Secretary, introduced what he called 'the most comprehensive package of measures to tackle crime ever announced by a Home Secretary'.[25] The proposed Criminal Justice and Public Order Act contained 172 sections, covering everything from anti-terrorist measures to recognition for male rape. Most pressing to the Gypsy and Traveller communities, Section 80 effectively tore up Lord Avebury's Caravan Sites Act.

The Labour party abstained from the debate. They would not be a party to such a draconian piece of legislation. It was left to the House of Lords to try to amend it. They proceeded section by section. They expected difficulty with Section 80, though, since the government had consulted on its plans for the bill and had received a huge response from local authorities against its plans to 'reform' the laws affecting Gypsies and Travellers – and still the government refused to listen. In their overview of the act, Luke Clements and Sue Campbell state 'ninety-three per cent of county councils, ninety-two per cent of London boroughs and metropolitan authorities and seventy-one per cent of district councils responding believed the government's proposals will increase rather than reduce the number of illegal encampments'.[26] The government stated that there was nothing useful in the replies to the consultation.

The Association of Chief Police Officers went public with their opposition to Section 80. They sent a letter to the Labour Campaign for Travellers' Rights announcing that, in their opinion, the general effect of the legislation would be to 'criminalise the act of living in a caravan'. The Country Landowners Association, the National Farmers' Union and the National Trust also joined the fray. Memorably, the *Journal of the Police Federation* described the proposals embedded in the bill as 'at best a knee-jerk reaction to the government's wish to be seen to be doing something about this year's particular problem. At worst they can be construed as direct discrimination against a minority – a discrimination that would not be tolerated if Gypsies were black, came from another country, or were homosexual'. There were massive demonstrations, local events and direct action to oppose the bill, but the government would not stand down. The number of vehicles needed to commit 'collective trespass' was reduced to six. Lord Avebury watched as his life's work was destroyed.

Yet some Gypsies, Travellers and their supporters couldn't decide to what extent they should mobilise against the bill. To many, the legislation was directed at New Travellers, not at them. 'The backlash against New Travellers affected all of them,' Avebury said. 'Yet there was a schizophrenia about it.' Would 'sticking up for the New Travellers … muddy the waters and cause greater hostility'? Avebury went on: 'People would say if anyone adopted this lifestyle as a voluntary decision then they should fend for themselves. There wasn't the same obligation towards them as to people who had traditional lifestyles that depended on living in caravans.' One diary entry from George Mackay, dated 1995, recalls a meeting with two Romani Gypsies on their way up to Appleby Fair. 'They are hard-working men who despise these [New Travellers] for their sponging, their laziness, their filthy lifestyles, their provocative flouting of the laws of the land, their drug taking, their music, the way they rip up hedges for firewood … I couldn't have got a more negative reaction from talking to the members of a Conservative Association or the National Farmers' Union in Wiltshire!'[27]

This annoyance at the attention that the New Travellers had brought on nomadism was understandable, but the Criminal Justice Act threatened the survival of all nomads. As Michael Howard said, as the bill passed into law on 3 November 1994:

'New powers will [now] be at [police] disposal for dealing with public order such as raves, gathering of New Age Travellers and mass trespass, which can be a blight for individuals and local communities.'[28]

The act, predictably, was a disaster for all of Britain's nomads. Even the shortest of stays at a traditional stopping place was now a criminal offence, potentially leading to fines and even prison sentences for the convicted. Lord Avebury had 'strenuously opposed' Section 80 since it did not provide accommodation for Gypsies and Travellers anywhere in the country. 'I kept asking what was going to happen to the construction or development of sites. I kept receiving vague assurances that the government knew that the provision would be looked after by private enterprise but of course there was no evidence for that and that didn't happen.' His fears proved right. There was a long period after 1994 when, apart from the few sites that were already in the pipeline, there were no developments at all. It was, as the writer George Monbiot termed it, the modern equivalent of an act of enclosure.

With the Criminal Justice and Public Order Act in place, the battered remnants of the New Traveller convoys regrouped as they could. Many moved abroad, to live and work in Ireland, France, Spain, Portugal, even as far afield as India and North Africa. Others, Tony Thomson said, found alternative ways to get by. 'People who were still together, they survived, they found quiet corners because they had the social skills to keep the peace. They found quiet corners in the UK, more tucked away,' he said. 'They are more static now, and really there is only any movement over the festival season' – especially for events such as the Big Green Gathering, the Endorse-it and the Levellers' Beautiful Days. But for the most part, the convoy days are long gone. 'Now you can't travel in a group so easily because you are visible,' Thomson explained.

Some have chosen to live more visibly, despite the complaints they sometimes encounter. The Horsedrawns use horse- and human-drawn transport and run some small festivals frequented by settled people. The Boaters have taken to the water and live on canal boats, reviving the ancient customs of Britain's Water Gypsies. Some, such as the Dongas Tribe, became key figures in anti-roads campaigns, particularly at Twyford Down, where they protested the extension of the M3 motorway in 1992, and Solsbury Hill in the late 1990s, after which most of the band emigrated to France in order to continue their travelling lifestyle. Others have inspired low-impact living with developments such as the Tipi Valley in Dyfed, Wales, which was first established in 1974, and Tinker's Bubble in Somerset.

In 2000, fifteen years after the injunction, English Heritage finally reopened Stonehenge to the public at the Solstice. Seven thousand people attended. But the monument was under strict control. New Travellers would not be given free rein.

By then, another group of nomads was drawing the baleful eye of Sauron. Gypsies and Travellers still needed places to live and work. Essex, in particular, was home to many of England's Gypsies as well as a growing number of Irish Travellers who were dealing in scrap and trading, often between the UK and Ireland.

Scrap dealing was quickly identified as an undesirable business. In 1992 Basildon Borough Council brought proceedings against Ray Bocking, the scrap-yard dealer whose property abutted Crays Hill. The scrap yard was illegal, the council alleged, and infringed on the green belt. In 1994 the council won its case, and Bocking had declared himself bankrupt. Irish Travellers – including the Sheridan and McCarthy families – were already visiting the area, looking for work and places to live, often just finding a place to stay for a few days at a time. The former scrap yard was already covered in much hard standing, because of its previous use – a great convenience when pulling on with a caravan. Some of the Travellers were eyeing up the land. This did not go unnoticed by beady-eyed local politicians.

In 1995, in an adjournment debate, the subject of these Essex-based nomads was raised in Parliament – the first time anyone had raised the issue of Dale Farm there. Teresa Gorman, the MP for Crays Hill, the nearest village to the settlement, proclaimed that Gypsies were a 'great problem' in Essex. 'The public clearly wanted something done about the menace of these itinerants, or gipsies [sic], or *didicois*, or tinkers, or new age travellers, or mobile totters, which is what they are. There was a huge sigh of relief in November last year when the Criminal Justice and Public Order Act was finally passed, because it seemed as though something was to be done at last. We were grateful in the part of Thurrock and Billericay that I have the honour to represent.'[29] She went on to share her version of their history: 'They travel from southern Ireland, in particular, and spend their summer holidays visiting the tips in Essex. They collect and sort garbage and leave the detritus behind them on the fields. Essex is invaded by Travellers in the summer, and we fear that the police may continue to refuse to deal with the problem.'

In reply, the junior minister, Robert Jones, thanked Gorman for raising the issue of the Travellers who have 'purchased land at Crays Hill, Basildon' and also acknowledged Eric Pickles, who represented neighbouring Brentwood, 'who has tirelessly campaigned for his constituents on this and other issues'.

The moral panic over New Travellers affected all of Britain's nomads. Irish Travellers were now firmly in the firing line. The first few years of New Labour's government, from 1997 onwards, didn't make things any better for them.

5

THINGS CAN ONLY GET BETTER

In 1997 a Labour government was elected. At Stringfellows night club, ashen-faced Young Conservatives watched the results come in: their party had lost power for the first time in nearly twenty years – for many, the Conservatives had been in power for their whole lives. As the mood in Britain changed, so did the soundtrack. DRream's 'Things Can Only Get Better' became the anthem of Tony Blair's new Labour government. The question would be, Better for whom? As a way of making a swift point of their answer, 'New Labour' began a campaign to rebuild Britain's battered public sector and welfare state. But over the next five years, they did little or nothing to help Mary Ann McCarthy and the other families at Dale Farm. Making things better for Britain's nomads, it seemed, was a policy step too far.

In the first years after the turn of the millennium, the rhetoric against Gypsies and Travellers was becoming hostile – including in Parliament. Numerous debates were held – including seven debates and written questions between November 1999 and March 2000 alone. In one legendary 2002 debate, Conservative MP Andrew Mackay, who would later step down from Parliament after being embroiled in the parliamentary expenses scandal of 2010, referred to the Gypsies in his Berkshire constituency: 'They are scum, and I use the word advisedly. People who do what these people have done do not deserve the same human rights as my constituents going about their everyday lives.'[1]

It wasn't just the Conservatives who were making it clear that the Gypsies and Travellers who had come to live in Britain were unwelcome. Jack Straw, the Home Secretary, launched a wide-ranging attack on what he called 'fake' Gypsies in an interview for BBC Radio West Midlands. 'There are relatively few real Romani Gypsies left, who seem to mind their own business and don't cause trouble to other people,' he said. 'And then there are a lot more people who masquerade as Travellers or Gypsies, who trade on the sentiment of people, but who seem to think, because they label themselves as Travellers, that therefore they've got a licence to commit crimes and act in an unlawful way that other people don't have.' Straw later wrote of Gypsies going 'burgling, thieving, breaking into vehicles, causing all kinds of trouble, including defecating in the doorways of firms'.[2] He differentiated between 'real' Gypsies – people, it seemed, who were never seen, living on air like the fairies and leaving their neighbours in peace – and 'fake' Travellers. And just as it had been forty years earlier on the outskirts of Birmingham, it was the Irish Travellers who were coming under scrutiny. As Straw peddled his views on the radio, Patrick Egan and John Sheridan were buying up the land that would become Dale Farm, and starting to raise a fuss among the villagers of Basildon.

It seemed to many in the Gypsy and Traveller community as though old Victorian morals were being resurrected under New Labour. They had saved up money – a lot of money – to buy the pitches for their homes, and now many, particularly the women, were desperate to settle down and make some kind of home. New Labour might as well have 'reinvented the Victorian concepts of the "deserving" and "undeserving" poor', in the words of Irish Traveller scholar Colm Power.

In May 2003 Gypsies and Travellers were horrified when a fifteen-year-old Irish Traveller boy, Johnny Delaney, was killed by two other teenagers – motivated, it appears, according to witness evidence, by hatred for his ethnicity.[3] It was a grievous, unprovoked attack, but unlike the murder of Stephen Lawrence, a black teenager, almost exactly a decade earlier, it did not cause a national outcry. The people at Dale Farm took note. Even more frightening, however, was the rejoicing found in many newspapers when Tony

Martin, who had shot a young English Gypsy in the back as he was running away after a bungled burglery, had his sentence reduced by the Court of Appeal in July 2001 and was set free in 2003.

Just four months later Gypsies and Travellers were left reeling in horror when residents attending the Firle Bonfire Guy Fawkes celebrations in 2003 burned a caravan with pictures of Gypsies inside painted on it.[4] The vehicle's number plate read 'P1KEY'. The caravan was at the centre of a dispute with Travellers that had started earlier in the year. They were further dismayed when the bonfire participants were to some extent excused by their local MP, Norman Baker, at the time a member of the parliamentary Joint Committee on Human Rights, who said the Sussex residents were upset because 'itinerant criminals' had damaged local land and property; a degree of anger was understandable, he explained.[5] The organisers, Firle Bonfire Society, denied any racism was involved, and in a statement published on the group's website, the chairman, Richard Gravett, said their intentions had been 'misunderstood and misrepresented'. Their target was not Gypsies, but local authorities, 'whose lack of action had caused so much frustration locally'.[6] (Baker later worked hard with all sides to try and increase understanding of diversity issues.)

Around the same time that the Firle Bonfire Society was putting flame to Gypsy effigies, the National Farmers Union produced a report entitled *Britain's Rural Outlaws*, in which they described Gypsies and Travellers as 'well equipped, extremely organised and above the law'. The issue was urgent: 'the problem of illegal Travellers is now so bad that the majority of farmers have been affected in some way', the NFU said. The complaints were warmly praised by Conservative MPs.[7]

But the Commission for Racial Equality was not going to let that be the last say in the debate. Its chairman, Trevor Phillips, said the burning was a clear example of incitement to racial hatred, a crime carrying a maximum sentence of seven years. 'You couldn't get more provocative than this,' he said in a piece for the *Western Morning Press*. 'The UK for Gypsies is still like the American Deep South for black people in the 1950s.' The

next year he appointed the first ever Romani Gypsy commissioner, Charles Smith, to the commission, with the aim of creating a strategy specifically to combat discrimination against the
communities.[8]

Inside the Gypsy and Traveller movement, some remained furious
that some of the New Age Travellers had brought the fury of the
public, the press and Parliament upon them. Why should it be
illegal for them to use their traditional stopping places? It was the
New Age Travellers who were the problem, and for that reason,
many wanted nothing to do with them. Indeed, New Travellers
had been forced to form their own advocacy groups, the most
influential being Families, Friends and Travellers, which had
become a registered charity in 1999. (FFT is now much respected,
and supports Gypsies and Travellers from all backgrounds and
ethnicities.) 'It was left to the New Travellers to conduct their
own campaigns,' Lord Avebury, who had championed the Caravan
Sites Act in 1968, said. 'They didn't form part of any of these
movements really, so it was seen as a separate issue, because the
definition of Gypsies and Travellers for certain purposes is an
ethnic definition, although in planning terms it is a bit ambiguous.'
Government officials began to suggest that the various travelling
communities be classified. As Lord Avebury said, 'There is talk,
as you know, of harmonising the definitions, so they are the same
for planning and other purposes.' The confusion in the settled
community about those adopting the convoy way of life 'wasn't
helpful' to Gypsies and Travellers.

Meanwhile, in the Commons, there was both progress and
backsliding. In 2002 and again in 2003, the Conservative MP for
Bournemouth East, David Atkinson, introduced the Traveller Law
Reform Bill as a Private Members' Bill — with the best of intentions, but obviously in hopes of generating debate rather than
of changing the law. The bill called for the reintroduction of a
statutory duty on local authorities to provide sites for Gypsies
and Travellers — including New Travellers.

Atkinson and Lord Avebury helped to mobilise the Gypsies and Travellers as one combined movement. An umbrella campaign group, the Gypsy and Traveller Law Reform Coalition, was formed to support Atkinson's bill. This was soon followed by the establishment of the All-Party Gypsy and Traveller Law Reform Group. Still, New Labour was too nervous to adopt the Traveller Law Reform Bill as draft government legislation. Instead, the government continued to pursue their own 'bi-partisan approach' to the Gypsy and Traveller accommodation problem.

In 2005, Tony Blair met John Baron, the local MP from Dale Farm, to discuss the situation there, and New Labour ministers made noises about the need to control anti-social behaviour around Gypsy and Traveller sites. They were willing to make one small concession, however: they would issue new guidance to force local authorities to strengthen their policies around identifying suitable sites. There was good practice embedded within this policy reform – but it did not please everyone. For instance, in the Housing Act 2004 the government required local authorities to tackle the reasons behind unauthorised encampments and establish an inventory of pitch needs. This enraged many local Conservative politicians, particularly when the government issued the first directive based on the new guidance to Brentwood Council, which was in many ways 'next door' to Basildon, with its largest Traveller settlement in the nation.

Brentwood Council had been avoiding identifying alternative sites for Gypsies and Travellers through what was known as a 'criterion-based policy'.[9] It had been challenged four times by local Gypsies about this stance. Essex Conservatives were further irked when a Brentwood Gypsy Support group, first founded in 1987, was re-formed to take up the fight. The Brentwood Gypsies were pursuing new sites with energy under the aegis of Thomas Acton, who had become such an influential figure in the activist movement, alongside Grattan Puxon and Donald Kenrick. For years Acton had charted the social, political and artistic growth of Britain's Gypsies and Travellers from his post at the University of Greenwich. He had also watched the rise of Roma activism in Europe.

That one small Labour initiative spelled the end of bi-partisan strategy towards Gypsies and Travellers. Essex Conservatives had friends on high. Eric Pickles, the Brentwood and Ongar MP, was a rising star in the Conservative Party and by 2002 had been named the Shadow Local Government and Regions Secretary.[10] He had long campaigned against what he saw as special privileges for Gypsies and Travellers, and now he had the ear of the party elite. Gearing up for the next general election, set for 2005, the Tories, led by Michael Howard, took up the Gypsy and Traveller 'problem' with fervour. Public opposition built up, as the tabloid press came in line as their loud hailer.[11] Howard took out full-page advertisements on the matter in every national Sunday newspaper: 'I believe in fair play,' he said in the adverts, claiming that in Britain there was 'one rule for Travellers and another for everyone else'. He criticised Travellers for using human rights laws – something that many Conservatives deplored (and still deplore) with a passion – to use their right to family life to protect their right to live on illegal sites.[12] Howard went on: 'I don't believe in special rules for special interest groups.' But then, in an almost farcical turn, he proposed a 'Gypsy law', which would make trespass a criminal rather than a civil offence, and promised that he would give police new powers to evict illegal occupiers fast. He pointed to the example of the Irish Republic, where a similar measure had led to a drop in illegal sites. Of course, after the Irish law had passed, many Travellers had moved to the UK, looking for a place to live. A law like that would leave the McCarthys and Sheridans at Dale Farm with nowhere to go.

Labour could have backed down, but instead it found new courage. By now the government was coming under increasing pressure from the Commission for Racial Equality, where Charles Smith had recently come on board and soon began to push the cause of Gypsy and Traveller rights. There were complaints to the Metropolitan Police and other forces that the media campaign may constitute illegal incitement to racist violence.[13] In May 2005, New Labour won the election, but with only sixty-six seats – a far cry from the huge majorities of 1997 and 2001. They were still in power, but they needed to find a way forward on the issue. Demands were now also coming from the European courts, after the successful win of Connors vs UK, which observed that Gypsies and Travellers, as a vulnerable ethnic minority, needed 'special consideration' for their needs before eviction proceedings were taken.[14] For his part, Pickles was promoted to Deputy Chairman of the Conservative Party.

John Prescott, by then Deputy Prime Minister, recalled: 'As early as 1997 I had Rodney Bickerstaffe [general secretary of the trade union Unison], saying to me, "Here's a job you need to do." I also knew from my own constituency that there was a shortage of sites. And then there was Dale Farm, and I knew that the temporary stay there wasn't enough, we needed to get all councils to provide spaces for our mobile populations. A lot of people in those communities wanted their children to have an education. So I got on with it, I was the planning minister so I had authority to do it, I couldn't be challenged on planning.'

Prescott had some sympathy with Basildon Council, feeling that it had provided more places for Travellers than other, neighbouring councils, such as Brentwood. 'They had a legitimate complaint, but we needed to try and solve the problem properly. I had John Baron [the local MP] coming to me, saying, "Let's send in the troops, move them on." I didn't think that was the way to solve the problem. This was a housing problem, and a job that needed to be done.'

So Prescott, along with a junior minister in the Department of Communities and Local Government named Yvette Cooper, started to take soundings among Gypsy and Traveller organisations about the possibility of reviving the policy of forcing local authorities to provide sites. The new plans would be consummated in Circular 1/2006, released in February of that year. Maggie Smith-Bendell, a Romani Gypsy, was one of those consulted by the government's Gypsy and Traveller Unit. 'We had many more meetings before the new circular came into force, but finally it did,' she said. 'There would be no more retrospective planning applications ... This new guidance gave councils no quarter and had to be abided by. The only things that worried me were that there was still a shortage of suitable, affordable land, and that the opposition of local communities seemed to be stepping up all the time.'[15] It had taken New Labour three terms – nearly a decade – to get to this point, despite the fact that the party had opposed the repeal of the Caravan Sites Act 1968.

Gypsy and Traveller advocates were delighted, nonetheless. Circular 1/2006 didn't just require local authorities to allocate sufficient sites for Gypsies and Travellers, it budgeted around £150 million over five years to pay for the process. It also emphasised that action should be taken only where unauthorised sites were the source of anti-social behaviour. The first step would be to commission 'Gypsy and Travellers Accommodation Needs Assessments' (GTANAs) in local authorities across the country. At the same time, the Equality and Human Rights Commission published a report, 'Common Ground', arguing for an assessment of Gypsy and Traveller pitches.

Progress was slow, but a few families started to win planning appeals under the new guidance. A small number set up their own new, private sites, although local people often objected vociferously to these sites being built in their back yard.

Around this time, another nomadic enemy was appearing in the sightlines of Middle England – Roma from the 2003 EU Treaty of Accession countries, including the Czech Republic, Hungary, Poland, Slovakia and Slovenia. Romanians came later, starting in 2007, when the nation joined the EU. They were even poorer than the Czech and Slovak Roma. Some of these new migrants made their way to Govanhill, in the south of Glasgow, and there are now thought to be around fifteen thousand Roma in Govanhill.

Govanhill is one of the poorest areas of the city. Over the past century, it has received several waves of immigrants – Irish, Pakistani and Somali being the most numerous among the newcomers. But the rapid arrival of Roma from the Slovak Republic, where many had been deprived of the right to citizenship and had experienced persecution and violence, was particularly difficult for the already stretched local services to accommodate. In the span of three years, around 2,500 Roma had arrived. 'The people on the ground hadn't really experienced it – I mean all the services on the ground,' said Chief Inspector Steve McAllister of Strathclyde Police. 'We had previously seen an influx of asylum seekers in the north end of the city, and initially that was managed really poorly, then we got a grip on it in terms of support, which helped integration. But the Roma exercising their rights as EU nationals under European migration rights just turned up.'[16]

McAllister described policing the subdivision as challenging. 'I'd say that at least forty per cent are non-white, and out of the remaining sixty per cent a substantial amount are from a minority group. It sometimes feels like the current situation in Govanhill was created as a malevolent social experiment to see how the service providers would cope.' There were unmistakable social and cultural issues at the outset, McAllister said. 'The Roma came with a different, *al fresco* lifestyle, with large family groups and singing and dancing in the middle of the night.' The people who had for years made their homes in Govanhill were disconcerted by such behaviour. 'On Allison Street [the centre of Govanhill] it can be like walking into a different country in the summer, with around four hundred, five hundred people out in the middle of the street … mainly young men. They are usually just shooting the breeze, but if you are a middle-aged white female and you have lived all your life in Govanhill, then you turn into a corner and all you see is foreign faces, your natural reaction is, "I don't like this."' He estimated that in about twelve blocks of the town's housing, some forty different nationalities were represented and fifty-one languages spoken.

In March 2007 violence erupted on Dixon Avenue, also near the centre of Govanhill. It had apparently started when some local white youths racially abused several newly arrived Roma teenagers; some locals said that the violence had been building for a year previously.[17] All sides agreed that things were calmer now, but McAllister reported that (unfounded) rumours about criminality in the Roma community still swirled. 'It almost became acceptable to blame the Roma for all the ills of Govanhill, with some of the rumours being utterly ridiculous, relating to baby factories and children being sold on street corners for prostitution, and people buy into these rumours. You know it's rubbish but there is a lot of very negative mood music and we spend a lot of time at public meetings challenging them.' The crime rate, police confirmed, had in fact gone down since the Roma came to town.

McAllister pays tribute to the strength and vibrancy of the communities, which are somehow managing to come together despite their extraordinary diversity. The Roma, for their part, have started to settle. 'You don't get any really significant issues with racism. There were complaints about the *al fresco* singing and dancing, and the people out on the streets, but they have reduced. Having said that, the Roma community have moderated their behaviour. They accept now that it's not really the thing to do at 1am in the morning, out in the back court.'

The real problems came from their living conditions. The Roma were almost immediately preyed upon by slum landlords and gangmasters. Many found accommodation in overcrowded housing; they had little access to public funds. 'They often live twenty to a household, that's almost all they can club together to afford. They have almost no recourse to any type of means, they are almost destitute but they would prefer to be destitute in this environment as opposed to Romania or Slovakia,' said McAllister.

Alan McDonald, the housing manager for Govanhill Housing Association, said that when the Roma arrived in Glasgow, they were poor and very disadvantaged. 'So not only did we have large numbers of Roma settling in the area in a short time, but they were the new kids on the block. They always, incorrectly, get the blame when things change. They were coming from really poor housing, where there were often no windows in the buildings, no proper sanitary systems and there was a completely different approach to policing then. They were afraid of us, of officialdom, they thought we were going to persecute them.'[18]

Officials from several of the local agencies visited the housing in which the Roma had lived in Slovakia before emigrating to the UK, in order to understand the conditions they had fled. 'In Slovakia they house the Roma within purpose-built accommodation, and then forget about them,' McDonald said. 'Most don't have functional toilets; in one settlement there was a common toilet and washroom block, with a police station on its upper floor. The waste disposal systems in that settlement was a skip, and what apparently happens is that they put the rubbish in and it rots away; the skip is seldom emptied ... Little or no running water. They do have electricity, some of them, and some residents burn the timbers, including part of their building's doors, windows and other fixtures to keep them warm, as there are no heating systems. Small wonder that they didn't know how to initially deal with Scottish tenement living in one of the most densely populated areas of Glasgow,' he said.

'When the Slovakian community turned up they weren't used to putting their rubbish in the common bins – they often flung it out of the window.' In one of the first cases he dealt with for the housing association, he recorded eighteen people living in a one-bedroom flat. 'There were nine children and the toilet was blocked, so the children were defecating and urinating down the stairwell.' McDonald's team moved in, and noticed that there was no food in the flat and there were cockroaches and bed bugs. They helped the family gain access to benefits and more appropriate housing.

One of those arriving in Govanhill at that time was a young Slovakian Roma woman named Marcela Adamova. Now a well-respected community worker for her people, and an employee of Oxfam, she recalled the difficulties of those early days. 'We were very vulnerable to exploitation around housing, slum landlords. Occasionally I will hear negative remarks about my community. But things are much better now.'[19] Last year Marcela helped to organise a community-led clean-up of Govanhill, picking up litter with a small team of Roma volunteers who received some free English lessons as a thank-you. Perhaps, she thought, the tide was turning: a small number of Scots decided to celebrate International

Roma Day in April 2012 by giving the Govanhill Roma flowers and chocolates – a much appreciated gesture, Marcela said, though many were slightly bemused by the unexpected kindness.

Despite Circular 1/2006, opposition to new sites to accommodate British Gypsies and Travellers continued. Yet again, government action was honoured in the breach. The Equality and Human Rights Commission reported that councils would need to double their speed to meet the target of 5,733 extra pitches in England by 2011 – a sluggishness of action that was destined to leave one-fifth of all Gypsies and Travellers with nowhere legal to live.[20] This, of course, led desperate, homeless families to double up on any sites where they had family connections. Some of those desperate families arrived at Dale Farm, even though the two-year permission to stay had expired the year before.

Tony Ball, the leader of Basildon Council, was growing ever more impatient at the delays – and annoyed that Basildon was tolerating the largest Gypsy and Traveller encampment not just in England, but in Europe. He was also exercised by the fact that the site was, in many ways, an extended family enclave – the Sheridans, Flynns and Egans creating a village that he felt was operating outside the law. 'It not only broke green-belt law on planning but on size as well,' he said. 'You were never going to get a site with fifty pitches in one place; we don't do fifty terraced houses in one site.' He batted off complaints that the move to evict the families from Dale Farm was 'Middle England' flexing its control over the less fortunate. 'We are, this country is, very tolerant, multi-racial, – [we have] a good record because we have managed to integrate.'[21] But neither the local community nor the Travellers themselves really wanted to integrate. A solution had to be found.

The Deputy Prime Minister, John Prescott, stepped forward with a proposal: a site at Pitsea was pushed as a new home for the community. He had been persuaded finally that the Travellers at Dale Farm could not stay indefinitely. 'The site clearance at Dale

Farm was inevitable. I had given them two years, but they didn't use that time to find somewhere else. They took the view that they were there, staying there and nobody was going to move them,' he said with some regret. In February 2007 Ruth Kelly, the Secretary of State for Communities and Local Government, turned down another appeal by the families to stay at Dale Farm (although the families won the right to a judicial review). Basildon Council promptly made matters worse, by turning down the Pitsea application.[22]

For their part, local MPs John Baron and Eric Pickles could not understand the continuing delays either, and their language hardened significantly. In May 2008, Baron took up the debate in Parliament. He alleged that Dale Farm had grown into something quite sinister. 'The problems locally, at least in my constituency, have gone well beyond fly-tipping; they include the intimidation of the settled community. I am copied in on a steady stream of emails to the police reporting a number of incidents, including vandalism and young people throwing stones and firing air rifles. I have had to deal with local people whose water supply has been diverted by some Travellers whose presence is illegal. We have complaints about the speed and volume of traffic going down narrow lanes, and even gas cylinders are being piled up around the entrance of an illegal site, as if to warn off unwanted visitors. Royal Mail refuses to deliver post to two of the illegal sites in question because it is unable to guarantee the safety of staff following an incident involving dangerous dogs.' Baron said he had tried to play the peacemaker, convening people from all sides to see if there was any way around the issues. The police had 'offered to provide an escort' to the postal workers, he said, but Royal Mail did not believe this was sufficient.

'We should not allow any part of the community [to] become a no-go area for public services. However, that example shows the problems generated by those illegal sites,' Baron went on. 'I am not attributing such problems to Travellers in general – I am talking about a minority – but I refer to the problem of anti-social behaviour because of the report's finding that illegal sites should be tolerated without resort to firmer enforcement action. That has to be wrong. Again, it is a question of fairness. My constituents cannot understand why it should be so difficult to take effective action against those who have so brazenly broken the law. It appears to my constituents that there is one law for the Travellers and another for the settled community. All my constituents ask is that the law be fairly applied to everyone. No one seeks to discriminate against the minority, but it seems that local residents are being discriminated against.'[23]

These were fighting words. But Julie Morgan, who was then a Labour MP and a key supporter of Gypsies and Travellers within Parliament, said that Baron had remained open to confidential negotiations at this time, however. In fact he was pursuing a twin-track approach, saying that Dale Farm must be closed while not denying the right of Travellers to appropriate housing.[24]

That approach would not help local Conservative councillors in Essex, who were also being challenged from the far Right on the Dale Farm issue. The British National Party was mobilising, saying that they opposed illegal Traveller sites – and that they were no longer willing to stand by, waiting for some government paper to be issued. One BNP candidate, Len Heather, attempted to gain a seat in local district council elections in the parish council of Noak Bridge, near Dale Farm, in May 2008. His bid failed, but the party came second. Then he stood in a by-election in September 2008. He lost again. But he clearly was not going to relent. He told the local paper: 'The feedback we got on the doors was they have the biggest illegal traveller site on their doorstep and want something done about it. Basildon councillors make a lot of noise about the issue, usually at election time, then it goes quiet. I would ask residents what they want done, then put pressure on the council.'[25]

Heather later set up street stalls in Brentwood to advance the BNP cause, putting yet more pressure on local and national politicians to take action on Dale Farm. John Baron denied, however, that the BNP presence had any effect on him personally. 'There were groups from both ends of the political spectrum involved – to my knowledge, they had no effect on policy. Our case in moving the Travellers off the illegal site was that the law should apply equally and fairly to everyone, Traveller or not.'[26]

Then, that November, Pickles vented his wrath against the unauthorised encampments. Reacting to New Labour's plans to have regional targets for new sites, he told the *Daily Express*: 'Communities across the country are going to face the bombshell of having a Traveller camp dumped on their back yard, whether they like it or not,' he wrote. 'Councils are powerless to resist these regional targets and are being bullied into building on the green belt or using compulsory purchase powers to provide the land for Travellers. It's not fair that hard-working families have to save up to get on the housing ladder while Travellers get special treatment at tax-payers' expense.'[27]

Notwithstanding such assaults, New Labour continued in their efforts to bring Gypsies and Travellers in from the margins. In June the government had introduced and funded Gypsy and Traveller History Month, which aimed to showcase the artistic, political and historical contributions that Gypsies, Roma and Travellers have made — and continue to make — to the UK. The magazine, *Travellers' Times*, was also founded, with funding coming from the National Lottery. But how would these pieces of PR, welcome as they were, counter the fiery words of an Eric Pickles or a John Baron?

Dale Farm, Julie Morgan was convinced, had become an iconic plot of ground. And it was shaping up to be the literal battleground on which Gypsy and Traveller policies would be fought out.

6
PAYBACK

In the run-up to the 2010 general election, the Conservative party released a 'Green Paper' with proposals to criminalise trespass – a policy that had been promised by Michael Howard some five years earlier. They also laid out plans to roll back all the guidance and directives Labour had previously issued in its attempt to give local and regional government incentive to provide sites. The Green Paper passed all but unnoticed. Just a few Gypsy and Traveller organisations, a handful of politicians, including Eric Lubbock, Lord Avebury, raised a quiet alarm. Meanwhile, much of the tabloid press, aided by smaller town and village papers that were unwilling to alienate the local people who provided much of their advertising revenue, helped to stoke the fires, by providing more stories about Gypsy 'invasions' and criminality.

Scrambling to hold on to their majority in Parliament, New Labour also joined the fray. The party issued pre-election guidance on anti-social behaviour, naming Gypsies and Travellers as offending groups. Local authorities, police and other agencies would receive strong powers they could use to deal with the alleged anti-social behaviour problems associated with Gypsy and Traveller sites.[1]

A week before the general election, on Friday, 30 April 2010, one small group of Romani Gypsies, Scotch and English in heritage, moved on to land they owned, but for which they did not have planning permission, in Meriden. The villagers mounted a twenty-four-hour blockade to prevent the Gypsies from bringing building supplies into the field. The courts later forced them to

allow sewerage works, but this was a small concession and did
not signal a mood change. The chair of the Residents Against
Inappropriate Development protest group, David McGrath, was the
nearest neighbour to the new site. The Gypsies, he said, had damaged 'a designated wildlife site' in a precious 'green lung'. He went
on: 'We are sympathetic, but the Gypsy and Traveller community,
fundamentally, are … adopting a cavalier approach to development. What they are doing is unethical and inappropriate.'[2]

The country's compass had turned rightwards. On 6 May,
the Conservatives won the largest number of votes in a general
election. Less than a week later, the Coalition Agreement was
approved by both the Liberal Democrats and the Conservative
Party.[3] Overnight, nomads lost almost all of their friends in high
places. Eric Pickles, a sworn foe of illegal Gypsy and Traveller sites,
became the new Communities and Local Government Secretary,
able, at last, to put his vision of 'fair play' into practice. Candy
Sheridan, who herself had once been a Liberal Democrat councillor
in Norfolk, was horrified. 'I turned my back on national politics
and chose to work for my own community. I couldn't believe that
the Coalition would choose to pick on an ethnic minority within
days of the agreement being signed. I was disgusted.'

Just as the Coalition's policies were being debated (and agreed
on), the *Sunday Express,* the *Express* and the *Daily Mail* reminded
their readers of the Conservatives' pledge to crack down on
Gypsies and Travellers. The papers conjured up the spectre of
unwanted Gypsy camps in the Conservative heartlands, mentioning specifically the threat to William Hague's seat in Ripon in
North Yorkshire, an Area of Outstanding Natural Beauty that was
also the setting for Jane Austen's *Mansfield Park* and the so-called
'Battle of Hemley Hill', a much-loved local beauty spot.[4] As the
Institute for Race Relations put it, in a summary of the overall line
of the articles at this time: the Gypsies and Travellers, according
to the Tory media, 'threatened the beauty of rural England and
could invade at any time'.

Testing the waters, on 28 May Eric Pickles issued a press release
warning local authorities to be on their guard against Gypsies and

Travellers shifting to new spots over a weekend, as the Gypsies at Meriden had done the month before. 'Communities and Local Government Secretary of State Eric Pickles is taking pre-emptive action to prevent unauthorised development over the coming bank holiday weekend. Mr Pickles is writing to all Local Authority Chief Planners to warn them to be alert and ready for action if any significant planning applications get submitted before the bank holiday ... Mr. Pickles is encouraging Councils to have planning officers on call over the weekend' to prevent 'a small minority of people' 'illegally developing their land' over the holiday.[5]

He then set his aim at policies that would bear a real impact. He withdrew all funding for new sites, though he was later urged to restore some restricted funding, which he did grudgingly. He also scrapped Labour's plans for regionally approved targets and announced he was considering limits on retrospective planning permission.[6] He also announced that he would legislate to bring in his new vision through a Localism Act, with which he hoped to strengthen the hand of people to influence policy at the local level. This, of course, would also strengthen the hand of those who wanted to resist Gypsy and Traveller sites – legal or otherwise.

Resistance, however, was building on the other side too, from the grass roots of the Gypsy and Traveller communities. Most of the organisations that claimed to represent them continued to lack both capacity and money. Committed people, both from the travelling communities and from the settled community, had been working with the Gypsy Council from 1966 onwards, but the body had little money and had even endured the scandal of its one-time president, Richard Sheridan, being jailed briefly for cigarette smuggling. It had also lost its charitable status. In 1999 the Irish Traveller Movement in Britain was established, with a brief to lobby MPs and produce evidence-based policy proposals, but it chose not to combat individual site clearances. Families, Friends and Travellers, which had been set up mainly by New Travellers to combat the 1994 criminal justice reforms, was also cash-strapped. The Commission for Racial Equality had spoken out on behalf of the communities, and its successor body, the

Equality and Human Rights Commission (EHRC) was still offering support. But as key people, most notably Chris Myant, Emily
Gheorgiou and Sean Risdale, left, the EHRC's backing melted
away. One prominent insider, when questioned about the shift,
said, off the record, that the EHRC would take up disability issues,
which were then less controversial, but weren't going to 'put their
heads on the block' for Gypsies and Travellers.[7] Members of the
All-Party Group for Gypsies and Travellers voiced concerns about
the new Conservative approach, but many of the most influential,
such as Andrew George and Lord Avebury, had their hands tied.
Their party, the Liberal Democrats, was now in coalition with
the Conservative party.

Small wonder, then, that some Gypsies and Travellers, rather
than relying on hamstrung allies or weak and poorly financed
organisations, took matters into their own hands. Occupying land
illegally was a kind of self-help resistance campaign. As Colm
Power noted in *Right to Roam*, modern mobile phone connections, more media savviness and, among the younger Gypsies and
Travellers, growing literacy meant that they could now increasingly do what they needed to do for themselves.[8]

Of course, some in the Traveller community were looking for
outside help by that summer, because the threats to the encampment at Dale Farm were hardening. The Travellers had lost legal
skirmish after legal skirmish and were now making plans to resist
a full-throttled eviction. The site was growing scruffier month
by month as the residents' focus shifted from making a home
to making one last desperate stand. Litter drifted around the
empty pitches. Wasps hovered near bins very obviously in need
of emptying, and dogs yelped outside the embattled caravans.
Yet indoors the homes remained spotless. What was the point of
fighting for a site that might soon no longer be home?

Mary Ann McCarthy was depressed. This was not the way she
had expected things to go. Her eyes glanced towards the statue
of the Virgin Mary in the corner. 'They call us nasty thieving

gypsies, but we are Christian folk. They want to destroy our way of life. Everyone has rights, except for us.'[9]

Her mood, and that of Grattan Puxon, who was visiting whenever his health permitted, had not been improved by the recent headlines. Nomads were under fire throughout Europe. In France, President Nicolas Sarkozy had begun a crackdown on Roma migrants, ordering their expulsion. He had tried to sweeten the 'deal' by offering a small resettlement benefit in cash. Some saw it was a bribe – and perhaps even a way to reinforce the stereotype that the community was only interested in grabbing money. Some of the Roma, unhappy in France, took the offer and returned peacefully to Romania and Bulgaria – but others resisted. In one town that August, a Roma was shot dead, and others had rioted.[10] A month later, a row about the French expulsions erupted during an EU summit, with some representatives denouncing the policy and even threatening legal action. Sarkozy had powerful allies, however, including Italy's then president, Silvio Berlusconi, who had himself deported Roma from his country the year before.[11]

Tony Ball, the Conservative leader of Basildon Council, publicly said he sympathised with the residents of Dale Farm, but all avenues except eviction were exhausted. The council had offered 'bricks and mortar' accommodation to all those it was obliged to house, he said. When asked where the Travellers were to go if they turned down the offers for such accommodation, he replied: 'They came from somewhere. One has to draw the line at some point. All our authorised sites are full up.' After the eviction, he mused, perhaps the encampment might well become allotments – productive ground for the villagers of Crays Hill.

In fact, Ball was at that time holding secret meetings with several groups, including the McCarthy family, the church, the Equality and Human Rights Commission and the Gypsy Council, in an effort to resolve the situation some other way. Then the eviction of Irish Travellers from the nearby Hovefields site on 7 September 2010 shifted the ground.

Father Dan Mason, who had taken over as parish priest that May, had spent his first few months getting to know local Traveller families at both sites before experiencing the eviction at Hovefields. He reflected. 'Hovefields was like Dale Farm in miniature; it didn't get the publicity that Dale Farm did, but there were many of the same issues, there were families threatened with eviction who had been there for some time, for instance. Many of us saw Hovefields as the dry run for Dale Farm, just a year earlier. The way the police mobilised, for instance, it felt as if they were getting ready for the big one … it felt as if the drum beat was beginning … after Hovefields the pressure was rising.'[12] The same bailiffs who were lined up to clear Dale Farm – Constant and Company – were in charge of the job at Hovefields.[13]

Grattan had been excluded from the partnership meetings thus far. From his outsider's view, he believed the Dale Farm residents were quickly running out of options. In desperation, he had started to put out feelers to people he thought might form into a group of supporters, mainly students from Cambridge University. Some, like Jonathan Oppenheim, a nuclear physicist originally from Canada, had been visiting Irish Travellers at a site outside Cambridge, Smithy Fen, since 2004. 'The local paper was running a campaign to get rid of the illegal nine plots onto which Irish Travellers had moved,' Jonathan explained. 'The local people didn't object to the English Gypsies, and I wasn't sure why, but I took it as a way of justifying that it was not prejudice against Travellers, just against *this* lot of Irish Travellers; it provided a cover for prejudice. There was a Rhodesian guy running the campaign – he had a homeland policy, and his group was called Middle England in Revolt. He ran a campaign to get the council to evict these guys. The papers made it sound like "a mass of Travellers", and then you go there and there are just nine families, [and] Patrick McCarthy, this old guy, this harmless guy – there is such a dichotomy between the image people had and what was there. We started going to council meetings and speaking to them. We were trying to come into contact with people who were working on this.'[14]

Others started to join the nascent campaign in 2010. One such was Jacob Wills, who was now a prominent member of the resistance at Dale Farm. Jacob had been drawn into the campaign through his involvement in anti-racism groups in Cambridge. 'The first time I visited Dale Farm was when Essex Human Rights ran a legal workshop about Dale Farm, and I thought this was a good way to get involved. That must have been before Christmas 2010 ... that built up throughout the spring ... and Grattan was a key figure in it. Without him, there wouldn't have been any mobilisation.'[15]

Grattan and the others started to put out more feelers, canvassing for more bodies to come out to Dale Farm. As early as January 2011, the charity No Borders Brighton advertised for 'solidarity action' against the funding being sought by the local authority to clear the site, and the London Freedom Bookshop held a meeting that same month to 'plan the resistance to the threatened eviction of the Dale Farm Traveller community', according to Superintendent Iain Logan, who, as the senior police officer for Essex Police, had been appointed to plan the tactics for eviction day.[16]

Logan had been canvassing for support of a different sort, gathering information about any and all activities related to Dale Farm. 'In the months building up to the site clearances at Dale Farm, a considerable quantity of material began to appear on open sources that suggested that protestor activity would become a significant additional factor during the site clearances. Intelligence more specific to the site clearances suggested that activist groups, such as the No Borders Network, and Earthfirst/Climate Camp, were attaching themselves to ... the protest group at Dale Farm,' the Essex Police would later disclose.[17]

This intelligence campaign was in no small part a response to the joint lobbying done by the local MP, John Baron, and Basildon Council as they started to put together the funds they needed to evict the site. The wrangling behind the scenes between various parties stumping up for the eviction of the Irish Traveller families at Dale Farm was getting complicated.[18] Civil servants had reluctantly agreed to hand over an 'unprecedented wad of cash from national coffers' to pay for Basildon's little local difficulty.[19] Essex Police at that time estimated the policing costs alone could cost up to £9.5 million in a worst-case scenario.

The first letter from Basildon asking for cash from central government was turned down. On 7 February 2011, the Under-Secretary of State in the Department for Communities and Local Government (DCLG), the Liberal Democrat Andrew Stunnell wrote: 'Local authorities are independent bodies who are responsible for local statutory and discretionary services … We have carefully considered your request but believe that these are costs that councils would normally be expected to absorb within their existing budget.' John Baron and Tony Ball would not relent. They took their collecting hats right to the heart of the government. On April Fool's Day, of all days, an unnamed official from DCLG wrote to the Treasury, saying that the department wanted to make a grant after all. 'Our Ministers wants [sic] this treated as a top priority.' Another unnamed official added that the grant should be 'finalised before Purdah as a matter of urgency'.[20]

In mid-April Bob Neil, another Under-Secretary of State at the DCLG, performed an about-turn. In a letter to Ball, he said, 'The government has decided to make this financial contribution because of the need to resolve the marked planning enforcement and community tension issues that have arisen around Dale Farm … This exceptional situation requires support from government, but should not be seen to set a precedent.' Money, too, was extracted from the Home Office, for what was named Operation Cabinet. But the chief constable of Essex Police, Jim Barker McCardle, was worried that he would end up with a significant shortfall, because of the Treasury's obsession with match funding – their first offer was to cover just fifty per cent of the policing costs up to £3.5 million.

McCardle was not happy. The money for the eviction was partly coming out of police reserves, he wrote back to the Home Office, and could leave Essex Police with 'a significant shortfall'. A couple of weeks later he received a reply from the Home Office. They would not seek match funding in this case, but cash was still limited to £3.5 million. McCardle thanked the government for the extra cash – but he informed them that there was at least a ten per cent chance that the cost of the eviction would exceed the cash budgeted. 'At the moment that risk is not covered,' he wrote to the Home Office. It seemed that nobody wanted to pay for the eviction that everybody wanted, primarily because nobody knew how much it would cost.

Baron met with David Cameron to secure the funding necessary. 'Guaranteed funding had to be put in place to cover the contingency of a worst-case scenario when it came to the clearance,' he later said. 'After lobbying various government departments, and with the help of Essex Police and Basildon Council, a meeting with the Prime Minister finally led to the securing of a near £10 million contingency fund.'

In May 2011, as pressure was ramping up at Dale Farm and other trouble spots such as Meriden, the annual Stow Horse Fair, the ancient Gypsy horse fair in the Cotswolds, was held as usual. Candy Sheridan, the vice-chair of the Gypsy Council, was there, along with Vera Norwood, a former Tiller Girl, artist and at one time mayor of Stow-on-the-Wold, who was a doughty defender of Gypsy rights. Candy was hosting a stall for the Gypsy Council, and was in celebratory mode. Smiling, she surveyed the teeming fair grounds. The Gypsy fairs, she said, were their chance for 'putting ourselves on show, trading with each other and having a sense of pride'.

It was a contented scene. Gypsies and Travellers had come to deal their trademark horses, piebald or skewbald cobs – highly prized beasts said to have calm temperaments. Ted Chaney, a horse-dealer, was sure that buyers this year were looking for a glossy mane, a nice size and (the main attraction) finely feathered feet. Another dealer, Loretta Rawlings, and around ten other Gypsy families, including her husband's, were selling cobs to Australia, Brazil, America and Eastern Europe. 'They have become luxury items,' she said.[21]

Not far away, Gypsy women were trading and buying Crown Derby china, elaborately smocked dresses for their girls and tweed for their boys, bedding, pots and pans. The younger set were clearly on the lookout for love, the girls, with their beautiful long hair, eyeing up the boys, who were showing off by riding cobs bareback across the fields, or cantering their horses and carts among the crowds, scattering them as they came by.

But as Vera sat down at a stall to have lunch, it was plain to her that not everyone in Stow, a prosperous market town in the Cotswolds, was as positive towards the fair as she was. Edward IV had granted the event a royal charter in 1476, giving it legal protection from closure that remains in force – and a good thing too. In 1995 the district council took out an injunction to restrict the number of nights that Gypsies and Travellers could stay in the area before and after the gathering. Many local shopkeepers close their doors during the fair. Robin Jones, then Stow's mayor, was quite chilly about the fair, claiming that petty crime at fair time was commonplace, though the local police report that the event is usually peaceful.

Soon enough, everyone's attention turned back to Dale Farm. Attitudes on both sides were hardening in the run-up to eviction day. As tensions increased, the Dale Farm Supporters sent out an email alert, asking people to come out for a 'think-in' on Sunday, 29 August. It would be held at 'Camp Constant' – the growing activist encampment at the back of Dale Farm that was named in an ironic nod towards the eviction bailiffs, Constant and Co.

Dale Farm was changed beyond recognition. At the gate to the site was an old trestle table, behind which stood a young 'supporter', as she called herself. She asked each visitor for their name and why they were there and wrote the details down in a book. Journalists were proudly offered a press pack. Dale Farm was now being policed by outsiders. The activists had moved in.

A well-known veteran of previous Traveller support campaigns was testing and fortifying a scaffolding tower at the front gate. He had previously been high on the Met's most-wanted list, though on the whole he favoured non-violent resistance, and it seemed that this was the plan for most of the activists who had arrived.

This was corroborated by the Essex Police Force's intelligence: 'It was very clear from open source intelligence such as internet traffic that the majority of protestors associating themselves with Camp Constant were planning peaceful, non-violent protest.'[22] But it wasn't true of all who were gathering there.

Some of the activists had taken to wearing raggedy face-masks and the black clothing often linked to anarchism. The Essex Police had noticed: 'As the date of the site clearances approached, specific intelligence was also gathered that suggested that known activists connected to a variety of protest movements, including some previously linked to movements with a history of extreme action, such as animal rights protests, were present on the site or appeared to be making plans to attend. In some cases, the activists were reported to be planning tactics which could represent a significant risk to the personal safety of bailiffs, police officials or other persons on the site.'[23] Other intelligence suggested similar groups being involved: 'Intelligence received suggests that extreme anarchists who were evicted from Notting Hill, London, will also be in attendance and that their aim is to cause havoc for the police and bailiffs.'

Camp Constant had been set up on vacant plots at the back of Dale Farm by a group of some fifty activists. They had put up sleeping tents, built a kitchen for preparing vegan meals, and erected a big tent to serve as a meeting area. They were now digging holes for compost toilets, and getting to know the Travellers. They were settling in. But the influx of so many new people had changed Dale Farm.

The place looked as though it was no longer cared for. Litter was swirling about, even near Mary Ann McCarthy's tidy chalet. While the Traveller women remained deeply house-proud about their spotless pitches, the custom of getting together every few weeks to tidy up the access roads had fallen away. Now, as demoralisation spread among the residents, those areas had grown dirty and rubbish-strewn.

Candy Sheridan was in the wooden hut where all meetings at Dale Farm were held. Grattan had got it erected in 2008, using money from Essex County Council — much to the fury of the councillors from Basildon District. A few stray dogs wandered in and out, their puppies clambering onto the laps of the people assembled. A dryer was going at full speed. Richie Sheridan was busy clearing out drawers in an old dresser so he could sell it. Candy didn't even know about the activist policing the gate; the press pack about Dale Farm hadn't been cleared with her or anyone else on the Gypsy Council (in fact, I gave her my copy).

This was an ominous and early sign of the two camps that were taking shape at Dale Farm. One camp, led by Candy and the Gypsy Council, was pursuing a legal route of resistance, filing paperwork with Basildon and other authorities in protest of the eviction threat. The other side was run by the activists, particularly Grattan, who had stepped down from the Gypsy Council that he had founded forty years earlier. The split would prove to be tragic.

Candy remained hopeful that they could stop the eviction through legal devices, or at least delay it indefinitely, as they had done so often in the past. But she was beginning to see that an eviction was growing ever more possible, and she wanted the residents to face up to it and prepare for some neat legal footwork that she thought might save at least a few pitches. In these efforts she felt thwarted by Grattan and the activists.

She had attended meeting after meeting with Basildon Council, the police and other officials (including some secret negotiations), feeling that Grattan's presence hindered her chances of finding a resolution. After years of working together, they had become wary of each other. Most of all, they disagreed about tactics. Candy had spent weeks trying to get healthcare workers to visit the residents, and had watched in dismay as it had fallen apart during a meeting. 'They say, "you stay nice and calm" and you keep doing it, but I'm not calm when I get home in the evening, I get very upset. I was extremely upset with Grattan. I finally invited him into a meeting on Thursday and he threw a cup of water over me and the man from the Primary Care Trust. So those meetings have now stopped, because they feel at risk. And there was almost a breach of the peace – last time I saw him he was out there wrestling with a policeman! The policemen said, "Do you want him arrested?" I said, "No, just ask him to leave the log cabin and calm down." I've got all these agencies coming out and I haven't even had the chance to talk to them yet. The primary issue here is health, the Primary Care Trust, a complete lack of duty of care, and he's gone away and I want him back again, with that health bus. They've stopped coming because of the eviction. It's issues like that.'[24]

Candy was under pressure from all sides, so much that she was now nearly weeping. 'I'm told that this is going to be no ordinary eviction, this is the biggest site ever to be evicted, it's got the most people, the most support, it's the most watched nationally, internationally. I feel like Alice at the Mad Hatter's tea party. People are telling me things, and it all sounds sensible, and then I agree with them, and when I go out of the tea party people say, "You're a stupid eejit, you're listening to the police, you're completely mad, you are on a different planet." But I am listening and I am hearing – what else can I do? How far do I have to stretch my role? I'm beginning to question how far I can go.'

Everything, she felt, had gone downhill since the general election and the Coalition Agreement, especially her attempts to find alternative living sites for the Travellers at Dale Farm. From early on, she had been looking for land that might be suitable, often with the help of local officials. 'I've been identifying land behind closed doors for two years, and researching brown-field sites. I put in the last two planning applications; we have a public inquiry about [a site on] Pound Lane on 21 November. I keep saying to Basildon, "You can solve this; if you identify the land, I will put in a planning application." It was fine until the election. After the election, they weren't even able to meet with me.' She added, bitterly, 'Welcome to localism and the new Coalition government, where they can't even meet with you.'

She reported that Pound Lane and another nearby site, on Gardiners Lane, had looked particularly promising. Authorities had identified them as places for planning applications. 'But then Basildon refused to "determine" them because local residents didn't want them there,' Candy said. Until the council approved the sites for residential use, she had to wait. 'I want to deliver that site. Even if Dale Farm is saved, it's still overstretched.'

This made the presence of the activists all the more disturbing to her. Like many of the Travellers at Dale Farm, she lumped them all together as 'the students', though a tiny handful came from the New Traveller community and others from church groups and political action collectives, and one, named Phien O'Phien, was both an activist and an Irish Traveller. 'We need to keep everyone calm,' Candy reiterated, 'and try and get the scaffolding down. But it keeps getting higher, although the women don't want it! It's become a war zone. We don't know what the students are doing because they are not talking to us.' Now it was time to open better communications – Camp Constant weekend, the meeting between the Gypsy Council and the activists, was set to start.

Johnny Howorth, a film-maker working with the *Guardian*, was there to film the day's events. He pointed out a few faces he knew as he made his way to the large white tent. 'Hunt sabs,' he said. A number of activists had put on their masks. A few Traveller women had decided to attend the meeting with their children. This did not bode well for a meeting of 'like' minds.

A tall, thick-set woman was videoing the proceedings. I was recording audio. She turned to me as Candy was speaking and snarled, 'Who the fuck are you?' This kind of intimidating aggression – by a small number of activists who clearly thought they were now in charge of Dale Farm and wanted to control journalists' access to it – was an unpleasant new development. Sebastian Hesse, a radio journalist for ARD, a German radio network, had been visiting the families for the past year. Now, suddenly, his access was barred. 'I had been to Dale Farm several times and for me it was easy to go and knock on doors, it was charming; they were very approachable once they trusted you. One day I came in August and there was a "press officer" there, and he tried to deny me access to the site.'[25]

Hesse didn't investigate the activists or their history – in fact, he tried to ignore them. Still, he found their presence inconvenient and distracting. 'In hindsight I don't think [the Travellers] did themselves a big favour by getting the activists in, because the way in which they occupied the ground was very aggressive. They infantilised the Travellers and didn't let them make their own decisions. They were so suspicious of media and everybody; they treated every media inquiry as an attack, almost, on their cause, and that backfired.'

Hesse used his contacts to bypass the 'press officer' and visit people he knew, but many other members of the press were significantly hampered in their work. Jackie Long, the social affairs editor from Channel 4 News, recalled: 'We had been to the site in the run-up to the eviction, and then we came one day, and the activists had set up a kind of press office. They said they were running 'tours' of the site at 1 p.m. and 3 p.m. and that we would have to wait.' When Channel 4 turned up again as the eviction loomed, the activists attempted to bar them from entering the site. 'We ended up breaking in, which was quite ironic, having to break into Dale Farm, just as the Travellers were about to be evicted from it. We dug our way under fencing and climbed in. Then the person who had barred us saw us. She was furious, but luckily Pearl McCarthy came over, calmed her down and let us stay.'

In the big white tent, Candy was trying to soothe the Traveller women and reassure them about the timetable of events before any eviction might occur. Yet she was also trying to get them to face the fact that most of the legal avenues available to them were now basically exhausted. It was time to address the restive crowd and lay out what she had learned.

The police had warned her, she explained, that they might have to close off the access road, except to named residents. The reaction was fierce. 'I'm not giving them my name, I'll roll over them [in my car],' one of the Traveller women said in defiance. This set off a firestorm of other fears. The women were worried about sending their children to school during the eviction and then having them taken away by social services. The authorities could not be trusted. Candy reassured them that she would be given the date of the eviction in advance. 'You are so lucky. They will give me the date – Dale Farm is heavily watched and monitored. I work at all the other evictions, and they just come on without any notice'. Not everyone who heard her thought their life was so lucky.

The activists were not keen on this turn of events either. 'We do not want to give our names to the police,' came the reply. One activist asked, 'Do we have to give real names?' and another wondered whether it would be possible to get on to the site some other way, perhaps by cutting across the fields. The meeting was spiralling out of all control.

Then Candy began to reveal her fledgling secret plan – to get emergency injunctions to stop the process. This would allow time to move people from illegal plots to legal ones, doubling them up temporarily on those pitches, if necessary, before any eviction went forward. 'The eviction is planned for late September, October. The eviction will give us twenty-eight days. Bailiffs do not have the lawful right to go for lawful removal of all pitches – one-third is lawful,' she said. There was so much paperwork that it was almost impossible to track it all, and the disarray was starting to hurt the Travellers' image with the public. 'It's a patchwork quilt of over one hundred enforcement notices. It's a mess. Basildon is looking more and more unreasonable. We need to make them look unreasonable.' She was clearly annoyed about the activists, and the effect their presence was having on the process. 'The issue here is that the police are extremely concerned about the scaffolding on the front gate and the sheer number of people here.'

As she spelled out what was coming, Candy's reasonable voice was literally drowned out, however. Activists and Travellers alike were taking issue with her version of the events, with her ideas for getting around the roadblock, with everything she said. She became more insistent: 'This is going to be hell on earth without knowing the date, but it could be slightly more managed hell with the date … I need names for legal monitors to get through the gate if it's put up, I need to put it on the list and activists need to give names so they can come and go as visitors.'

Candy asked whether any of the activists, who now numbered between fifty and seventy strong, were ready to be trained as legal monitors. Only six raised their hands. She could not believe it. 'This is really crucial; here you are building scaffolding towers and only six of you will become legal monitors.'

An activist retorted, in an obvious attempt to undermine Candy, 'I want to ask the residents, Is there is a plan that you are counting on? We will support it. Candy has come into this meeting, to tell us what she is doing, asking for UN observers,' she said. 'This is different to what we are doing. We don't want to give our names to the police.'

Some of the activists asked for the cameras to be turned off. Suspicion was taking over. It was at this point that a Traveller tendered a direct enquiry to the activists: 'We are going to protest and put up a fight. If we are doing this, are ye willing to stand behind us?' A shouting match followed. Eventually Candy left, shaking her head. She had not got the legal monitor names she needed in order to manage the hell of an eviction.

Jacob Wills, aka 'Jake Fulton', was by now one of the de facto leaders of the activists. He was good at putting on a brave face, stressing in interviews how optimistic the group was that they would be successful in supporting the Dale Farm residents and halting the eviction.[26] But in reality, he had been ambivalent about setting up Camp Constant. In his words, they were 'definitely tentative'.[27]

At first, he said, he and his friends in the activist camp had been 'quite worried – we didn't think it was appropriate to impose ourselves on this community'. They moved forward, in a 'definitely tentative' manner, because 'it seemed like people would be quite in favour of it, that they wanted to see more practical forms of solidarity. And it doesn't seem so useful just to wage a media outreach form of campaign. So I'd say by the late spring we were focusing in on what was possible, trying to let more people know about it.' To recruit more activists, they used the internet. A 'Dale Farm Solidarity' email mailing that had been almost dormant was resurrected.

With knowledge of the activists' early doubts about their role at Dale Farm, the break-up of Candy's meeting wasn't surprising. But former social worker and Catholic peace activist Ann Kobayashi, who had been visiting Dale Farm since her priest had asked her to help with benefit forms in the late 1990s, was just as disturbed as Candy by the emerging rift between the two camps. Tensions were clearly simmering. 'Candy got it from both sides in some cases because she has done her best for the cause of people not being put out,' Ann explained. 'In court she never agreed on a safe eviction which resulted in them being on the road, that was her bargaining chip to get somewhere else. But it didn't work. If only there had been more transparency about what different peoples' agendas were – Candy, Grattan – if we could have all met together, and had some means of uncovering some of the difficulties, for example, around the ways of decision-making ...'.[28] Things could have gone so much better, Ann felt.

The Travellers at Dale Farm had not been entirely cut off from the local community, after all. Indeed, as former EHRC staffer Sean Risdale, who was now with the Irish Traveller Movement in Britain, recalled: 'There were different strands of activism at Dale Farm in the time leading up to the eviction. Long before Camp Constant, and in some cases going back to the original Dale Farm settlement, there was a group of local women giving continual practical support to Dale Farm families – largely in terms of accessing healthcare, education and other services. Most of these supporters were peace campaigners and active parishioners from Our Lady of Good Counsel, the Catholic Church in Wickford. They got to know and like the Traveller families through their joint involvement in the Church and attendance at Sunday Mass. And some had joined the women from Dale Farm when they held night-long candlelit vigils of prayer for the preservation of their community. Sister Katherine, Ann Kobayashi and others worked tirelessly to support and comfort the families at Dale Farm, operating in a non-judgemental way with everyone involved in the struggle. Father Dan Mason, the parish priest at Wickford, has been continually supportive to the families of Dale Farm – along with his housekeeper Anne Matthews, providing the only real opportunity for them to feel valued as part of a broader Wickford community.'

Another key volunteer, much loved by the Traveller women, was Susan Craig-Greene of the Washington-based Advocacy Project. Susan was compiling the first inventory of health and housing needs at Dale Farm, working quietly away in the background in order to provide evidence that might underpin the legal challenge to the eviction and the Travellers' right to accommodation.

Ann believed that the problem had been the uneasy mix of activist and Traveller culture, particularly the sort of horizontal decision-making that had become a hallmark of anarchist and other activist collectives. Much of activist culture, in Ann's view, 'was never going to work at Dale Farm. It wasn't familiar to the Travellers, and from Candy's point of view it was ineffective, weird, hippyish – threatening. The activists were in the main a fairly articulate, educated group, they were able to explain why they were doing things in a certain way … and that was very tough for Candy. Because there wasn't enough space or time to sort it in a helpful way … it placed a huge burden on the residents at Dale Farm, who were stuck with conflicting loyalties.'

Candy's strategy, to cede some ground to the council, was undermined by the presence of the activists, Ann said. 'Candy sincerely thought this was the best option, to give a little and then when things had died down to go back, wait till the dust died down – very much the idea that he who fights and runs away lives to fight another day … That's very much a response of nomadic groups, that they learn that you can go back once things have settled, whereas face-to-face confrontation, in the Traveller experience, has never worked in their favour.'

Sean Risdale understood the risk that Candy took of alienating the Travellers in order to save Dale Farm. 'Candy was courageous in the run up to the eviction – working almost without sleep towards the end to try and avert what everybody else was anticipating would be a violent outcome. She knew she would get little thanks from anyone for dealing with the "enemy", unless by some miracle it led to a last-minute reprieve for the residents. Of course she was as sickened as anyone else when Basildon officials involved in the negotiations talked about this decimation of an entire settlement as complacently as if they were discussing a greenhouse extension. Many of those affected were her cousins, uncles and aunts, but she couldn't afford to lose her temper with the officials in case of a possible breakthrough.'

Crucially, however, Grattan disagreed with Candy's approach. He saw no point in standing back – you had to confront the forces that were against you. According to Risdale, 'When Grattan was angry, his anger was generally focused on the evil of the eviction process – both as a matter of principle, and ultimately as it overshadowed and then took away the peace of Dale Farm. He might lose his temper with individuals who contribute[d] directly or indirectly to the eviction process, but he [didn't] sustain personal feuds or harbour grievances. He has witnessed the bitter intolerance shown towards Irish Travellers and Roma over a lifetime, and has got beyond politeness in discussing the issues with anyone who lacks goodwill towards Travellers.'

Grattan felt, quite sincerely, that if he could attract around a thousand activists to Dale Farm, there was a chance of saving it through direct action. But the police never believed that such numbers could stop them doing what they needed to do, according to Iain Logan of the Essex Police. 'This was not a life and death situation. If there had been a thousand protestors there, it would just have taken longer. This wasn't the town centre of Croydon; we didn't need to seize control. If safety was jeopardised because we were outnumbered, we would have withdrawn and regrouped. There was no time imperative.'

The activists didn't know that, however, and were busy

demonstrating, rather proudly, their various resistance techniques to the bemused Travellers. 'There were all these techniques that were being introduced … They were going around the caravans, having tea, having a chat, and then saying, "By the way, this is a tube, you can put your arm in it, and sit in one van and stick it across to another van and you'll block the road." And this is the first time people had heard of this way of resisting,' Ann Kobayashi recalled. 'And I always felt it was unrealistic to ask people who are used to depending on mobility to avoid trouble to mobilise themselves voluntarily. I mean, I've done it over the years for blockades out of choice, because I've seen it work for short-term purposes of blocking a base for demonstrations – Faslane, for instance. It does work, but in a different context, when you are trying to keep traffic out – here we were trying to stop the police coming in. It was a different situation.'

There were other issues too. Travellers are polite and don't like to offend, especially to offend people who are offering a help-ing hand. 'There were difficulties with the vegan diets,' for one. The Travellers, too polite to refuse the vegan stew on offer, fed it discreetly to their dogs, who lapped it up. For another, 'The horizontal decision-making … this underlying principle that the Travellers had the right to say yea or nay … to suggestions,' Ann said. 'The difficulty was that though the Travellers did feel they could contribute, and that was helpful, they felt under an obliga-tion to these young people who had come to help them … They may not have felt that it sounded a great idea, but how could you look a gift horse in the mouth, and what else was being offered?'

Careless talk, from a small number of Travellers suggesting that they had access to guns, didn't help matters. One Irish Traveller boasted to local newspapers that he and other residents would fight any eviction and had firearms on the site. Essex Police intelligence took this in: 'Information … suggested individuals associated with the site, whether members of the travelling com-munity or protestors, had access to firearms or other weaponry, were connected to violent incidents or other criminality or due to previous criminal history would be likely to involve themselves in actions that would endanger others. This would have obvious relevance to any police activity on the site.'[29]

The police were preparing for a violent confrontation. Intelligence gathered in July 2011 stated: 'Some residents have started to make a move ahead of the eviction, but the vast majority are intending to stay and are fortifying the site in an attempt to make the eviction lengthy and dangerous. Gas cylinders are being built into walls and buried into the ground in a crude attempt at creating explosions and likely harm to bailiffs, police and contractors connected with the removal ... Intelligence suggests that petrol bombs are being prepared on Dale Farm.[30] Other intelligence suggested that activists would be wearing rucksacks containing 'ammo' (rocks and stones), and that they had access to homemade shields, cricket pads and motorbike helmets.

The activists, for their part, were feeling under pressure. Some were taking or had just taken their exams at Cambridge; others had work commitments. Jonathan Oppenheim said that recruiting people to join Camp Constant was a hand-to-hand job – lots of work, lots of time, lots of persuasion. 'Grattan ... had this email list [and] he was sending out these reports, and there weren't many people [showing up]. It was difficult because they felt it was a constant state of emergency, so people just lose energy. Also, it was one of the most difficult things to mobilise for I've been involved in, compared to migrant stuff, climate, World Trade Organisation. You had to explain the issue more with Dale Farm; there were lots of questions, lots of barriers ... it just wasn't on the radar for some reason ... It's a bit outside of people's vision. Climate change was a huge task we have to engage with, and I don't think that people saw Traveller rights in the same light.'

Given the increasingly desperate email alerts that were going out to garner support, it's no small wonder that there was little 'quality control' around the sort of activists who were allowed to take up at Camp Constant. 'There was a lot of restraint being exercised and there were people going by principles. But there were some who came on the site, for instance on the night of the first eviction day, who were unknown,' Ann remembered. 'They were telling different stories to different people, purporting to be Travellers, and they vanished again, after causing trouble. They scared people; some of their talk was very violent. They were unpleasant to some of the women. There was talk about the IRA and stuff.'

Father Dan Mason was also troubled by the lack of scrutiny of the activists. 'The women welcomed the activists because they saw them as support and [because] they are naturally hospitable, but one of the concerns for those with young children was that there were all kinds of people turning up, some with concerns about alcohol and drugs. And they felt really uncomfortable about this group of people they didn't know. There were child-protection issues.'

A few well-known activists came on board, notably Jonnie Marbles, who had famously thrown a custard pie at Rupert Murdoch during a parliamentary hearing in connection with phone-hacking, and Marina Pepper, a former Liberal Democrat mayor for Telscombe in East Sussex, and an articulate climate-change campaigner. Jonathan had approached some of these 'celebrities' to raise the profile of Dale Farm. 'I targeted Marina because she was great, she was perfect, she was good at talking to people, having cups of tea with them.' But the core group remained tiny, with only a half-dozen able to stay put for the duration, organising the larger group of people coming and going at Camp Constant.

'We needed people who could stay,' Jonathan explained. 'It was great when Jake could stay; initially it was a rotation of five people. I set up a text alert: sign up for days at Dale Farm ... we had a month to fill.' Starting from no one had been a challenge, but eventually things had improved. 'We were lucky it was so many people ... It did ramp up, but I didn't think we had the capacity to sustain the camp for three months. Cooking meals three times a day – people have jobs, they can't commit to it. It was a nightmare having a three-month-long presence for people who had limited capacity. We had a constantly changing group of people; they would put in a week, and then they were gone.'

'It was literally friend by friend, mobilising other friends. So Tom and Sam said they would do the kitchen, Natalie volunteered to do media, and it was very slow, person by person. It was hard. It wasn't something where you could send out emails, say there was an info thing in London, and people would come; we had to recruit people ... A lot of it was that it was hopeless; you don't know when it's going to happen, and then it's a lost cause. People don't have months to sit in Essex. You know that when the bailiffs come there will be five people.' He knew that wouldn't be enough.

The activists had been hit almost immediately by very hostile media coverage, even in these days before Occupy had taken over the area in front of St Paul's. This carried the risk of doing more harm than good, encouraging even more hostility towards the Travellers. Jacob Wills disagreed. 'We were running quite a successful media campaign as part and parcel of a much bigger thing,' he said, and he and others thought that this very hostility towards them might be of some use. 'I think, to be honest, sometimes we did quite well in deflecting adverse media attention away from Travellers to us ... We were used to that sort of denigration, not that Travellers aren't, but considering all of the other strains on them, I definitely don't think it would have been all right to leave.'

Many of the residents, Jacob said, were welcoming, despite the ill will forming in the media. 'The Travellers really ensured that we were aware that they had never really experienced this sort of solidarity before, or even this interaction with the settled community before, and obviously few of us ... were Travellers. But to my knowledge there has never been any comparable situation where a large number and a large kind of varying population of people from the settled community end up staying on a site. So we were amazingly well welcomed, cooked for, given bedding, we had our clothes washed, we built up really strong friends – that is part of the strength now of the national network. Some of the people who were at Dale Farm are now at Smithy Fen, and I think it's those links with those Travellers that have provided us with some sort of passport to other areas of the Traveller community.'

Indeed, Mary Ann was pleased that the supporters were there. 'The students are absolutely beautiful. I have never met nicer people in my life. I said, "Thank you very much for coming, for showing so much support." There are good people in the world. They are here to help. They are living in tents, everywhere, so they are here for our support,' she said. 'I was shocked, really and truly: they came from all over to show their support, which was very nice and thoughtful. I was speaking to some of them, and they were saying, "Look, Mary Ann, we don't know what's going to happen to us one day, but we would like to help." We all need a friend, a friend in need is a friend indeed.'

By this time, her chalet was almost bare. 'I packed up my china — in case they come and break it up,' she said. 'I've got a lot of sentimental things I've got over the years, I wouldn't want them to come in and break them. I've just got my Bible out now.'

Quietly, she then added, 'We are just living in fear.'

7
'WE WILL NOT LEAVE'

By now, the residents were outnumbered by the activists. A swirl of rumours and complaints built up. Some Travellers, for instance, complained that the activists were fed vegan food and drank endless cups of tea flavoured with 'oat milk' that were partly paid for by the residents, who were accosted through a series of (what they felt were not completely) voluntary collections.[1] Photojournalist Sebastian Hesse had heard similar stories. 'They took money from the residents, which I found appalling; they were not only taking food and drinks and living there for free, but also asking for money.' The activists countered that they were contributing to a communal pot and that all donations – from Traveller families or the cosmetics chain Lush, which they had approached successfully for funds – were freely given. Some activists, like Jonathan Oppenheim, had donated a lot of their own money to the cause – in his case from a successful damages claim against Kent Police for numerous stop and searches during a previous action.

The amount of money the activists managed to raise infuriated groups such as the Gypsy Council, which had little to no money for its own campaigning. Candy had paid all of the costs of her trips to Dale Farm out of her own pocket. She was driving from North Norfolk, a round trip of 250 miles, and had lost many days' work as an antiques trader. She'd also had to leave a school-age child home alone during her many visits. The activists, for their part, said that they offered to set up a PayPal account for the Gypsy Council to help them with financing, but that the offer was rejected.

The high point for Grattan came on 30 August, when the actor Vanessa Redgrave visited Dale Farm, in part inspired by her brother Corin's visit some six years earlier, not long before he died. The Travellers were due to be evicted two days later, barring the success of any of their pending appeals. A phalanx of print and TV reporters had gathered to record the events, and Redgrave posed with Grattan for photos outside Mary Ann McCarthy's neat chalet. 'A big society is a human society where everybody takes care of each other,' Redgrave declared for the assembled press, cameras clicking away. 'Corin wouldn't be disappointed coming here. Here is a warm place.' She called Dale Farm 'a strong, wise, warm, gentle community'.[2] She and Grattan then went inside the chalet for a bowl of Mary Ann's Irish stew, washed down with mugs of strong tea.

Pressure was also heaped on the council by a visit to Dale Farm from an advisor to the United Nations, Professor Yves Cabannes, two weeks later. Standing outside Mary Ann's chalet, he accused the council of 'violating international law' on three counts, notably, 'the right to adequate housing, the right to be defended from forced eviction and discrimination'.[3]

The Redgrave visit, and then the UN advisor's slap, along with the relatively positive media coverage both engendered, had Basildon Council worried for the first time in months.[4] Their communications director, Cormac Smith, was a highly experienced PR operative; he had previously worked for Westminster Council – an iconic and powerful local council. He had been recruited to handle the press in the run-up to and during the eviction.

'The amount of publicity it created, and along with a well-choreographed narrative around Nazis, racism, discrimination ... drawing comparison with half-a-million Gypsies that had died in concentration camps ... The Travellers and their supporters, who were very media savvy,' he said, 'got a certain amount of support from the United Nations; they got a certain amount of support from Amnesty International; they also made attempts to get involvement from the International Red Cross. There were very well repeated accusations around Nazi death camps and discrimination, and this was a huge reputational risk to the council. This really did at one stage threaten to throw Basildon Council in a very bad and unwarranted light. And now, reputation for a local authority is a very valuable thing, because if our reputation suffers then our ability to work with and engage with and deliver day-to-day services suffers. That was my biggest concern, that there was blatant – I hesitate to use emotive language, but certainly "untruths" – being propagated in parts of the national press, both print and broadcast, that were threatening the good name of Basildon Council. At the end of the day, in the local government world we are recognised as a high-performing local authority that does a good job for its local residents, so that was difficult. That was what Vanessa Redgrave brought to it for me.'

It didn't help Smith's case that the Traveller women were keen to talk to the press at this stage, and worse, they came across as they were – vulnerable wives, mothers and children. Very few men ever agreed to be interviewed, which helped to keep some unhelpful complications out of the Travellers' side of the story. The council couldn't adopt this personal touch, so it was a rather unequal battle for public sympathy – despite the fact that they were, after all, in clear breach of planning law.

Still, the presence of the activists was useful to Smith's PR strategy. A number of newspapers – the *Basildon Echo*, the *Daily Express*, the *Daily Mail*, the *Telegraph* and the *London Evening Standard* – published exposés about members of the activist community, some of them funny, many of whom had concealed their names or hidden their rather prosperous family backgrounds.[5] Jacob Wills was one of those dissected. 'Stories about me, personally – the exposés were generally harmless ... Why would you say that someone who is in a structural situation that gives them an education can't have a conscience? That's quite laughable to me,' Wills said in reply to them.

The leader of Basildon Council, Tony Ball, saw this as good news indeed. 'I had no negotiations with the activists; I saw them as being irrelevant to the issue and were not doing the Travellers' cause any good at all, to be honest. They were a distraction and detrimental to the Travellers ... From my point of view it gave me a target. It was very difficult for me to be against the lovely McCarthy sisters ... [but the activists] gave me a target which others would support.'

PR operative Smith concurred. 'I think there is a huge question as to what value the activists added to the Travellers' cause, and we were clear from the very start that anybody who had the Travellers' interest at heart would have got them to comply with the law and move away from the site – because that was always going to be the ending.'

Grattan, however, was convinced that the presence of the activists was essential in galvanising media coverage. He could look back to his experience of resisting evictions in Ireland for useful lessons. 'We put on the same resistance at Cherry Orchard but we didn't have supporters back then. What we hoped by having supporters here and resisting was to cause a delay until something sensible could be negotiated ... I had asked some of them to get involved at Smithy Fen. It goes back several years. It was unusual to have so many supporters, in an organised way. We had a handful of Traveller supporters in the past, but never so well organised and prepared to resist to that extent.' Would the international media have shown up in such numbers without Vanessa Redgrave or Professor Yves Cabannes providing sound bites?

While the battle played out in the media, the police and the Home Office were continuing to gather intelligence, mostly about the activists. The date for the site clearance had been set: 19 September. The authorities were convinced that violence could well be employed during the eviction. Officers were worried that a wave of 'left-wing activists' would soon arrive to add to the numbers at Camp Constant.[6] Emotions among the local villagers were also running high. At the end of August Len Gridley, who was at the end of his tether, had been arrested for threatening Travellers with a shotgun, and his firearms seized.

The atmosphere at Dale Farm grew ever more tense. Many more of the activists put on masks, and now even a small number of Travellers were joining them. The site itself was less open, even compared to the 'security' check on the gate during the Camp Constant weekend. One day the entire site was blocked off and barricaded, only accessible with the help of a well-known activist or resident, and even then requiring some subterfuge and navigation under barbed wire and over high brick walls to get in or out. Gas canisters had been piled up near the front entrance, and makeshift barricades had been installed on some of the small side streets inside Dale Farm. Some youngsters were experimenting, trying to make homemade Molotov cocktails. Unknown journalists – any outsiders – were immediately suspect. This was not surprising, as it was quite possible that police had infiltrated the activist community. Two *Sun* reporters had already posed as activists to 'infiltrate' the camp, although their revelations were not enlightening, certainly not worth the effort to which they went.[7] Still, it had put people on guard.

Mary Ann left Dale Farm shortly after the photo opportunity with Vanessa Redgrave. Candy told me: 'She had lost a lot of weight. I used to sleep in the same bed as her when I visited, and I watched her getting worse and worse. In a week her family got her off, and I was pleased for her. But she had in some ways held us all together. When her chalet went, there was just that emptiness at the centre of what had been Dale Farm.'

There was another reason behind Mary Ann's departure, and the sadness of many of the Dale Farm Travellers about it. The evangelical Gypsy Christian church, Light and Life, had visited Essex in July during one of its large conventions, and had held a number of tent meetings to support those at Dale Farm. A small number of Irish Travellers, all previously devout Catholics, had converted to Light and Life – including Mary Ann and other members of her family.

One of Mary Ann's daughters, Pearl, remembered the chain of

events. 'Light and Life started to do meetings at Dale Farm, and I had been a devoted Catholic, along with all my family. They came out here every week. We were the only family who welcomed them in, the others thought it was a money-making game ... I started going to the new church, and reading my Bible, and one of the things it said was that we shouldn't worship false idols. We had been worshipping the Virgin Mary and the saints, although when I asked him, our priest said we weren't taught to worship them.' At a convention in Woodham Ferrers that same month, Mary Ann, Pearl and other relations converted.[8] The statue of the Virgin Mary in Mary Ann's chalet, once so lovingly dusted, was no longer such a cherished object.

This had added yet another note of tension within the embattled community whose common Catholic faith had once held them all together. It was especially problematic given Mary Ann's role as one of the community's anchors – one of the public faces of Dale Farm. 'It was very difficult, because it wasn't just about our religion, but we had come from a lot of tradition, as a community. So we got, and still get, a lot of stick for it,' Pearl said. Yet the blowback at Dale Farm did not dissuade them. The new church was a sanctuary at a time when many of their friends had deserted them. They could not fault the local priest, Father Dan, who always tried so hard to support them. They just felt as though they had found a new spiritual home in Light and Life.

Father Dan felt that in some ways the split over religion hurt some of the Dale Farm residents more than the actual eviction. 'When I arrived in the parish Mary Ann and Pearl were both very active parishioners, and Pearl was actually a Eucharistic minister – she would assist at the Mass,' he remembered. 'So when they moved to the Light and Life church, initially Pearl, and then Mary Ann, that was a real blow. A number of the other families were saying to me, "I thought they were such good Catholics." And Pearl had approached me and said she was worried about other family members joining Light and Life and they were saying all sorts of things, and I said, "Well, you need to be strong in your faith."' The big shock was yet to come, however. 'The next thing I know she has cleared off and saying, "The Catholic church gave me nothing." My perspective on this is that it is not about "market share". I don't mind what religion people choose, but I resent when people are told lies about my faith to persuade people to join this church. That's what I resent, being told, "We are not allowed to worship false idols," for instance – these are arguments from the Reformation, like whether or not the priest should be called Father or not. Some of the Travellers were more concerned with the [division between the] Light and Life Church and our church than about the eviction.'[9]

Around the same time, several powerful supporters had stepped away from the Travellers' fight. The EHRC was no longer putting its head above the parapet, fearing that protecting Gypsies and Travellers was too much of a direct challenge to the new government. It needed to dig in for its own survival. Sean Risdale, still then the policy officer for the East of England office, had helped to run the behind-the-scenes mediation process between the Travellers and the local authorities. 'The aim was to try and identify a site or sites in the Basildon area for families on the disputed part of Dale Farm. The residents from Dale Farm co-operated in this process, and we seemed very close to identifying potential sites just before the general election of 2010 – when Basildon Council suddenly pulled out of the process.' The EHRC lost heart. Officers stopped returning media phone calls or giving in-depth comments from around 2011 onwards, during the run-up to the eviction.

Labour lost heart as well. The new party leader, Ed Miliband, came out in support of the eviction, saying: 'The law does have to be upheld right across the country, whatever background people are from, wherever people are.'[10] His approach was not adopted throughout the Labour ranks. In Wales, the Labour administration put out the 'Travelling to a Better Future' policy document, described a 'new deal' for Gypsies and Travellers on services, sites and stereotyping and was strikingly positive in tone about the place that the communities should have in society. It went almost unnoticed outside of Wales.[11]

The residents at Dale Farm had some allies – the activists gathered at Camp Constant, some bishops and rabbis in the area, the local Member of the European Parliament and officers at Amnesty International. They even had the support of a few sympathetic individuals in Crays Hill. But for the most part, they were on their own.

Candy kept her promise and delayed the site clearance as long as possible. She worked closely with Keith Coughtrie, the lawyer for the Dale Farm residents, and Marc Willers, who was instructed as barrister for the residents to prepare the legal niceties of their case against Basildon Council. She also worked with her long-time ally, the planning expert Stuart Carruthers, a thorn in the side of many local authorities who opposed Gypsy and Traveller site provision. But her position as interpolator for the Irish Travellers was not secure – sometimes the people at Dale Farm favoured her tactics, sometimes they preferred Grattan's. Towards the end, the site was split, individual families fighting for individual policies and their own homes.

The Sheridans and their relations, the Flynns, supported Candy and her tactics to a large extent. But they also managed to maintain a cordial relationship with Grattan, who they counted as an old and dear friend. The McCarthy sisters joined forces with the outside activists, although Pearl stressed that what sustained her most during these last bitter days was her revived Christian faith. 'God had opened up my eyes. I felt I could talk better to the council because I wasn't bitter. I saw that there was so much hatred in the world, but also so much love and kindness from our church. They offered us everything – even money, and there was always someone to pray with you as well.'

At one time Candy was even informally banned from the site by a small number of the Traveller families. This meant that her ability – or anyone else's – to negotiate with the council was fatally compromised. 'There were private meetings in pubs [with Mary Ann McCarthy], formal meetings with ministers, with MPs,' Tony

Ball said. 'I also remember Richard Sheridan telling us that they would move for a couple of million. Really, I couldn't have done that.' He claimed that the shifts in powers made for confusion – it seemed that every week there was a new person to talk to. 'First it was Grattan, then he was sidelined by Candy, then she was barred. Then Richard Sheridan said I should talk to him. Then Patrick Egan, who owned the cottage, came back and he said if the council turned a blind eye to them moving onto the legal site, he could make that happen … Candy was banned from the site and not talking for them. Kathleen [also known as Pearl] McCarthy was speaking for them at the end. It was difficult. I wouldn't say that the Gypsy Council or the Irish Traveller movement as such were that influential, it was more individuals.'

Essex Police Superintendent Iain Logan also found the ebb and flow of responsibility difficult to deal with. It made negotiations in the run-up to the site clearance all but impossible, he said. 'There was no homogenous group and there was massive frustration for us, in that there was a lack of an identifiable leader or somebody who could influence events. We talked to great people from the Gypsy Council, Candy in particular, and we would have a conversation with them and think, these are really wise people. They listened, they probed, they were challenging, and you have that thought, maybe this might make a difference, but then they went back into that environment at Dale Farm and nobody seemed able to influence, mitigate and negotiate.'

The media interest in Dale Farm was, by this time, intense, and some of the Travellers enjoyed the attention. This was a conversion of a type – both Gypsies and Travellers had until recently eschewed such attention, as they had found it to be negative, for the most part, and they prized their privacy. But that had changed after the series *My Big Fat Gypsy Wedding* became a hit on Channel 4. The wider public had got used to seeing Irish Travellers, and to seeing them presented as big-hearted, generous, flashy individuals who sometimes liked a tipple. The publisher of the *Travellers' Times* criticised the show, saying, 'They're made to look totally feckless, not really to be taken seriously as an ethnic group.'[12]

The spectacular, unbelievable wedding dresses featured – including one weighing fourteen stone and featuring electric lights – were admired, sometimes mocked. The McCarthy sisters themselves took pride in colour-co-ordinating their outfits for the press at this time and, perhaps rather tongue in cheek, as court dates came and went, suggested that Candy Sheridan should have a makeover. Candy, who favoured modest clothes, wasn't interested. But the stereotypes bolstered by the TV programme shaped much of the reporting from Dale Farm – and some of the families chose to play up to what was expected of them.

As the first date for the site's clearance grew closer, Candy and other legal supporters had watched as the balance shifted at the site, making the potential for violence more of a real threat. Only a handful of residents – perhaps forty in all – were left behind on 19 September. Over a hundred activists were there.

Margaret Gammell was one of the Travellers left behind. 'We have nowhere to go and we don't even have a van to drive away in. This is all we have. I never thought we would come to this,' she said, weeping, in her modest chalet. Margaret was worried about a heart condition as well as her diabetes; she didn't know where she would get next month's medication, or where her blood tests would be taken, if she had to go on the road again.[13] 'I never thought we'd get to this point. I was going to paint my home, fix it up nice. There's no point now. Will things ever change for us?' she asked. She and her children had been evicted from Borehamwood eight years earlier, at four in the morning on a January winter's day. She had come to think of Dale Farm as her sanctuary, and now that sanctuary was under threat. Her children had got the education she never had, while living at Dale Farm. She said, quietly, 'We thought our travelling days were over. I'm fifty-six, I'm not well, I want to settle down.' Her daughter Mamie had been at Dale Farm since the age of one and was now studying hair and beauty at a local college.

Not far away, some masked activists had chained themselves to various obstacles they had erected near the gates to Dale Farm. Anarchist slogans were neatly scrawled above two activists who had locked themselves to site's main entrance. One, a young Belgian woman who would give only her first name, Emma, chained herself by the neck to the gate. The other, a putative film-maker, Dean Puckett, locked his left arm to an oil barrel. They were positioned to ensure that if Constant and Co. attempted to enter the site from the front, the activists would be harmed.[14]

It was a long-standing protest tactic, but it wasn't guaranteed to work, especially if the bailiffs were antagonised. Superintendent Logan was at the gate that first day and saw a mug of tea thrown into the face of one bailiff. (The temperature of the liquid remains, to this day, a matter of some dispute.) 'That concerned me, in terms of violence; the imagery around that wasn't good,' he said. 'We watched what was happening that day; there were the young people with D-rings round their necks at the front, warning that if we came in they would die, and such hostility. The media didn't help either, it was a real scrum, and conversations were happening by megaphone.'

Earlier that day Candy had condemned the action of the activists on Radio 4, saying that they were doing 'nothing useful' for the cause of residents at Dale Farm. Then she took court papers first to Basildon County Court (where by chance the judge was not sitting that day) and then to Chelmsford, in a last desperate attempt to try and halt the eviction. She and Stuart Carruthers, without any legal help, had crafted an emergency injunction in the name of Mary Sheridan (aka Michelle Sheridan), to halt the site clearance, arguing that Basildon Council was exceeding its enforcement notices. The sitting judge sent her immediately to the Royal Courts of Justice, where Justice Edwards-Stuart was sitting. Nobody thought she had a chance of halting the eviction. Activists such as Dean Puckett were merely irked by her actions and her remarks. 'Candy needs to listen to the residents here. We're supporting them. She doesn't represent them,' was his retort. He defended the broad alliance, adding, 'I don't want to break the law, but this is the most diverse campaign I've ever worked in. We have come together, we are standing together; just because you are masking up doesn't mean you are violent. We always condemn individuals when they fight back against state violence.'

Joseph Jones, a veteran of the Gypsy Council, spent part of the day up near the front gate. He was eyeing the makeshift barricades and shaking his head. 'This isn't helpful,' he said. 'There is a solution, but this isn't going to get us a solution.'

Trish Bowey, a therapist, and worker with the Southwark Travellers Action Group had journeyed to Dale Farm to support some friends. 'Dale Farm is affecting all Gypsies and Travellers. They have spent a lifetime being moved on, to find somewhere where they feel safe.' She was ambivalent about the presence of the activists, and asked whether anyone had considered the child-protection issues of having masked anarchists wandering around the place. 'I don't know, maybe the media attention will make people ask questions,' she said.

But Grattan still supported the presence of the activists, masked or not. He acknowledged that 'different views have come to the surface' in the run-up to the eviction. But he believed then that the presence of the activists had put pressure on the local council to change its mind – and that the international media outside the barricades had focused attention on the plight of Gypsies and Travellers facing eviction throughout Britain. Differences within the Gypsy Council were a small issue compared to the eviction at hand.

Marina Pepper, one of Jonathan Oppenheim's celebrity recruits, agreed that bigger problems needed to be in spotlight. 'Candy needs to listen to the Travellers. She's Gypsy Council, and it's not good to have a split within it. We are here to support the Travellers.' She described what was happening at Dale Farm as 'institutional racism'.[15]

Ann Kobayashi had stayed in Nora Egan's trailer the night before the proposed eviction. 'We got up very early in the morning … Nora was very frightened and the others came in, some of the other women, and one of them suggested we say the rosary,' she said. 'I was dying for a cup of tea but we said the rosary first, a very long one, and we said the prayers, including a prayer that nobody came to any harm, including the bailiffs and the police and Constant and Co. I think that was generous and Christian of them.' Ann was locked on after that. 'It wasn't uncomfortable, but it was tedious,' she said. She defended the presence of the activists, even those in masks. 'This is a loose coalition of groups. But [the activists being here] has altered Travellers' perceptions that they are marginalised. They never knew that people cared.'

Father Dan was there that day, just outside the fortified site, to show his support; his bishop had asked him to come. It was a 'desperate, awful and undignified' situation, in Father Dan's view. He was joined by the local vicar, Paul Trathern. 'When the law ceases to be compassionate, it ceases to be good law,' said Trathern, who was devastated by what he was seeing. What good could come of the 'breaking up of families, the traumatisation of children'? At various patches around the encampment, some small Traveller children were trying to make makeshift cement bombs; a few protestors were carrying a leaky car battery towards the front gates; makeshift barricades were being erected. Their chances and their future were looking bleak.

Candy's legal tactics were about to pay off, however. Her last-ditch attempt to secure the emergency injunction to delay the eviction had succeeded. But the injunction included a quid pro quo. She had to secure the 'dismantling of obstructions and barriers at the site' immediately and activists should be discouraged from further protest. At around 5 p.m. Justice Edwards-Stuart decided that the clearance should be halted, as it seemed poised to go further than the enforcement notices permitted.[16] Activists were unlocked, and some semblance of normality returned to the embattled site. Few, however, were thankful to Candy for the hours of work she had put in. But at least the residents had a last-minute reprieve.

Outside the barricades, local parish council representatives were furious. They told the assembled media that they might withhold their council tax in protest. That was a much smaller price to pay than the feared-for bloodshed.

The activists never took responsibility for the threat of violence issued by certain among their number. Jacob Wills, for instance, was unwilling to use violence himself, but he believed that each activist needed to make that decision individually. 'I guess the first thing is that we never formulate rules, and even if we did we are always aware in an eviction that we are doing massive call-outs to lots of people, and we are not there to police the forms of action that people take,' he said. He also felt that the tactics for resisting the eviction had been decided in consultation with the Travellers – that the activists weren't acting on their own. 'We try to ensure that they are in line with what the Travellers' community wants … We had lots of really long conversations with Travellers about the forms of resistance that we might employ – "we" as a collective – and I think, through that process, began to refine our understanding of what was acceptable and what wasn't. And definitely there was no tactical differentiation based on ethnicity; the lines weren't drawn that way at all. There is support for different forms of resistance from each community, and I think that people wanted to be very clear that the safety of everybody was paramount. So, for example, there are clear rules about no forms of active resistance where there are people locked into things so they can't move … maybe approaches a rule.'

Such ambivalence, and at times confusion, about the use of violence almost ensured a confrontation. If there were no clear 'rules of engagement', then it would only take one person to change the tone on eviction day.

On 7 October the community police team walked up to Dale Farm for one of their last visits before the eviction. Intelligence recorded: 'As officers approached Zone 4, Plot 6, Camp Constant, large writing in paint could be seen on the wall by the entrance. The writing said "Vandalism, as beautiful as a rock in a bailiff's face".'

Such sentiments drew deep concern from longer-term advocates for the Gypsy and Traveller way of life. Lord Avebury observed from the sidelines that 'there was a definite split emerging at Dale Farm between those people [the activists], and traditional campaigners like Candy Sheridan, whose objective was to try and solve the Dale Farm problem by finding alternative sites to which they could move … It was two campaigns.' He added: 'I honestly think it was confusing to the residents to see two totally different approaches to their problem in which this battle was being fought over their heads, as it were, between the two wings of the campaign. The fact that they weren't united may have damaged their prospects of reaching a solution.'

He acknowledged that the activists' presence had brought useful monitors to the crisis at Dale Farm. 'It got so much publicity and attracted international interest – one thing you can say for it, maybe we wouldn't have had the High Commissioner for Human Rights visiting Dale Farm and making such a strong pronouncement on it; he wouldn't have been there if there hadn't been the degree of agitation. And Grattan Puxon would, I daresay, claim that was a positive result of his activities there. Indeed, the Committee on the Elimination of Racial Discrimination at the UN might not have noticed what was happening at Dale Farm if it had not been for the activists … Yes, they might be able to claim that these results were a product of their work. So I am not going to say that there isn't a role for activism, but my view is that, in the end, you have got to arrive at a political solution.'

On 12 October, Mary Ann's five daughters, the 'McCarthy sisters', turned up at Court 76 at Britain's High Court to hear Lord Justice Ouseley's decision. The sisters wore matching red blouses for the day, a sign of solidarity. They were joined by several older supporters clad in sensible suits, while the activists from Camp Constant had turned out in somewhat scruffier garb: jeans, faded T-shirts, piercings and other alternative-culture adornments.[17]

This was, at long last, the end-game of the legal machinations for Dale Farm. Lord Justice Ouseley turned down the three linked applications for judicial review of the decision to refuse belated planning permission for the residents. Some cried quietly as the decision sank in. Ann Kobayashi, sitting in the audience, went pale and shook her head. Dismayed activists held their heads in their hands. Ouseley said that there must be 'public respect for and confidence in' planning law, and that although Basildon Council had not identified alternative pitches where the Travellers could live, those deemed homeless had been offered 'bricks and mortar' accommodation. The decision by Dale Farm residents to decline such housing, due to, as he put it, their 'cultural aversion', was their own responsibility. He pointed out that the Travellers were breaching the law by remaining on site.

Ouseley's judgement took nearly three hours to read out, with the stenographer clearly flagging towards the end. In it, he seemed to rule out any chance of success for the final appeal.

As the audience filed out of the courtroom, the McCarthy sisters, Candy, other Travellers and their supporters followed their barrister, Marc Willers. Still in his wig and gown and halfway down the stairs, they gathered around him. He promised to do anything he could to mount an appeal. 'I was very disappointed. I thought we had good arguments, both under the Housing Act and about acting in the best interests of the children,' he later said. 'One problem was that those challenges were dismissed, partly because we had brought them late, as I had been instructed very late in the day. Lord Justice Ouseley just wasn't swayed by my arguments.'[18]

Press photographers and camera operators were waiting outside the High Court to capture the reaction from all sides. The McCarthy sisters and the activists had set up an impromptu tea party just outside the court's gates, and Candy sat down briefly at the sisters' table. While they took tea and the cameras snapped, Tony Ball gave his statement.

He took 'quiet satisfaction on behalf of local people that in all matters the council has been found to have acted lawfully', he said, although he acknowledged that the council had been criticised by the court on a number of minor points. He asked the Travellers to encourage their supporters at Camp Constant to stand down and not to engage in violence. Pointedly, he noted that this was not a moment for 'triumphalism' – though there was but one side that might claim triumph, and it was his own. The eviction of the site, he indicated, might start as early as the following week.

After Candy had taken her turn addressing the media, vowing to fight on and appeal, she and Stuart Carruthers left the High Court and walked up High Holborn to sit, shell-shocked, in a Costa Coffee. This was the end, there was no doubt, but Candy still spent time phoning round, telling people the result and exploring avenues of possible resistance.

The atmosphere within the camp quickly soured that night. More Travellers were leaving, with some pulling their chalets and caravans onto pitches owned by families and friends on the legal site next to Dale Farm so that they could not be towed away by the bailiffs. Some of the more peaceable activists were leaving too, frightened by the prospect of a violent tussle ahead. The place was nearly deserted. Officials knew it; intelligence at the time stated that 'the unauthorised site currently has about thirty adult Travellers and Camp Constant has between forty and fifty activists'. The numbers were going down, not up, as eviction loomed.

Just five days later, on 17 October, Lord Justice Sullivan of the Court of Appeal turned down Marc Willers' request and granted Basildon Council the right to commence with enforcement activity at Dale Farm.[19]

The true end-game would now play out.

8
EVICTION

'Update on black side, please?'

'People moving forward now, lights flashing, cameras are going off at the location.'

'Silver, you getting the downlink?'

'Negative from silver.'

'Fifty-five persons on the inside, black fence, closing in on the officers, confirm if missiles still being thrown.' ...

'Confirm if you have any hostility on white side?'

'Within the site, protestors are there, no hostility.'

'Black side. Extremely large lumps of concrete being thrown now, powder being thrown, along with concrete.'

'Move to right-hand side, please, quick as you can.'*

On Wednesday, 19 October 2011, the clearance of Dale Farm finally began. Around 150 police, clad in full riot gear, arrived at 7.18 a.m., according to legal monitors, and broke down a fence at the back of the site. The bailiffs from Constant and Co. followed some twenty minutes later.

At 4 a.m., Tony Ball, the council leader, was informed that the site was going to be cleared, and how the day's events would proceed. 'Standing in the field on the morning and seeing riot

---

*   Helicopter uplink, audio provided by Essex Police. Code: white side: front of site, black side: back (point of entry), green side: left (near Len Gridley and other settled homeowners on Oak Road), red side: right (near legal site on Oak Lane).

police lined up in a field in Basildon is not something I would ever have wanted to see, and certainly wouldn't want to see again anywhere,' he said later. 'And you go through, "How is this going to play out?" and the risks ... Something very serious could have happened.' The police had to take control of the operation, he said, because of the risk of violence. 'There were gas canisters ... The Travellers had made threats before to the bailiffs, that they would set them off, they had made those threats ... There were people on lock-ons, we weren't sure how to get them off safely, things like that. I believe in September there was someone with a noose round her neck. Of course, I didn't know that the police had decided to go in through the side. I wouldn't ask. Not a matter for me. I had to leave it to the professionals to be handled. I knew the date, but not how.'

Cormac Smith, Basildon's director of communications, sat on Gold Command, the body led by Chief Superintendent Tim Stokes, which was charged with determining the date of the eviction, but he was also not told of the operation till early that morning. 'Right up to the last moment, it was a council-led operation. The police, literally at the eleventh hour, decided, because of intelligence they had had, that they expected danger. The decision was taken for the police to take the lead, as opposed to the bailiffs.' That meant that at the last moment the council lost control of the operation, Smith said. 'The police would not have discussed the details with us, that was a strategic decision to catch the Travellers and supporters off guard so they could enter the site, to minimise the dangers ... to take primacy of the operation, to transfer that from the council to the police, due to the intelligence. When the commander of the police announces that, we have to agree.'

Ball added that the police had brought in trained negotiators to talk to the activists. 'The police took the view that there was too much of a risk to the bailiffs' for them to go in. Indeed, Essex Police had earlier released a statement saying that they had 'received intelligence that indicated protesters had stockpiled various items' with the intent of using them against bailiffs and police. They were taking the intelligence seriously.

Superintendent Iain Logan of the Essex Police was serving as Silver Commander, in charge of the actual operation to clear the site, and reporting up to Gold Command. 'Work was being done to reinforce the boundaries – we had all seen media images of people carrying stones and rocks up onto the gantry at the front of the site, we had seen bottles of urine going up. Nothing specific led us to go in on that night, but the court proceedings had concluded and the action could now take place,' he said.[20]

Police intelligence from just two days before the eviction had convinced him of the need for decisive action: 'Intelligence suggests that the activists have been preparing petrol bombs made of glass bottles with rags in the top. Intelligence suggests there are four to five large gas canisters on site. The residents and activists plan on attaching a form of piping to the canister and turning on the gas so that it pumps out of the piping. They will then light the end and move it around like a flamethrower, which will scare off the bailiffs from bringing vehicles onto the site. Intelligence suggests that the activists have made a number of devices that look like a ball of metal nails.'[21]

Logan had spent many hours inspecting the perimeter of Dale Farm, trying to assess what tactics would allow his team to gain control of the site on eviction day, particularly in light of the reports he was receiving about possible weapons. 'We knew that gas – in this case acetylene – was there, and it is an immense threat if it gets hot: it explodes. It is really dangerous … the Fire Service was watching very carefully. In terms of how we felt about violence, it really did concern me, after what happened on the previous move forward by the bailiffs' – he was now referring to the hot tea allegedly thrown in the face of one of the Constant and Co. officers. 'My view was that to force an entry through the front gate was too dangerous an enterprise for everyone,' he continued. 'I kept looking at the site, asking myself, How can we do this in a way that minimises the risk of injury to activists, Travellers and police officers?'

In the end, Logan decided that 'the old-fashioned way, using surprise' was probably the best option available to him. 'I spent a lot of time walking around, and decided we would approach this in a different way, and find the least risky way of entering. We were trying to be audacious, use the element of surprise.'

He was particularly concerned to avoid a direct confrontation between the bailiffs and the protestors. 'There are videos on YouTube of bailiff-led evictions of Travellers that are awful, heartbreaking, from around here, Essex, as well as further afield, Birmingham. These remain in people's minds and they [the evictions] were not dealt with subtly,' he said. 'Also, bailiffs only have tabards and helmets. If we identify there is a serious risk of injury or death, it is our responsibility [as] the police to act, because of our training and [the] kit we are able to deploy.'

Logan also had it clear in his mind that the police role would be limited – their job was really only to kick-start the process and to keep the peace. 'Our decision was that we would facilitate entry to the site and return it to Basildon Borough Council control,' he explained. Then the bailiffs and the council would take over clearance of the site. 'It is not our job to evict anybody. Our job was to create an environment that was safe.'

Around 4 a.m. that Wednesday morning the police had sent a text message to Candy Sheridan's mobile, suggesting that she come to Dale Farm immediately. 'I was packed up ready to go to Stow Horse Fair,' she recalled. 'Instead I drove to Dale Farm with my [fair] stock in the back, a long drive with residents phoning me, saying the electricity had been cut off. The police were ringing me, telling me to hurry … Residents crying … and [me] miles away.' She had always stressed how important the fairs were for celebrating Gypsy and Traveller culture when the rest of their life was so hard. Now, here she was, forced to detour from the fair to attend an eviction – hard times indeed.

Logan's team was preparing to enter the site in less than three hours. The site perimeter had been divided into four quadrants by the police. The front gate at the southern edge of the site was to be known as 'white'. The western edge, near Len Gridley's back garden and Oak Lane, was 'green'. The south-east edge, near the legal site with Patrick Egan's cottage, was 'red'. The north back of the site – the place that Logan had chosen as his point of entry, if the front gate proved impassable – was codenamed 'black'.

The Essex Police officers had remained in their own homes during the run-up to the eviction, but their numbers were going to be reinforced by officers from the London Metropolitan Police, South Wales, and elsewhere. These forces had been barracked at the local Ministry of Defence training centre at Wethersfield, in Braintree. Given the number of different units involved, Logan had appointed two trusted Essex officers to report to him – Bronze reporting up to Silver.

'They were ready to convoy in. My steer was that if they [could] open the front gate, we go in that way, if it was easy and safe to do so,' Logan explained. 'I had two Bronze Commanders there that day, one at the front gate, one at the back.'

Logan's plan involved the use of Tasers as a form of defence against any weapons on the site. 'The Taser is a very effective piece of protective equipment; we describe it as less lethal rather than non-lethal. The Taser is designed to provide immediate protection for officers if they come under attack … It is designed to deal with a close-quarter threat,' he said. 'The Taser was authorised for the officers to carry who were engaged in the first entry to the site … I think I authorised it to only the method-of-entry team, so in single figures; it was allocated just to them, as part of their protective equipment.'

'I took the decision to go in at 6.56 a.m. Everyone had already been briefed and the resources were in place. The time of day [was] important because I wanted the ability to get the officers in safely. The nature of the site, the way it is laid out, is hazardous, and we didn't know whether other hazards had been built in,' he said. There had been intelligence about booby-trapped walls, in addition to the various weapons. 'You need daylight for this, you can't do this with searchlights, we wanted the maximum number of daylight hours. I also wanted to get the officers into position without disrupting the community.'

The Bronze Commander at the front gate had reported that the force would not be able to gain easy access there. So the entry team in their full riot gear made their way to a rickety fence at the back of the site. As they approached, a bell went off, warning the protestors of their presence. At Silver Command, Superintendent Logan's video down-link had failed, and he was left to rely on live audio feeds to learn what was going on.

> *'Black side. We are getting extremely large lumps of concrete being thrown now ... also some sort of powder thrown over the unit at the front.'*
>
> *'Some foul-smelling powder, we don't know what it is.'*
>
> *'Some powder over units at black side.'*
>
> *'Yes, along with large lumps of concrete, about a foot square.'*

Logan recalled: 'The entry team came under attack from rocks. There was almost a hierarchy of ammo used. There were bigger rocks nearer the [back] fence and smaller rocks further back and we did sustain injuries. The level of violence we encountered was the worst I have ever experienced, in terms of the hostility – speaking to the officers who delivered that action, very close-quarters and a horrible level of violence. It was probably the close-quarter nature of it. We come from Essex, we don't get riots ... This was a wholly exceptional level of violence; the officers would have never have encountered that level of violent resistance before.' In the fight, a Taser was used 'against one male who was presenting a lethal threat with wood with a nail on it', said Logan. 'The piece of wood coming across, powder being thrown across, we didn't know what it was, there was paint being thrown at them during that initial very violent interaction.'

Len Gridley was hosting some of the media, who were covering the event from spots in his garden. 'About quarter to seven more police riot vans turned up, around 250 officers came down the hill to the bottom of the site. They made a hole through the fence – they were getting pelted by everything, by metal poles – that's why they used the Tasers. They broke into the site and within twenty to forty minutes they had control,' he said. 'It was very professionally done, hands up to the police – a job well done. If they hadn't done it in that manner, they would have hung the eviction in for months, maybe years. Sending the police in was the correct way to control the site; they came in through the back of the site, the legal part of the breakers yard.'

Jonathan Oppenheim had come back from working in Poland just the night before, and one of the first things he had done was talk with the other core Dale Farm residents and activists about when the council might move forward. 'We were trying to gauge when it would happen. The problem is that if you put out false alarms, you tire people out,' he said. As the eviction date kept moving, the number of activists at Dale Farm had dwindled to fifty from about two hundred. The week previously, a call had gone out for activists to converge on the London Stock Exchange on Saturday, 15 October, as part of the Occupy movement that had been launched on Wall Street in September. The activists had been pushed off the Stock Exchange's property by the police, and had relocated their protest to St Paul's Cathedral. Two hundred and fifty people stayed there overnight. Two days later, the Occupy London group – now numbering between 150 and 500, based on various reports – issued a nine-point 'initial statement' to the media and authorities. Point eight read: 'We stand in solidarity with the global oppressed and we call for an end to the actions of our government and others in causing this oppression.'

By the time of his return on 18 October, Jonathan and the others at Dale Farm felt sure that the eviction would come almost immediately. He tried to rally more people to the site, but it was not working. 'It was a sleepless night, trying to get vans to come from Occupy London, and then the trains were down so lots of people couldn't get there. I didn't sleep much – I was already in my climbing harness,' he explained.

Jonathan was one of the activists assigned to the gantry, the twelve-metre-high scaffolding barricade that had been erected at the front gate and become an iconic symbol of Dale Farm, for both those inside and the media gathered outside the site. Still, the activists knew that the gantry was their strongest line of defence – a highly visible barrier. They also knew that they would need to keep a watch around the entire site. 'I got woken up at five in the morning just to discuss whether we should sound the alarm. We could see some activity happening in the compound, but we weren't sure ... But then it became apparent that something was going to happen, so we sounded the alarm, the siren. We did expect them to come at the back, but we were the crew who climbed up the gantry, so that's what we did.'

The time at which the decision was made to enter Dale Farm is questioned by the activists, including Jacob Wills. 'They said they made that decision at three in the morning, but I totally don't buy that. I think, I'm very sure, that that decision was made a long time before that; that's not how operational decisions are made, at three in the morning with a map the night before. We all looked at the back fence, and said, "Ooh, that fence needs a bit of work," but so much stuff needed work. I think it's kind of clear why they ended up coming through there – it means we did a good job of barricading the front, I guess. We were obviously outnumbered. And then there was the use of the Taser, really immediately, and the sheer numbers of police was really difficult. Also, the previous day there had been quite a lot more people ... it was unfortunate, in essence, that we weren't able to mobilise more people to be there on the day.'

'Resistance would have been very different if there had been hundreds and hundreds of people there,' Jacob continued. 'If there had been one thousand people there, the eviction just wouldn't have happened and that's what we were trying to build towards, that's the sort of movement that we would like to have built ... [but we were] under a hundred. There were fewer of us than the police. So I think it was clear to people that it was a rearguard action, and we would try and stay there for as long as possible.'

There was another reason for the lack of support at the site on eviction day. The English Gypsies, particularly those from the stronghold of North-East England, had made a crucial decision not to support the Irish Travellers. Billy Welch, the organiser of Appleby Horse Fair and a much respected *shera rom*, an elder in the community, was ambivalent about the events at Dale Farm. He had watched as the activists had amassed there, he was in close contact with Candy during the whole campaign, and he had been persuaded that things would not end well.

'There were other Gypsy men round me, asking me, "Should we give them some support, should we stand with them?"' he recalled. 'I said, "No, I would do, but if you are watching the TV, there are no men there, just the women and kids. They [the men] should stand up for themselves, and then we would go and stand up for them." They should have followed protocol and the law. I do feel they have made mistakes.' He added: 'They had the wrong people there, [the activists] didn't do themselves any favours. You don't set up tea-party shots outside the High Court. And look at all the shouting, violence and abuse, being abusive is not good.'[22] Influential Gypsy families from East Anglia and the Midlands were also ready to pull on to Dale Farm and stand with the Dale Farm residents – but only if the activists went, they told Candy. She relayed this news to Grattan – but he wanted them all to stand together, travelling peoples and activist allies. It was an either/or situation for the English Gypsies. They didn't come.

Parishioner and peace activist Ann Kobayashi was away that day too, in Japan, and only a handful of her Catholic congregation gathered in solidarity during the eviction process. 'I was enormously disappointed that more local people from the Christian community didn't come,' she said later. 'I have seen the power of encirclement, and standing vigil. You won't stop a determined group of people, but it's hard for them to act rough in the face of people standing silently, if possible, or sitting. Very hard. The difficulty was … one, there weren't enough people to tip that balance.'

■

Despite the rocks and powder and barricades, the police quickly took control. According to Superintendent Logan, 'Once we were able to get in to the site, it was methodical. We just moved forward, the issue was to get hold of the gantry from the reverse side, slowly, safely and in as dignified a way as possible, so that the bailiffs could do the work they had to do.'

The few activists and residents who were left inside rushed to the back of the site, where the police were now streaming in too. Some protestors physically fought the police in hand-to-hand combat. 'Some Travellers were violent, and so were some women [Travellers] as well,' reported Logan. In the scuffle, one Traveller, Nora Egan, fell down after allegedly being hit by a baton. She was later taken to hospital with a back injury.

But any such resistance was futile. Constant and Co. were on the site around fourteen minutes after the entry team had breached the rickety back fence.

The police and the bailiffs moved systematically towards the front of the site and the gantry. Some activists had positioned themselves on fences, scaffolding and platforms around or attached to the gantry. Some now hurled bricks, bottles – some with urine in them – and other debris onto the police and bailiffs below.

When Candy arrived, she was allowed through the police cordon on Oak Lane. 'It felt like a war zone on a film set,' she said. 'A police officer told me, "I have orders to bring you onto the site ASAP." I told him I wanted to walk on by myself.' She was not allowed to do so. 'He said, "I am here to protect you and stay with you," so I was walked on with a police presence, past the jeering activists and past distraught women Travellers.' It was not how she had imagined her last day trying to save Dale Farm.

At about 9 a.m., teams of riot police, in groups of eight, moved at a swift pace to assemble in front of the main gate. Two fire engines stood by, and soon fire officers had entered the site as well. A smoky haze hung over the site – a caravan had been set on fire by an activist and a plume of evil-smelling orange smoke curled upwards into the sky. Ten minutes later, bailiffs wearing climbing gear started to go in at the front. A clinical psychologist,

Robin Jamieson, had come out to support the Travellers, and was watching the events unfold at the front gate. 'They are already having appalling problems; the children are having nightmares. The bailiff is the bogeyman for them. This will have a huge effect on the children.'

Three helicopters hung overhead. Inside Dale Farm's makeshift barricades, activists and some Travellers were shouting, 'Fight, fight, fight,' and then, from the gantry at the front, 'Dale Farm will never be defeated!'

On the police audio, there was chatter about the fear of greater violence:

> '99, you got a number of protestors by a barricade in Camellia Drive, they appear to have bottles, possibly petrol bombs.'
> 'Just confirm that location again.'
> 'Yes, Camellia Drive, towards red, on the main entrance.'
> 'Silver ta to Bronze 2.'
> 'Silver, for your information from the Air Support Unit, there may be petrol bombs near to the main gantry on white side so far.'

The bailiffs were by now pushing the packs of reporters back, away from the front gate, 'for security reasons'. The front gate was heavily fortified, with little space for the assembled media to get in for a closer view. There was Fergal Keane, reporting for the BBC; Jackie Long, the social affairs editor for Channel 4 News; Johnny Howorth, the *Guardian* film-maker – all the regulars from the eviction coverage of the past two months, among them Sebastian Hesse from ARD Radio in Germany and international press agencies. Two legal observers who had come up from the Occupy London camp, Ben Doran and Alex Bennett, helped some journalists to sneak into the site.[23] 'The ironic thing for me was visiting trailers and seeing the families watching a live feed of footage of the "scaffold tower",' Howorth remembered. 'They just needed to step outside to see it. They seemed amazed that they were a part of history in the making.'

This had once been a makeshift but fully functioning hamlet – a strong village community. Now it was being torn apart, plot by plot. Women were sobbing, but the police continued to move forward, step by step, calmly. It didn't feel quite real, more like agit-prop theatre designed for the cameras. Perhaps this was because, as Superintendent Logan later said – the 'real' confrontation had been avoided, the feared, violent altercation between the Traveller residents and the bailiffs. Instead, the outsider activists and the police were slugging it out. They were proxies for the real protagonists. The Travellers had become pawns in a much larger battle, a media war, staged for effect.

'In many ways, the activists relieved the Travellers of the need to do any hand-to-hand combat,' Long said. 'I remember seeing women sitting out in their yards, watching what was going on. There was a level of excitement there, and I think some of the children quite enjoyed it. The Travellers were very savvy, and the activists helped them in terms of physical elements, such as getting the barricades done, fighting for them. But there was a genuine relationship there as well.'

By mid-morning all eyes were on the gantry.

> 'Silver ta to Bronze one.'
> 'Urgent.'
> 'Gary, from other means, there are believed to be hostiles in balaclavas hiding within caravans on red side. Near to one of your access points.'
> 'Do you receive?'
> 'Yes, received that. We may need to come back to deal with that and stick to following the objective.'
> 'Objective is agreed, get to the gantry.'

And other exchanges:

> *'From the Air Support Unit, there may be petrol bombs*
> *near to the main gantry.'*
>> *'Males in blue boiler suits in white masks mount-*
>> *ing the gantry.'*
>> *'And also from other information males in blue*
>> *boiler suits wearing white masks are actually mount-*
>> *ing the gantry.'*

Jonathan Oppenheim, in his distinctive wide-brimmed hat, sat alone on one small platform attached to the gantry. Protestors were locked on all over the place – to cars, to fences. About a third of the activists were masked.

On the gantry itself, a number of people were delivering dramatic speeches. Hanging off the scaffolding, Marina Pepper addressed the bailiffs and media: 'This is their home. They have nowhere to go. You are evicting them for money. Why is there money for your cruel jobs, when there is nothing for schools and hospitals? I don't know how you will sleep well tonight.' As the police moved forward, activists gave a running commentary on their performance and the injustice of the situation. One masked activist standing on the gantry squeaked out a few irked observations about the police and their 'fucking weapons and shields', like a scene pulled straight out of Monty Python's *Holy Grail*, when the Black Knight has all his limbs chopped off but continues to fight to the last – an inadvertently light moment in a dreadful day.

The gantry had become the centre of the activists' media strategy. The activists had appointed a spokesperson – a student going by the name of Ellie Wilkinson – and she was standing on the gantry. She promised that they would stay there for as long as the Travellers wanted them to. The McCarthy sisters were also prominently featured, giving press interviews in front of the scaffolding inside the embattled Dale Farm. 'We stayed through the eviction, we were screaming. It was terrible,' Joanna McCarthy said later.[24]

At just before eleven the 'Save Dale Farm' banner was hauled down from the gantry by the bailiffs. In an interview with Sky News, Wilkinson stood firm: 'We aim to stay as long as we

possibly can to show the law is unjust, but we realise we can't
stay here forever. If the residents ask us to come down, of course
we would do that.'

Pearl McCarthy, who had for some weeks taken the lion's share
of the media work from the Traveller side, shouted at the massed
riot police, 'Shame on ye, shame on the lot of ye!' She was taken
aback by the overwhelming force of the police – the Travellers
had not expected that.

Susan Craig-Greene, a human rights advocate who had visited
the site many times over the previous three years, was stunned by
the force enlisted. 'It's tragic. I don't know how it's come to this;
I'm surprised by the force. It just makes it all more traumatic for
the residents, they are really distressed. This isn't a solution – for
them, local people or the government.'

Michelle and Nora Sheridan were standing among the ruins of
their old plot, trying hard to stay calm. Many of the Travellers
who had gathered at the back of the site looked pale with stress;
some were crying. 'I saw someone being Tasered, he fizzed, I tell
you,' Nora reported as she tried to prevent her three boys from
going near the police lines. Michelle added: 'He was properly
lifted off the ground, he was fitting.'[25]

'Yes, some of the protestors were throwing stones, but it was
inhumane,' Michelle continued. 'I was running away with a child
in my arms. I didn't stop to look. I was terrified.' Tom, Michelle's
youngest, who was just eighteen months, was wailing, being
passed between her and her husband, Pa, for some sense of comfort in the middle of the clearance.

'They just kept coming,' one of the activists said, clearly
shocked.

Michelle replied, bitterly: 'There's nothing great about Great
Britain.'

It was Nora's son Jimmy Tom's eighth birthday. 'In the midst
of this chaos and devastation, I felt powerless but tried to help
with the small things,' Susan Craig-Greene later recalled about the

celebration that day. 'Probably the most useful thing I felt I could do that day was to help Nora … who was determined to give him a little piece of normality on his birthday. The community police, who have always been helpful and well liked at Dale Farm, escorted Nora, Jimmy Tom and me off the site to my car so that we could go to Asda to buy him a cake and a few decorations … For a few moments during the small celebration, with his immediate family and cousins in his trailer, we shut out what was going on outside. Jimmy Tom, who had excelled during the last two years at the local school, was excited to read *The Gruffalo* (the book I'd got him) aloud to me several times. At one point, the generator died and he was so eager to continue, we read by the light of my phone screen. All I could think as we were reading in the dark was that this was not just about one phenomenally bad birthday for Jimmy Tom.'[26]

Nearby, Candy was trying to get two older, sick residents off the site. She turned for help to one of the Bronze Commanders, asking that ambulances be called to evacuate the sick and older people. When the ambulances arrived, just after twelve, she cried out: 'If anyone needs to leave, tell me. This is unbelievable. What's happening?'

She was angry, and justifiably so. An injunction had been filed with the court protecting certain fences on the site – fences that the police had broken down as part of their plan of entry. 'It's against all the notices. They have made a mockery of the injunction. Look at these people, two have already gone to hospital,' she said.

When the electricity to the site had been cut by the council, it had left some of the older residents without access to necessary medicines, in particular those given using a nebuliser. She'd requested that portable generators be provided for these residents – but they had not shown up. 'I asked for the generators, and the police and the head bailiff, Jeff, were endlessly helpful. I rang Dawn French [a senior Basildon Council officer] and asked her why the generators for the nebulisers were still in the pound. She told me she couldn't get them on, as the activists had blocked the gantry gate. I felt a huge swell of anger against the activists – they wanted publicity but had no care for the sick or the elderly. It was a huge task, all eyes on the students, while residents began to take in the reality of the eviction and what would happen next.'

Sean Risdale, who been an officer for the EHRC, but had since started working with the Irish Traveller Movement in Britain, disappeared to find Grattan. There was some urgent work to be done, far from the heights of the gantry. 'I spent some of the afternoon ... sitting in an abandoned chalet with Grattan, with a wall of acrid flames on one side of us and a line of riot police on the other, phoning every agency we could think of to intervene even at this stage,' he said later. 'I rang the Children's Commissioner – we were concerned about safety for the one hundred or so babies and children still on or around the site, or potentially on the road, that night. They initially said they wouldn't do anything, because the Travellers had brought the situation on themselves by inviting the activists into Dale Farm. Eventually they agreed to ring Basildon's Eviction Control Centre to remind them about child safety.'

Grattan had stayed in a private yard belonging to Jim Hegarty, an Irish Traveller from Dale Farm, the night before. 'I felt sickened by the amount of force the police used that day,' he said. 'I have been present at some forty evictions; [in the past] the police have been there to keep the peace, and they let the bailiffs do the dirty work. I couldn't believe that they let seven police officers advance with Tasers.' Grattan worked tirelessly behind the scenes with several lawyers in a last ditch attempt to stop the eviction, the efforts funded, he said, by Vanessa Redgrave. But it was hopeless.

Just before the one o'clock news reports went live, another cry went up from the gantry. 'Dale Farm, we won't go. We love you, Dale Farm!' Shortly afterwards, the cherry picker moved slowly up towards the platform on the scaffolding.

'Our objective was the gantry,' Superintendent Logan later said. 'It was slow work ... But the officers who deliver that type of work are trained and they had rehearsed it previously. They build bits of scaffolding to train on, they are trained in the use of the cherry picker, which we use for helping possible suicide victims as well. There is no technique we would use that hadn't been tried before. We had a bit of an issue with legal advisers taking their tabards on and off,' a tactic used so that they could melt into the crowd and become activists when it suited their purposes, and vice versa, the police claimed. 'But once we contained the gantry and prevented legal observers from getting on there, we knew we were in a situation where it takes as long as it takes … We felt it was important to take the people off the gantry ourselves. It was a health and safety issue.'

At this point, Jacob was on the top platform attached to the gantry. A cry went up, 'We won't go!' as a scuffle broke out between the protestors and the police in the cherry picker trying to remove them. 'It's very difficult to know how to deal with that situation when you are being charged by loads of cops,' Jacob said. 'You are just trying to shut gates, which is what loads of people were trying to do. Yeah, I certainly don't think that there is any forward planning of those kinds of tactics. There are just lots of bricks at Dale Farm, because it was a scrap yard, but I imagine also – I am guessing here – lots of people have had difficult and traumatic experiences with the cops, and those were definitely exacerbated by what happened at Dale Farm.'

He claimed: 'It is important to note that, not only at an institutional level was it a very racist act, but we experienced – and this is only me as a privileged player in this – we witnessed really racist behaviour and really sadistic and fascistic cops … There was both an utter disregard for any interaction with Travellers whose homes were being destroyed but also verbal racism against them, them being called "pikeys", during the eviction and clearance operation. That's the bailiffs.'

At just after 3 p.m. Jacob was brought down by police. He shouted to journalists: 'They're torturing people up there! We are trying to resist peacefully!' He was hospitalised later that day.

'I was the first one to get taken off, so I can't say for everyone else, although I knew it continued, the verbal abuse was really concerning. They were putting their hands over my mouth and nose, putting their boots down on my chest, so I couldn't breathe for a few seconds, using lots and lots of pressure points, shoving my head into the corner of the scaffolding clip, a very sharp bit of metal, and saying, "I'm going to keep doing this until you go on the cherry picker." I mean, I was entangled in quite a few people there, but I wasn't actively resisting,' he said. 'I had a seizure; I have a muscular condition that has never manifested itself like that; I have lots of tendon problems. I lost control of my limbs and was hyperventilating for a while there. I was arrested and taken to hospital with two cops by my bed, which was not good for my mental health.'

Jonathan Oppenheim was also removed from the scaffolding tower. 'We had the tripod ... in front of the tower, and that was needed to stop them from opening the gate ... I was on the tripod, so I was separated off from everyone. There were many bailiffs and police on me, so I was treated fine,' he recalled. 'I was running back and forth between the two poles.'

Later, he said, when they were taken into custody by the police at the site, the accommodations were objectionable. 'They put us in a portable jail and – there may be lawsuits about this, as they had to pee in their chairs, basically.' When officers tried to interview him, he 'just said, "No comment, no comment"'.

The skirmishes continued for most of that day. One activist shouted, 'No more racist evictions!' as she was detained.[27] Twenty-three people were arrested.

At the end of Wednesday the police and bailiffs scaled back their teams. 'Daylight was important for us,' Superintendent Logan said. 'We weren't keen to deal with lock-ons overnight.'

Darkness fell. With the electricity shut off, activists and Travellers stumbled around the site, trying to work out their tactics for the next day. Accounts about these discussions differ, with some Travellers saying that they were prevented from leaving with their caravans after the gates were locked shut after around

10 p.m. Grattan, for his part, said that there was much controversy about Candy's plan to leave the gates open, so that police and bailiffs could continue with limited action that respected the terms of the injunction she had won a month earlier.

'That night was the worst ever, as panic and fear grew,' Candy said. 'The police retired to guarding the gantry. The activists kept on building fires, tearing down fences to feed them, while those with breathing problems suffered. Most Travellers were saying prayers in their trailers.'

Candy herself had retired to Mary Flynn's trailer. 'Suddenly there was a large whooshing noise. A fire had been lit nearby. Michelle, Nora and I went down the gantry and begged the activists to open the gate. The police said it was too dangerous to prise off the locked-on protestors. We didn't even know if we would survive that night. My daughters were begging me to come home.'

Others said that some activists were talking in terms of more violent resistance, and of using petrol bombs. An Irish Traveller family, who had come from Wellingborough to support the Dale Farm residents, became hopelessly suspicious of everyone in the dark. One member of the family threatened Candy and punched an activist in the face.

Now everyone could feel that Basildon Council had won.

The operation to clear the site continued at daybreak, with the main objective among the police forces being to cut free the last six protestors, who were still locked on to various barricades inside. Around 8.30 three were arrested. Tony Ball released a press statement: 'Again, we have been made aware that there are residents who want to leave the site and are being prevented from doing so by the barricade and the actions of the protestors. Along with our contractors and partners, we want to do all that we can to help them to leave safely, and removing the barricade is key to achieving this.

'I hope that there are no repeats of yesterday's scenes of premeditated violence and disorder from the protestors on the site, and that we can get on with the job of upholding the law, and clearing the site in a safe, professional and dignified way.'

The press coverage from the day before centred on the use of the Taser and the efficient force used by the police. *The Times*, for instance, said that the use of Tasers had prompted accusations of a breach of guidelines about not using it for crowd control. But because the police could truthfully say that a Taser had only been used on one person, it never really took off as a story. It had, however, been pointed at others, and the threat of its use remained very clear.

By 10 a.m. the main gate at Dale Farm been reduced to rubble. By mid-morning the two last protestors, named Arran and Danya, who had locked on to a barrel, were also removed. Pearl McCarthy, finally defeated, told journalists that there was nothing more to be done. Just after lunchtime, Joseph P. Jones of the Gypsy Council said Travellers just wanted the Dale Farm eviction to pass without any more violence.[28]

At just after half past five, the last Dale Farm Travellers, three of the McCarthy sisters in the front row, marched peacefully out of the site together, along with the remaining few activists. Some of the activists chanted, rather quietly, 'Save Dale Farm,' as they went. Pearl McCarthy told journalists: 'It is a terrible moment, very sad, but the time has come' and added that they were walking out with dignity, with their 'heads held high'.[29]

Despite the police intelligence about weapons at the site, no guns were ever found. There were no booby-trapped walls or petrol bombs. However, two wheelie-bins of rocks were found near the Gate Tower.

Grattan said: 'I had thought we could hold on for a few more days, but Pearl's decision was right. It allowed all the caravans to move out into Oak Lane. It was a kind of victory.' But in many ways, the end of Dale Farm was a crushing blow that no one had ever expected would come to pass.

A week later, Candy too left Dale Farm. 'I walked into a garage on the A12 and the assistant said, "I saw you on the TV." I had forgotten about the "real world".'

9
CLINGING TO THE WRECKAGE

Dale Farm was a pyrrhic victory for Basildon District Council. It had cost local residents at least £4.8 million for the initial operation, and would later come to cost much, much more. Many of the Travellers moved over to Oak Lane, the nearby legal site, or just a hundred or so yards down the road. Others moved away for a few weeks, then came back shortly before Christmas. A number of local residents were incensed that so many Travellers were still around the site, calling for the council to explain itself. Radio phone-ins and comments to the local papers were rabid with frustration.

For the former residents of the site, the immediate problems were emotional and psychological, but physical problems soon presented themselves too. Dale Farm's cesspits had not been emptied before the site clearance had started, and the area rapidly became polluted. Soon vast numbers of rats – known as long-tails to the Travellers – appeared, frightening the residents. The roadside Travellers were living without plumbing and piped utilities and had to rely on the kindness of those who had found space on the legal site for access to toilets and drinking water. The winter of 2011 was a hard, cold one. As many as three-quarters of the evicted families had stayed on, or returned after being evicted from elsewhere.

Some twenty caravans lined the pot-holed road leading to the closed site.[1] Men were grooming themselves on the roadway, peering into tiny mirrors mounted on their caravan doors. The women were throwing cleaning water into the road, making deep puddles. Frustrated toddlers played behind closed caravan doors.

Parents had mostly kept their children inside after the eviction, fearing that they might fall into the deep trenches that had been dug by contractors to prevent any caravans returning to Dale Farm. 'I feel like a refugee in my own land,' said Michael Slattery, who had young grandchildren living with his family at the site.[2]

Among the few families with a legal claim to a pitch on the old site were Mary Flynn and her daughters, Michelle and Nora Sheridan. The pitch had been bunded, however, so they could not get back on it. Mary had both chronic obstructive pulmonary disease, which made it difficult for her to breathe, and brittle bones. At the pitch, her daughters had built a makeshift but accessible set-up for her condition. That was gone, and she had suffered many minor bone breakages since being forced to move her caravan to the roadside. Now she and her daughters had to rely on toileting that had been installed for friends on the legal traveller site at Oak Lane; they had to ask them for water too. Looking pale and drawn, Mary said: 'We were happy at Dale Farm. We were independent. Now we have to ask for every jug of water.'

Michelle reported that the residents had been struck down by chicken pox and a persistent stomach bug – small wonder, as four or five families were sharing a single toilet. The Sheridans were finding it particularly hard because a court order had initially protected their pitch, but they had been moved despite that shortly after eviction day. 'Dale Farm had been our sanctuary,' Michelle said. When they were soon moved off Dale Farm for 'health and safety' reasons, they found shelter next door on the legal site, in the hope that they would soon be able to move back home.

They tried to give the children a normal life, sending them out trick-or-treating on Halloween.[3] Two weeks after the eviction, on 2 November, some of the Sheridan children went back to school.

'We had made a home, that was it,' said Nora, as she observed just weeks after the eviction. 'We hadn't been on the roadside for ten years. We had our kids going to school, what I never had. I can't read or write, I don't want them to be like that. I've lived without a lot of things in my life. I wanted my kids to have an education, to make something of their life. They had all their needles, all their vaccinations, what I didn't have when I was growing up – I didn't have any vaccinations. Things would have been different for us if we had had an education.'

That day, Lorraine Brown, the solicitor for Basildon Council, came to tell the Sheridans that they would have to move off the site after all, so that the hard standing could be removed. The next day they also removed their caravan, shifting to the legal site on Oak Lane. Nora watched as the diggers began their work, telling a reporter from the *Guardian*: 'It's the end of our world … it's heart-breaking.'[4]

A few days later, on 8 November, Candy came back to try and negotiate for the families to move back onto their plot. Permission was denied.

Nora's children were struggling. 'The children don't understand. We wish they had moved off during the eviction now. It was too painful. My kids stayed on the pitch and she [Mary] was on the pitch and my sister was on the pitch, when the police came through and everything happened, we all ran out to see everything. Whenever they see the police they are frightened that they will come in and break up our homes, they had a fear they would come in and trash all of our homes. They trashed our caravans. My ten-year-old is too frightened to go to school, my seven-year-old won't sleep in his own bed, it's a living hell for us, that's what they have done to us.' Both Michelle and Nora hoped at this time that they could move back onto their pitch, saying 'at least we will be clean if muddy'.

But that was not to be. Nora's voice turned bitter: 'They thought we would vanish into thin air when they evicted us, but we have nowhere else to go. And we are still saying, "If there are authorised pitches, we will go elsewhere." I have travelled my whole life, I have never been evicted – it was my first eviction … I was used to the bailiffs coming to the door, at the roadside, knocking and saying, "Pack up, you have two hours," I was used to that. So unfortunately I didn't think the eviction would be like it was. I wanted to stay for my kids. My mum was sick. I'd lost my dad here, I didn't think it would ever come to this.'

The makeshift path that the council had grudgingly provided as access to their pitch made its way between deep, dangerous trenches. The path itself was just crumbling muddy earth – not fit for their mother's wheelchair. They hoped that perhaps the council might be pressurised to create a wider, more suitable pathway.

The next morning, Nora phoned, crying with pain. The family had a washing machine set up in their utility room on their pitch and often had to resort to washing school uniforms there by candle light, asking other families if they could dry the uniforms for them overnight. They found it excruciating and embarrassing. The night before, she had gone up to the pitch in the dark to wash some clothes and fallen into the trench.

'I kept saying it was not safe ... I wasn't worried about me, I was worried about my kids falling down the trench, and my mum. And then I fell down. I went up at five o'clock to put diesel in the generator in the washing machine, to wash the kids' school uniforms ... My sister came and my youngest little boy [Jimmy Tom] was with me, and I was watching him, I had him on the inside, I was saying, "Watch the stones. Don't fall. Be careful." Then the bank gave way and I fell in and it took an hour and ten minutes to get me out ... Next thing I was in A&E. All I could picture was that I was in the hole and I couldn't move.'

Nora had injured her back and was now on anti-depressants. 'I am still on pain tablets for it.' Her mother had been to A&E eight times since the eviction.

Nora could not understand how the council had broken their side of what she thought was a clear agreement. 'They signed up for wheelchair access, the fire people told us. We had the fire brigade out and they said, "It's not safe wheelchair access." This is not what we agreed. Basildon said they were giving us access to the pitch. It took four security guards, three ambulance crew and three policemen to get me out of that ditch.'

Nora had tried to pull herself out of her depression by decorating cushions with diamanté work for her caravan. They were beautiful, dainty pieces of work. Candy had encouraged her in this, saying that perhaps they could be sold at the horse fairs. But

Nora had no car to get to the fairs and could see no way forward beyond a day-to-day existence. 'You have to do something. You have to keep their home nice for them. That's the most important things: the kids are washed, cleaned and fed, and their home is clean that they have to go into. Make it positive,' she said. 'They don't want to see you stressed-out and crying. I hide all that. We cry when they are asleep or at school, or say I have something in my eye or – always an excuse for the kids. If I fall apart, then they fall apart. [The council] have made our life a misery. It's really hard.'

Being back on the roadside wasn't an answer, in her mind. 'It was a very bleak mid-winter.'[5]

Ann Kobayashi was also increasingly worried about the conditions on the roadside. 'I remember one of the women saying, "I go up every evening to my yard and cry, I just cry," and after six weeks, she said, "I've cried all I can, all the tears have gone, I won't go up there again, it upsets me too much." Their whole way of life has disappeared. Local people see them moving back to Dale Farm as defiance or awkwardness,' she said. 'They don't see the enormous hardship involved with living in the conditions they are now living … They have been reduced to the stereotypical awful conditions that people always imagined they lived in – but of course they didn't. They always live in very clean conditions. Their own yards, they keep them clean. The public bits eventually get cleaned up. The yards are neat and tidy, and there is lots of internal criticism of a woman who doesn't keep her yard clean. Now that business of having your own bit of territory has been taken away from them.'

The more vulnerable members of the community were hit very hard, Ann observed. 'The impact on the elderly has been quite profound. The loss of speaking to their own peers, passing the time of day, being able to keep an eye on the children, grandchildren at the same time – they can't sit out on a private road and do that. The parents and carers have it tough, looking both ways, there is lots of latent depression hanging around, but at least they can work it out. The young children have been deprived of their yards, their homes.'

She had seen how the women, including Nora and Michelle Sheridan, were straining to keep their families together. 'Their relations have vanished, and also their whole feeling of territory, being moved from where they were, squeezing down onto the authorised bit, on sufferance ... It's not the same as having their own place. They have to send a child out to get a jug of water, sanitation."

She persuaded the Red Cross to visit and make an assessment — an almost unprecedented occurrence, and one that the Red Cross wanted to keep discreet. As Michelle explained, when they arrived on 21 December, it was an 'undercover kind of thing ... There were just two of them. They were shocked, when they saw the conditions outside on the road ... One lady had her Christmas tree outside the door; she had no space – she had this massive Christmas tree, and she had had a nice home for it at one point, but not any more. They felt for us, they thought that was so sad; they took loads of photos of that.'

Ann had arranged for the Red Cross inspectors to be joined by the Irish Traveller Movement on the confidential mission to the site. 'They asked about the sanitation, the water, and at that point we were asking for toilets, the electricity, Portaloos,' Michelle said. 'We use whatever toilets are nearest to us,' she had told them. The timing could not have been more poignant. 'The ones on the road really had a bad Christmas of it. They did the best they could, did a pot roast, but it wasn't easy. We are managing for the shops, all right; my biggest worry is where we will pull on to now.'

Christmas, the women emphasised, had been really bad. 'The eviction was bad, but Christmas was even worse,' Nora said quietly, almost forcing herself to say it. Her sister added: 'They took our pride away from us when they evicted us.'

Another Traveller woman said it had been a nightmare for them. 'I'm at the back of the site, on the roadside. It's not very good. I have three kids; they are too sick for school. It was bad over Christmas. Very bad for them, they were playing up. They are used to Christmas trees, fairy lights outside, proper things they have every year [but] they couldn't get them out because the bailiffs destroyed them. They were born and raised up [at Dale Farm], and this was the worst Christmas for them.'

Nora, like other mothers, had stored her Christmas decorations, but they were ruined during the clearance. Now her children, who used to be able to play safely within the gates of her pitch, were locked inside the caravan. The road was too dangerous, too cold and muddy.

Indeed, up and down the pot-holed lane, the sound of frustrated children could be heard coming from inside each and every spotless caravan. Other mothers were also frightened to let their children out. 'They were lovely kids, really good, but they are not the same any more,' one woman said. 'They are so unhappy since they left Dale Farm. It's like a third-world country here. We are terrified as mothers. They dug up our yards, and it's like a big swamp, with the rain coming – what if our kids going missing for a second? We are screaming, having a nervous breakdown, because we are thinking if one of the kids are falling in there, it is a death trap. Kids are kids, I have got a three-year-old, a six-year-old and I am panicking … Tony Ball is saying, "The law is the law. They should have moved on." What good is that to me, to any mother?'

She thought about her toddler and keeping an eye on three children at once. 'We are terrified … I get the shakes in my body; I trembles, for every mother, thinking that they could be up there, dead. It's a death trap. Life is never going to be the same.'

The McCarthy family had scattered before and after the eviction. Mary Ann, who needed medical treatment, had moved to live with her sister on a site at Leighton Buzzard, in Hertfordshire. One of her five daughters, Joanna, went with her, to care for her: 'We miss seeing our nieces and nephews, it's so hard. Our whole world has been shattered. We never thought the eviction would actually happen. My mum was ill with the shock of it.' But Joanna felt she and her mother could not stay at Dale Farm after the clearance. 'It's a health hazard there; we were lucky to find this. But it's nothing like what we had before. We felt so safe at Dale Farm: we had no hassle, no problem, we got along fine with everyone else in the community.'

Joanna had vivid memories of the aftermath of the eviction. 'After the cameras had gone, the women and children had it bad, there was nobody recording the terrible names the bailiffs called us. It was terrible to watch all the grounds being dug up and the bailiffs were laughing at us. And when the children went back to try and find balls they had left, they would be hauled off,' she claimed.

The effect on the Dale Farm children, she said, would last generations. 'Our nephews and nieces, they have a stigmata [on] their heads now – it has ruined their lives. We tried to bring [up] our children without prejudice to nobody, but they have grown up now hating and disliking all settled people. They say, "They have broken up our homes, they are the ones that hurt us." They don't trust country people [the settled community] any more. It's hard to explain who are the good ones among them now.'

The eviction was devastating for many of their activist friends too. Said Jacob Wills: 'I think a huge number of the people who were involved, both in the eviction and the people who were there for most of the couple of months but not there for the eviction, are suffering quite a lot of post-traumatic stress ... A lot of that is to do with the specifics: the physicality of the eviction and ... the knowledge that the community at some level put a large amount of faith in us. Our link with that community, although still very strong, has been ripped apart by forces outside our control ... I'm in counselling now. And even now some people are in a very bad situation, and of course that goes for the families as well.'

Feelings of failure and defeat haunted some of the activists, he acknowledged. 'Most people did see it in a deterministic way – and that's not to negate the act of resisting; it's not to say that it was futile. I don't personally feel, at least not consciously, that I, or we, failed the Travellers, and I know that they don't feel that. It's really saddening, the situation … I think that people's trauma and sadness was because of the unutterable horror of people who you were very close to losing everything.'

Jacob and the other activists did not give up on their support for the residents, however. After the eviction, they established a fledgling organisation, the Traveller Solidarity Network, to lend support to other Gypsies and Travellers under threat of eviction and to raise awareness of their plight. The experience, Jacob said, 'spurred a lot of people on to the creation of the new national network – moving beyond solely doing support sites, trying to address how government policy is formulated'. The group went on a limited tour of Britain in March 2012 to raise awareness of Traveller rights. They had received a ring of endorsement for their efforts from none other than Grattan Puxon, who continues to support the network.[6]

It was perhaps ironic how determined the former nomads were to stay near the ruins of their one-time home. But they were telling the truth when they said they had nowhere else to go. They also wanted to stick together, as there was safety in numbers. More terrifying threats might emerge if they shifted elsewhere, where they were not known and where they felt vulnerable. They all remembered the case of Johnny Delaney, a fifteen-year-old who had been kicked about the head after an altercation between his friends and a group of local teenagers on a playing field, just a few miles from his home, in Ellesmere Port, Cheshire, back in May 2003.

Johnny and his friends had tried to run away from the other youths. Johnny fell and was kicked as he lay on the ground. Witnesses reported that one of the attackers had stamped on Johnny's head with both feet and said he deserved it because 'he was only a … Gypsy'. A girl at the scene said that, if she had to rate the kicks for force on a scale of one to ten, she would have given them a nine. One of the two defendants charged with the attack said he heard Johnny groan as he lay on the ground before his accomplice walked back and stamped on him with both feet.[7] Johnny was taken to the Countess of Chester Hospital, but died shortly afterwards.

The two defendants, Louis McVey and Ricky Kearney, were sixteen at the time. They were found guilty of manslaughter in November 2003. The judge lifted a ban on reporting the youths' identities as a deterrent, but said he could not increase the sentences for racial aggravation as it was unclear who had made the racist comment. This disappointed the investigating officers. Detective Chief Inspector Jed Manley of Cheshire Police said: 'It was recorded as a racially motivated incident on the first day of the inquiry ... because of certain comments made at the scene of the incident. I believe that the incident still falls within the definition we would use for a racially motivated incident, and we believe that is appropriate.'

According to his family, Johnny had faced prejudice before, and hated being picked on for being 'a Gypsy'. After the verdict, his father, Patrick Delaney, said: 'There is no justice here. They were kicking my son like a football. Are they going to let this happen to another Gypsy? Every travelling person is going to be upset by that verdict. As far as we're concerned it was a racist attack. I have lost my son for life. This has left a big hole in our family. He was a very polite lad who never did anything wrong. He didn't deserve this.'

Johnny's mother, Cuzzy, and his older sister, Nan, still keenly feel the pain of his murder nearly ten years after Johnny was killed. They live in a small, tightly knit Traveller site on Liverpool's Oil Street, behind the local Costco and in sight of luxury apartments along the city's waterfront. A large photo of Johnny hung on the wall of the neat utility room that the family had built next to Cuzzy's caravan. A simple cross and other family photos were nearby. Much like Mary Ann McCarthy's chalet, well-dusted china fruit and flowers decorated the room. Cuzzy tried to summon up a smile as she remembered her son. 'We never got justice for my son; the judge didn't give us justice. And then I lost my husband a year afterwards. What they did took two lives from me.'

With a mournful note to her voice, Nan added that she had lost her baby to cot death soon after Johnny's death. 'It was very hard and it gets harder every year.'

'That day I knew something was going to happen to them,' Cuzzy said. 'I said to him, "Stay here. Don't move off the site." He said, "Iron me a blue shirt, and black trousers" – for my sister's party – and then he went out. Then I got a phone call saying that he had a broken nose, and we went down to the hospital. It was that packed with Travellers, they had all heard. The policeman just told me, "Your son is dead."' Her husband was too upset to identify Johnny's body, and Cuzzy had to do it instead.

Most upsetting was that the family never had a chance to say goodbye to him. He was dead before they had arrived.

'Not a day goes by when I don't think about my Johnny,' she said. 'I've kept all his clothes, his socks.' When visitors came calling, she would show them the many photograph albums she had put together of his short life and awful death. Inside one, she kept two of his most precious possessions: his rosary and his mobile phone. He loved his phone so much, she said, that some of the flowers at his wedding were shaped like mobiles.

Cuzzy said that the murder had stolen her future away from her. 'His birthday was every June, so he just didn't make his sixteenth birthday. His youngest brother misses him. He has had a hard time. Him and Johnny were very close, being the two youngest boys, sometimes he would sleep with Johnny in the caravan.'

Nan remembered her strict brother with affection. 'He wouldn't let me go out to a disco on my own, he didn't want me to get grabbed' – kissed without permission. 'He would ask me where I was going, even though I was older than him!'

The Chief Constable of Cheshire Police, Peter Fahy, said they were aware of underlying tensions between people in Ellesmere Port and the Travellers. Fahy's sister, then a young schoolgirl, was campaigning tirelessly to raise awareness of hate crimes against Gypsies and Travellers. That campaign, along with internal pressure from police insiders and the Crown Prosecution Service, was having some positive effects. One was the creation of the Pride not Prejudice project, which brought together police officers and members of the Gypsy, Traveller and Roma communities to tackle racism. John Cole, from Liverpool Council's support team for Gypsy and Traveller families, was one of the founder members; another was a former police officer turned academic, John Coxhead. Before his death, Johnny's father, Patrick Delaney, had also been an important figure. Working with the Derbyshire Gypsy Liaison Group, the project members developed training for the police as well as a DVD, *Del Gavvers Pukker-Cheerus* ('Give the police a chance'), created by the Gypsy Media Company in co-operation with the police.[8]

The Crown Prosecution Service was also changing. In November 2011 the first ever CPS guidance on hate crimes against Gypsies and Travellers was released. It was written by the local hate-crime prosecutor, Rosemary Thompson, who had previously worked on raising awareness of disability hate crime.[9] At the launch of the guidance, Joseph Jones, the chair of the Gypsy Council, spoke vividly of his memories of hate crimes and general discrimination in the Birmingham area from the 1960s onwards. Thompson said: 'The CPS regards any element of prejudice, discrimination or hate in any type of crime as totally unacceptable. Travelling communities have a right to equal access to justice, safety and a right to live their lives without fear. We want victims of hate crime, their families, communities and the general public to be confident that the CPS understands the serious nature of these crimes and is committed to playing its part to bring these offences to justice. We are determined to play our part in tackling racism against Gypsy, Roma and Traveller Communities.'

But progress had been painfully slow. In her research in preparing the guidance, Thompson had been unable to identify a single successful prosecution for a hate crime perpetrated against a Gypsy or Traveller.[10]

John Cole, who makes frequent visits to Johnny's family, asked what Cuzzy and Nan would like to see happen on the tenth anniversary of his death. Cuzzy said: 'I don't want Johnny to be forgotten. I don't want Johnny hidden away and forgotten. That's all.'

Leaving the safety of Oak Lane – even if it wasn't the old Dale Farm – wasn't a move to be taking lightly.

By mid-January, Grattan was trying to dig a path to the Sheridans' pitch, so desperate were they to move back on. He, too, was visibly shattered by the events at Dale Farm that autumn. Knee-deep in the mud and the wreckage, he supervised a small digger manoeuvring to try and level out a path to the lawful pitches on the site. 'It is devastating for me psychologically, and I am trying to put the bits together again. I would much rather have gone the other way: I wanted to save Dale Farm ... That would set a precedent for this country, but it has gone the other way, and it has set a precedent for violent action against Travellers. We are still hoping to reverse that, through the law and planning applications. Put Dale Farm back and show that what Basildon Council did was futile as well as brutal. If we can do that, I would be pretty happy I had done something towards the end of my life.'

He did not regret involving the activists. He remembered back to the fight at Cherry Orchard, in Ireland, nearly fifty years earlier. 'We put on the same resistance at Cherry Orchard, but we just didn't have enough supporters. What we hoped by having supporters here and resisting was to cause a delay until something sensible could be negotiated,' he said. 'I do believe that Constant and Co. bailiffs would not be able to carry out the eviction without this huge initial, violent assault by the police, using Taser stun guns. We probably would have been able to hold back Constant and Co. until, as we thought, we could negotiate something with the council, a settlement.'

The residents quite clearly adored him, despite the wreckage surrounding them. 'My husband just loved the man,' Mary Flynn said. When Grattan had his bypass operation, if my husband saw him doing anything, he would stop him, and say, "You can't do

tings like that! Take it easy.''' Nora added: 'He had those operations, but he would still come back and be here all day and he
had a rough time of it, and we would press a cup of tea on him.
We really do like him, all our families like him.'

They appreciated what the activists had tried to do too.
Michelle stressed how important it was that they had come back
to see them since the eviction. 'Every one of them has been back
to visit us. As soon as ... the injunction was lifted, they came
straight here. When the ban was up, they reported to the police
station at three and they landed here at four o'clock. Their court
orders were up and they were allowed to return.'

Tony Ball was disappointed that around half, if not more, of the
families were still at Dale Farm just yards away from the old site,
living roadside. He claimed that some of the families were new
arrivals, something that the residents said was untrue. 'The illegal
site is clear of all residential caravans, which was our primary
objective,' he said, holding on to some small sense of victory.
'There were ninety caravans and up to four hundred people on
the site. There is no doubt that, although I am disappointed, the
clearing of the illegal site was the first and most important step.
We are now in the process of working up enforcement notices. It
will be this month. It is a matter for our legal officers.'[11]

He had not been down to Oak Lane himself in the weeks after
the eviction. He had heard reports about the living conditions
down there, however, and said he had 'grave concerns' about
them. 'The public health issues around sewerage ... There are
fire issues ... It's just absolutely unacceptable for any residential
developments to be there.' He also understood that there had been
requests for the provision of temporary Portaloos, to help make
the situation less desperate. 'I would not condone people living
in those conditions by assisting in temporary toilets,' he insisted.
'We have made the offer of appropriate and better accommodation.'

He went on to claim that the situation on the roadside was
the responsibility of the Travellers themselves. 'I feel that some

of the Travellers are victims of being used by the hierarchy of the community to try and prove their point. The Travellers Support Network has lots of individuals, and some are extremely well meaning and good-hearted. But there are others with their own agendas. It is very hard to make a sweeping statement, but my concern is that there are people being used as pawns by whoever is advising them.'

What about the frustration felt by local residents at the lack of progress in actually getting the Travellers to leave? 'The general view has been supportive of [our approach]. There is frustration, but we are clear that the objective of clearing the illegal site is done and we will now move onto sorting out the legal site.' He stressed that he had done his best to offer those in housing a decent place to live.

Ann Kobayashi didn't agree. 'Some people say they brought it on themselves! It's an outcome of a number of different groups resulting in this, because of a refusal to look for [a solution]. This hasn't resolved anybody's problem – the residents, or the settled community, or the authorities, all looking forward with dread to spending more money and having more headlines, more traumas.'

By now, the Red Cross was compiling its confidential report based on its pre-Christmas visit and another in the new year. Its findings were damning. 'The immediate concerns of the community centred on the health of their children due to raw sewage seeping from the illegal part of the site and the limitations of one temporary toilet block serving thirty caravans. Coupled with overcrowding, this poor sanitation is causing illness, with the risk of more serious health problems arising.'[12] Other concerns were raised, such as an upsurge of fly-tipping on the illegal portion of the site, which had triggered an increase in the rat population. Polluted water was standing in pools on the illegal site too.

The report was submitted to the council, which said it would remove the rubbish as a matter of goodwill. But it took no responsibility for the lack of sanitation, and Tony Ball stood firm on the 'no toilets' policy – hoping perhaps that the bleak winter would smoke the Travellers out.

On 27 January 2012 an enforcement officer turned up from Basildon Council to serve breach of condition notices on the Sheridans and all the other families living on the roadside. The residents, despite the terrible conditions, were determined to stay. But there would be no last-minute reprieve for the residents — just more and more misery, not only at Dale Farm, but elsewhere as well.

10
CAUGHT

Operation Netwing had been launched to investigate allegations of slavery at a Traveller site just north of London, run by
Bedfordshire and Hertfordshire Major Crime Unit, and aided by
the UK's Human Trafficking Centre.[1] It followed many months
of undercover work observing possible slavery at the site in
Leighton Buzzard, Bedfordshire. By chance, Mary Ann McCarthy
had moved to a site adjoining Greenacres, to avoid the mayhem
of Dale Farm's eviction day – and found herself caught in the eye
of a harrowing media fire-storm.

Not all Travellers were as upstanding as Mary Ann and her
five daughters. A small number were known to have committed
crimes – including some very heinous ones. At 5.30 a.m. on 11
September 2011, around a hundred officers from the Bedfordshire
and Hertfordshire Major Crime Unit executed search warrants on
several residents of Greenacres, arresting four men and one woman
on suspicion of slavery, under the Coroners and Justice Act 2009.[2]

Four men from one Irish Traveller family, the Connors, were
charged with 'conspiracy to hold a person in servitude and requiring them to perform forced labour'. They were Tommy Connors
Snr (thirty years old), Patrick Connors (nineteen), James Connors
(thirty-four) and James Connors (twenty-three). A fifth member
of the family, thirty-year-old Josie Connors, was later charged
with similar offences. They were all accused of keeping dozens
of people – mostly alcoholic, drug-addicted and homeless men –
captive at the site. The Connors controlled and exploited their
alleged victims, verbally abusing and beating them, in order to

take advantage of their free (or low-cost) labour on the site and various jobs, such as clearing rubble, prosecutors said. One of the alleged victims claimed the family had treated him 'like a slave'. Another said the family lived in 'luxury' in contrast to his own horrible accommodation – the police called the conditions 'shockingly filthy and cramped'. The men had been recruited from homeless centres, soup kitchens or 'simply off the streets'. The case would be put to Luton Crown Court in Bedfordshire.

'Men were targeted because they were vulnerable, and kept on sites like camps under orders not to leave. Their heads were shaved. They were paid little or nothing for their work. They were on occasions verbally abused and on occasions beaten,' prosecutor Frances Oldham QC said. 'They may not in the strict sense have been "slaves", but they were not free men.' She continued: 'The evidence suggests that the Connors family made very substantial amounts of money through the exploitation of the servitude and forced labour of their workers.'[3]

The captive men had been moved around a succession of sites, before finally arriving at Greenacres Caravan Park, jurors heard. One of the men told police he regarded the site as 'like a concentration camp', the court was told. Some days the victims were given 'no food at all', nor were labourers allowed to leave work to get something to eat, it was alleged. The jurors were told that bedding was changed roughly every four months; the workers' quarters were 'smelly' and the roof leaked; there were no shower facilities, and labourers were taken for showers at most once a week but sometimes only every few months; the area where they slept was 'freezing cold'; they were at times given food so old that 'flies were crawling over it'. One man claimed that the dogs at Greenacres were better fed than he was. Others described sleeping in a converted horse-box kitted out with eleven tightly stacked bunks, or a caravan 'so cold and damp that mould grew' in it.[4]

Some contemplated escape – and a few had succeeded in getting away in April 2011. But everyone lived under the Connors' threat that they would be 'pulled back' and 'cracked' if they tried to leave Greenacres, according to testimony before the court.

On 11 July 2012, four of the Connors – Tommy Snr, James John Connors, Patrick Connors and Josie Connors – were convicted of some of the slavery charges.[5] In another case in 2011, sites in Gloucestershire, Leicestershire and Nottinghamshire were also raided, and several people from another Irish Traveller family by the name of Connors, as well as others, were charged and convicted of conspiracy to require a person to carry out forced or compulsory labour between April 2010 and March 2011.[6] Police maintain that these slavery cases are not linked.[7]

The story was covered with great gusto by the press, according to Jake Bowers, a well-respected Romani journalist. But the revelation was not entirely a surprise to him – most of all because, like any group, there are going to be a small number of individuals who take advantage of others if they think they can get away with it. 'There are some extremely nasty people out there. When the slavery case kicked off, it didn't surprise me ... I've known for some time that people, particularly Irish Traveller families, have kept people as dossers' – or more precisely, casual workers – 'to do their bidding. It would [also] be unfair to say that it's just the preserve of Irish Traveller families – a number of Gypsy families are involved in keeping dossers. But it ranges from the blatantly exploitative to something benevolent. It can be a kind of an institution – so it's not that simple to write about.'[8]

Bowers's assessment was borne out in observations by other scholars and activists. The Romani studies scholar Donald Kenrick has often encountered homeless people on sites that he has visited but in his experience they are not usually treated badly. 'A lot of sites I go to, you interview the family, and then there's John or someone,' he explained. 'They have picked him up on the way, and he's also always part of the family. [The dossers] usually have their own caravan and are free to go and come; often they have no other family. They are picked up from dole queues and doss houses, or turn up by themselves, but most of the larger family groupings have got one or two attached to them. But it's very unusual for them to be treated in that way, to keep them in a dog kennel.' Similarly, the anthropologist Judith Okely observed in 1975 that many Gypsy and Traveller families in her study of the South of England had homeless work-mates living with them; again, she found no evidence at that time that they were treated badly.[9]

Deputy Chief Constable Janette McCormick, the lead officer on Gypsy, Roma and Traveller issues for the Association of Chief Police Officers, is keen to point out the complexity of the Greenacres prosecution. 'This case does not mean that Irish Travellers as a community are linked with slavery and exploitation. There have been cases and we are now looking at the triggers for them, such as: "Do we have a closed community here?" "Are there vulnerable people who are ripe for exploitation?" If we focus on the race, rather than the triggers for the crime that have enabled it to happen, we further alienate the community,' she said.[10]

'We have identified groups of Irish Travellers and English Gypsies who are involved in serious organised crime. But that doesn't mean to say that the entire community is involved in serious organised crime,' she added. 'There tends to be an association, in terms of both perception and reality, with some crimes, such as doorstep crime, because they lend themselves to travelling criminality. But that doesn't mean to say there is a propensity for doorstep crime in that community.'

McCormick acknowledged that the difference is subtle but important. 'There are some issues, say, around the top ten wanted list that we put out,' she said, considering the fact that there are several Roma and Irish Travellers on it – more than one would expect given their numbers in the population. 'Sometimes, people who travel are the hardest to arrest, and also in any enclosed community, such as the Irish Traveller community, it is hard to get the intelligence to arrest them, so they end up on those lists. Having said that, we get a lot of support in the community to arrest some individuals. It would be a huge leap to say there is … a propensity to … criminality among Gypsies and Travellers. It's simply that anyone who is on the move is harder to track down, whether or not they have committed a crime.'

Gypsies and Travellers account for around 0.6% of the general population but at least around 1% of the prison population.

This differential is not a result of a disproportionate likelihood to offend, however, according to scholars of the criminal justice system. Instead, it is a product of the way in which their offences are viewed by magistrates and judges – and how they may lead to a tendency to punish the lifestyle in addition to the crime. One study, conducted in 1994, found that Irish Travellers were largely over-represented in the criminal justice system because they were targeted for minor traffic offences. They were often held overnight so that the police could request bail restrictions from magistrates when the courts opened for business in the morning. The Travellers were then more likely to be remanded in custody.[11]

Research carried out by the now disbanded Association of Chief Police Officers of Probation, published in 1993, found that young Irish Travellers were also significantly over-represented in Feltham Young Offenders institution – a staggering thirty-eight per cent of all young people classified as white by the courts at the time of their imprisonment.[12]

Yet another study from Manchester found that many pre-sentence reports on Irish Travellers used discriminatory and racist language. 'Irish defendants are more likely to receive custodial sentences than any other group even when they have committed the lowest rate of more serious offences,' it also reported.[13] Those who were deemed to be nomadic were seen as particularly suspicious. As Colm Power said: 'nomadism (rather than transience), and the criminalisation of nomadism are barely recognised structural factors, though they underpin much of the negative stereotyping applied to Travellers.'[14]

Although it is reasonable to expect a bail address, there are culturally sensitive ways to address this – rather than banging up people who are inclined to claustrophobia inside four walls for offences that, for the rest of the population, would be dealt with outside prison walls. A devastating report by the Irish Chaplaincy in Britain, surveying almost one hundred prisons in the UK, noted that Irish Travellers in prison had difficulties accessing services, partly because of lack of literacy, experienced racism by some staff and other prisoners and had a lack of confidence in the complaints system. The study, *Voices Unheard*, was launched in 2010, to investigate the experiences of Irish Travellers in prison. Travellers in prison were commonly subjected to racist treatment from other prisoners and from some staff, but they were not specially monitored.[15] There were also no official figures for Gypsies and Travellers in prison, despite the concerns about their ill treatment.

Strikingly, over half of all Irish Travellers in prison were there for property offences, compared to thirty per cent of prisoners from the general population. 'All forms of theft tend to occur disproportionately in poor, isolated, socially disadvantaged neighbourhoods … In criminology, the rationale for this occurrence lies in "strain theory" which, put simply, suggests that a lack of legitimate opportunities to achieve material success will lead to criminal activity as an alternative method to achieving it,' *Voices Unheard* explained. '[I]n Traveller communities, where employment is scarce and the prospect of moving out of poverty seems remote, one would expect to find higher rates of offences involving misappropriated property. This results from the fact Travellers have one of the lowest levels of legitimate opportunities, and therefore unlawfully obtaining the property of another becomes a conceivable means to success.' While this analysis does not excuse any crimes, it does expose a powerful motivator for criminality. It is striking too that the Chaplaincy learned of few Travellers who had been convicted of crimes of violence, drugs or sexual offences, in comparison to the general population.

Many of the Irish Travellers in prison also had mental health issues of some kind, which, in many cases, were compounded by their incarceration, with nearly one-third reported to have learning difficulties and nearly two-thirds of female Travellers (and one quarter of all Travellers in prison) having mental health problems. These were staggering statistics. Why were so many disabled Travellers being imprisoned and why were so many of them being imprisoned for offences for which a member of the settled community would receive a non-custodial sentence?

In Ireland the Irish police, known as the Garda Síochána – 'Guardians of the Peace' – were dealing with increasing anti-Traveller racism, some of it tracing back to 1996 and the murder of three elderly people in a rural area. Other attacks on elderly people in rural areas were soon pegged on Travellers as well.

Irish journalists were not coy about the murder allegations, despite lack of proof. Jim Cusack from the *Irish Times* splashed: 'At least forty elderly farmers were attacked in the West of Ireland during the autumn and in most cases, Gardaí believe, criminals from Travelling communities were responsible.'[16] Kevin Myers, in the same newspaper, wrote: 'A hugely disproportionate amount of rural crime is by a handful of Travellers ... they have generated an atmosphere of terror in rural areas unlike anything Ireland has experienced since the 1920s. Rural life is being transformed and nobody dare speak the truth in public. In private, everybody acknowledges that certain Travellers are responsible.'[17] Kevin Moore referred to police intelligence in his report: 'Garda intelligence reports show that an estimated twelve gangs of Travellers and mobile traders – up to eighty people in all – are responsible for most of the murders and vicious attacks on elderly people living alone, in the past year,' he wrote, then quoted an anonymous garda, who had told Moore that: 'We will know that ninety-nine per cent of the time, Travellers are responsible for these crimes in the rural area. But you can't always prove it and you certainly can't say it publicly.'[18]

The worst comment, however, came from journalist Mary Ellen Synon, who wrote in the *Sunday Independent* that the travelling way of life and its culture was 'the culture of the sewer', describing it as 'ungoverned by intellect'. She continued: 'It is a life worse than the life of beasts, for beasts at least are guided by wholesome instinct. Traveller life is without the ennobling intellect of man or the steadying instinct of animals. This tinker "culture" is without achievement, discipline, reason or intellectual ambition. It is a morass. And one of the surprising things about it is that not every individual bred in this swamp turns out bad. Some individuals among the tinkers find the will not to become evil. For the poverty and brutal life of the Travellers' camps does not force anyone to become a criminal: it simply presents a life in which virtue has no reward and lawlessness is acceptable. Every man in every tinker camp who becomes a criminal – like every man anywhere who becomes a criminal – becomes evil by choice. Crime is volitional. So consider what ought to be done with these breeding grounds of crime. Simple: stop petting tinkers and start treating them like all other citizens.'[19] One Travellers' rights group attempted to prosecute Synon, unsuccessfully, for inciting hatred.[20]

The country had been gripped by a moral panic. Many people at Dale Farm didn't want to go back to Ireland, despite the exhortations of the English tabloid press, in the resulting blowback. Synon was not the only public figure to state that Travellers might be inherently criminal. One such even suggested electronic tagging for all members of the community. 'In 1998, the Fine Gael county councillor John Flannery proposed that all Travellers be 'tagged with microchips like cattle' in order to monitor their movement. Travellers, he claimed, 'expected everything to be done for them while giving little in return', according to Irish authors Ronit Lentin and Robbie McVeigh.[21] Other local councillors went further. One suggested mandatory birth control to limit the number of Traveller children.[22] Another said that his area, Killarney, 'is literally infested by these people' – as if they were vermin.[23]

In *Prejudice in Ireland Revisited* Mícheál MacGréil explained: 'Irish Travellers are still seen and treated as a "lower caste"' and attitudes towards Travellers have deteriorated since the early 1970s, soon after the start of the Troubles, with the rural murders simply providing a new flashpoint.[24] He concluded: 'Irish people's prejudice against Travellers is one of caste-like apartheid.'[25] In the mid 1990s, the Irish government set up a Task Force on the

Travelling Community, including actual Travellers in the consul-
tations. By 1998, the conclusions were clear: an equality law to
protect Travellers' rights to employment and access to services
and goods needed to be created. However, in the law, which was
immediately passed, Travellers were not offered protection on
racial grounds, giving them less ability to fight back against much
of the discrimination they experienced.[26] By 2000, forty per cent
of people in Northern Ireland said that they believed a Traveller
lifestyle was invalid; fifty-seven per cent did not want Travellers
to live in their neighbourhood – the quintessential Nimby position. A 2004 survey similarly found that 'Travellers and asylum
seekers are the minorities viewed most negatively by the majority
population', with the researcher reporting that attitudes towards
Travellers were 'more instinctive, more deeply ingrained and less
subject to correction by liberal sensitivity'.[27]

By 2001, twenty-four per cent of all Irish Travellers in the
Republic were living on unofficial sites – without electricity,
refuse collection or running water. According to a survey commissioned as part of Traveller Focus week in 2001, although
Traveller respondents said they were 'satisfied with life in general', and although conditions had improved, they still faced
serious discrimination. Seven out of ten reported that they had
been discriminated against by pub owners and four out of ten by
owners of clubs. The authorities fared little better: thirty-eight
per cent said that they had been discriminated against by gardaí,
thirty-three per cent by county councils and twenty-six per cent
by the Department of Social, Community and Family Affairs.[28]

This was the climate of fear and distrust that made the Dale
Farm Travellers so desperate to stay put, even though they were
not welcomed into Crays Hill. They were 'unwanted economic
migrants' – perceived as being in England to make some quick
money, legitimately or not; they were not 'real Gypsies'. 'The
fictional *didikois*, renegades or ex-housed dwellers from abroad,
alleged to be radically or ethnically closer to the sedentary society
without any redeeming exoticism, are alleged to have the most
"anti-social" behaviour,' wrote Judith Okely in 1975. They are 'a

Mary Ann McCarthy in her chalet at Dale Farm, near Crays Hill, Basildon, Essex, in summer 2011. Photo by Sebastian Hesse.

Michelle Sheridan prepares tea in her Dale Farm caravan while her son looks on. Photo by Sebastian Hesse.

Father Dan Mason prepares for an open-air mass to be held at Dale Farm in the run-up to the eviction. Photo by Sebastian Hesse.

The McCarthy sisters – left to right, Margaret, Maria, Nora and Pearl (also known as Kathleen) – take tea at a protest outside the High Court, London, after the last appeal against the eviction failed on 12 October 2011. Photo by Peter Macdiarmid/Getty Images.

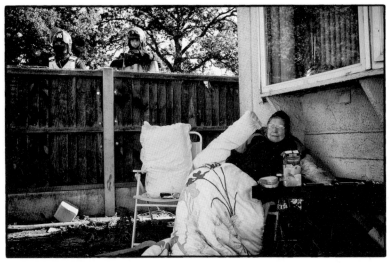

Eviction day, 19 October 2011: an activist settles in at Dale Farm while police scan the perimeter. Photo by Sebastian Hesse.

Left: The leader of Basildon Council, Tony Ball, gives an interview to the international media. Photo by Oli Scarff/Getty Images.

Right: Former social worker and Wickford resident Ann Kobayashi became a vocal supporter of the Dale Farm community. Photo by Katharine Quarmby.

Metropolitan Police, dressed in riot gear, walk around the site as a caravan burns. The fire was set purposefully by an activist. Photo by Sebastian Hesse.

A Traveller boy stands atop a van painted with protest slogans. The gantry, erected at the front gate of Dale Farm as a defence against the eviction, can be seen behind him. Photo by Katharine Quarmby.

Co-chair of the Gypsy Council Candy Sheridan (left, pointing) at Dale Farm on eviction day. Photo by Sebastian Hesse.

Michelle and Nora Sheridan stand on the site after the clearance amid mounds of dirt and trenches, the product of 'bunding'. Photo by Katharine Quarmby.

Left: Noah Burton in his caravan on the field he owns at Meriden, near Birmingham. Photo by Katharine Quarmby.

Right: Senga Townsley moved to Noah's site in 2010. The families there were facing eviction in spring 2013. Photo by Katharine Quarmby.

Cuzzy Delaney holding a photo of her son Johnny, who was killed because 'he was only a ... Gypsy' in 2003. Photo by Katharine Quarmby.

Billy Welch, the English Romani Gypsy elder who organises Appleby Horse Fair, with his granddaughter outside the family caravan. Photo by Tom Green.

Haggling for a fair deal on horses at Stow Horse Fair. Photo by Katharine Quarmby.

The 'flashing lane' at Appleby Fair. Photo by Sebastian Hesse.

Siddy Biddle, a member of the evangelical Gypsy Christian church Light and Life, recites a prayer before the beginning of Stow Fair. Photo by Sebastian Hesse.

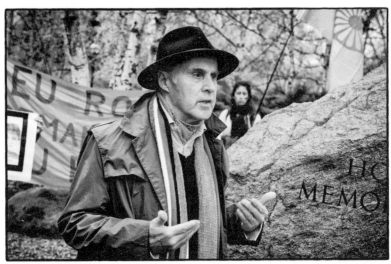

Activist Grattan Puxon at a Holocaust memorial. He and others are working to gain greater recognition of the experiences of the Romani people during the war and across Europe today. Photo by Sebastian Hesse.

disturbing mixture of "us and them", a reminder that Gypsies can cross racial and hence social boundaries. The alleged drop-outs are denigrated, because they have abandoned and rejected sedentary society of their own free will. The "foreigners" – also alleged to be "drop-outs", usually from Ireland, are potentially the most nomadic, and considered to have the least rights in the locality.'[29]

This doesn't mean, of course, that individuals from the travelling community never commit crimes. A small number do – including very heinous ones, as the Connors case had proved. And those were the stories that were making headlines as the Dale Farm eviction was reaching crisis point. In fact, some more conspiratorial voices even suggested that the arrests were timed to reflect a poor light on the Dale Farm Travellers – a charge vigorously rejected by the police.

The media, reflecting society's values, all too often reports only one side of the story when it comes to crime and Gypsies and Travellers, observed Romani journalist Jake Bowers. 'I think we need to say, "Every community commits crimes and is the victim of crimes," but our society has only looked at one part of that with any enthusiasm. It has never looked at criminality within the community (and its effects on the community), [or] criminality experienced by the community. If it did that, it would find a community with *lots* of victims and *some* rogues.'

Some of this is a matter of historical accident. In the 1920s and 1930s, academics were keen to unravel the power of propaganda during the First World War. Their theory was that messages in the media were delivered with the effectiveness of a hypodermic needle (or a 'magic bullet', depending on the theorist) directly into the brain. In 1938, they were able to examine an isolated case of infection: Orson Welles' Halloween radio broadcast of H.G. Wells' *The War of the Worlds*. Here, they said, listeners accepted the 'news bulletins' of the programme as though they were fact, responding en masse to the information with panic, then outrage. The audience was passive and moved in lock-step. Although the theory was discredited by subsequent research, it remained (and remains) popular in the media itself, where commentators often directly link the increased popularity, for instance, of violent video games to episodes of aggression in children, such as school rampage killings.[30]

Another theory comes from Paul F. Lazarsfeld's book *The People's Choice*, about the 1940 presidential election. Lazarsfeld argued that peer-group influence was far more powerful than that of the media – but the media still had a role. He stated that so-called 'opinion leaders' interpreted for others the facts reported by 'mass media' in a process he called the Two-Step Flow Theory.[31] People like Mary Ellen Synon take on an outsized voice in shaping how facts are understood.

This is why the routine use of certain descriptions is so troubling. Words such as 'criminal', 'dirty', 'sponger', 'tax-dodger' and 'flooding into the country' are often used; Roma are often labelled as 'illegal', or 'prostitute' or 'beggar', Irish Travellers as 'unwanted economic migrants'. Even if the media doesn't inject stereotypes directly into the brain, the public may read these reports as 'fact' and lap up the interpretations presented by members of Parliament, residents' association chairmen, and other community leaders. Analyses by the MediaWise Trust and the Irish Traveller Movement in Great Britain suggest that such archetypal 'brands' are alive and kicking, even if they are no longer burned into the skin.

The MediaWise analysis in particular shows how certain language is inextricably linked in the mind of the public to Gypsies, Roma and Travellers. Starting with the arrival of some European Roma in 1997, the charity tracked words used in the major broadsheets – 'invasion', 'tide', 'deluge', 'handouts' and 'scams' were pervasive. This language, the report's author, Mike Jempson, observed, helped to spur a British National Party demonstration at the international arrivals port in Dover. Asylum seekers were physically attacked. Under pressure, the government eventually restricted visas for Slovakian Roma. MediaWise took special interest in a campaign in the *Sun* and other newspapers in the run-up to the 2005 general election. The 'Stamp on the Camps' campaign used similar language, as well as terms like 'living hell' to describe the conditions of people living *near* Gypsies. It was also keen to push the line of 'one law for them and one for us'. The heated rhetoric may have been connected to bullying of Gypsy children at school, suspicion at and around workplaces and an increased police presence at their sites, in Jempson's view, a position backed by investigations conducted by the Advisory Council for the Education of Romani and other Traveller organisations. The human rights of Gypsies and Travellers are trampled over, Jempson observed, 'too often with the complicity of media professionals'.[32,33]

When the Leveson Inquiry into the culture and practices of the British media was convened in July 2011, the Irish Traveller Movement in Britain decided to make two submissions – the first on how Gypsies and Travellers are treated in the press and a further one, during the second phase, which investigated the relationship between the press and the police. The twenty-two-page document listed examples of name-calling, unbalanced stories and unmoderated comment threads that put into question many newspapers' objectivity. Bridget McCarthy, a member of the group, was quoted: 'They [the press] say "Gypsies" and "Travellers" when they are speaking about a single Gypsy or Traveller … I mix with people from the settled community at all levels. When a big story about a Traveller doing wrong is in the papers and they say "Travellers are doing this", I wonder about what the people I meet that day will be thinking.'

The testimony also made clear that the police and the media sometimes become enmeshed in a pernicious camaraderie when it comes to reporting criminal proceedings involving Gypsies and Travellers. The Irish Traveller Movement went so far as to call it 'public lynching'. Their evidence involved coverage of the slavery raid at Greenacres and elsewhere in Bedfordshire; press releases from the Metropolitan Police regarding 'Operation Golf', the investigation and prosecution of 'a Roma Romanian-based Organised Crime Network operating in London, Romania and elsewhere';

and a British Transport Police investigation into 'Romanian metal theft gangs' given the project name 'Operation Leopard'.

The press briefings on these subjects amounted to an assumption of guilt, according to the advocacy group. On the day of the Operation Netwing raid, Deputy Chief Inspector Sean O'Neill suggested there were links between the Traveller families at the site and an alleged slavery ring in Scandinavia; the BBC picked up this line and reported on it as though it were fact, to the shock of the Irish Traveller Movement, which filed a complaint. In Operation Golf, the Met Police claimed that one thousand Roma children had been trafficked to the UK to commit street crime. One hundred and thirty Roma were arrested, but only twelve charged with an offence; only eight of those arrested were eventually convicted. No children were trafficked, but press releases, said the Irish Traveller Movement, 'built an illusion that child trafficking was common among Roma'. Finally, when it came to the London Transport Police's metal theft investigation, the newspaper headlines suggested that Romanian gangs were responsible, at a cost of £770 million per year to the British public. The reporting was based on an interview with Detective Sergeant Chris Hearn, head of Operation Leopard, who was quoted as saying that Romanian gangs were behind it, as well as 'the high-street begging scams and other criminal enterprises'. The *Daily Mail* took his statement as inspiration, illustrating a story with 'a picture of a Roma child begging', according to the Irish Traveller Movement's report. 'This link to begging by DS Hearn and the *Daily Mail*'s use of a picture of a Roma child begging once again frames the Roma community as a criminal problem that needs to be solved,' the group said.[34]

They concluded: 'The Irish Traveller Movement in Britain (ITMB) are alarmed at the sensationalist and prejudicial nature of the police press briefings and statements about Gypsy, Roma and Traveller criminal proceedings. We believe that these briefings are encouraging reporting that both prejudices criminal trials of Traveller defendants and stirs up racial hatred towards the Gypsy, Roma and Traveller communities. We believe that the cause of this is the press's need to deliver sensationalist stories interacting with the Police's need to justify their particular operation by provoking media interest and coverage. This interaction – between the Police seeking publicity and the press seeking sensationalist stories – is driving a "race to the bottom" and means that a police statement or briefing will seek to "tick" news values and pander to the media's need for moral panics and folk devils. This, we believe, has a disproportionate affect on the Traveller community, as most media organisations will always splash criminal proceedings involving Travellers.'

In 2010 the European Commission against Racism and Intolerance released a report on Gypsies and Travellers in the UK. They, too, concluded that the media were stoking the flames of prejudice – sending out what they called 'racist and xenophobic messages'. 'Gypsies and Travellers are regularly presented in a negative light in the mainstream media, and in particular in the tabloid press, where they are frequently portrayed, for example, as being by definition associated with … sponging off British society, making bogus claims for protection and being troublemakers.' The commission was particularly troubled by reports that when Gypsies and Travellers were targeted in the media, it seemed to encourage people to focus on them for 'violent attacks'.[35]

The power of the press cannot be ignored in the case of Gypsies and Travellers. Bridget McCarthy's worries about 'what the people I meet that day will be thinking' were well founded, according to Rachel Morris of the Traveller Law Research Unit of Cardiff Law School. 'As most members of the public don't know any Gypsies or Travellers, their view of the communities is filtered through press reporting,' she has written. In this way, 'racist invective by the press infects society in a widespread way' – rather than receiving an injection of belief from a hypodermic needle, readers were catching a virus that could 'confirm existing prejudices and create new ones'. But, she said, the media also repeatedly report on Gypsies and Travellers as though they are all cut from the same cloth. '[The] print media commonly suggest to their readers, in their representations of Travellers, that this category of people routinely display certain negative characteristics not only typical of but essential to the group: that is, they represent Travellers in a stereotypical and prejudicial fashion. The relationship of the representation to the real is the same as it would be for any societal group: some Travellers are dishonest or lawbreaking, some don't clean up after themselves. The difference is that while some settled people also have those characteristics, other settled people are not assumed also to possess them, as is the case for Travellers.'[36]

When the Dale Farm eviction became a circus, it was not the only depiction of Gypsies and Travellers in the media. There was the Greenacres slavery raid, of course, but there was also *My Big Fat Gypsy Wedding,* which had become a bona fide pop-culture phenomenon since it first aired in February 2010. Approximately seven million people tuned in each week.

Ask anyone in the street what the word 'Gypsy' means to them and they will almost certainly come up with *My Big Fat Gypsy Wedding* (and its spin-off, *Thelma's Gypsy Girls,* which follows the so-called Gypsy dressmaker Thelma Madine). Big dresses, spray tans, skimpy outfits and make-up slathered on with a trowel became the emblems of Gypsies and Travellers as a result. There is, of course, a grain of truth in the images. Some young Gypsy and Traveller girls and women do like to put on the Ritz, gild themselves with tan and totter into town and back on high heels. But then, so do a number of young women from the settled community. And while some Gypsy and Traveller girls aren't accustomed to the trappings of education and employment, this is a political issue as much as anything, with Gypsy and Traveller children lagging way behind in educational achievement, as borne out in statistics. Pinning a few radiant butterflies onto a board for the amusement of the public and claiming they are a representative sample may not be cricket, but it was the media conducting business as usual – especially the business of entertainment that had dominated much air time during the 'reality TV' boom.[37]

The coverage of the series was joyously voyeuristic, separating Gypsies and Travellers from 'normal' society. Here were the residents of a strange, unstable world in which girls could be 'grabbed' (forced to kiss) boys and would be married off young. After the big wedding day, the girls would be allowed to do nothing but clean; the boys in the series all seemed to be blurred out, giving the impressions that they were criminals, or at least didn't want to be identifiable. In a recent advertising campaign for the programme, hoardings were plastered with 'Bigger. Fatter. Gypsier'. They were eventually ruled 'offensive and irresponsible' by the Advertising Standards Authority, the industry's independent regulator (supported by advertisers themselves – so not a whiff of government correctness involved).[38]

Many Gypsy and Traveller families felt the negative effects of these damaging stereotypes – and experienced direct action against them. In June 2012 Helen Jones, chief executive officer of Leeds Gypsy and Traveller Exchange, told parliamentarians: 'Directly coinciding with the airing of the programme, we at Leeds Gypsy and Traveller Exchange have had ongoing hate crimes, including dog excrement being directed at our office. The office was subject to an arson attack in 2011 which destroyed one end of the building, the end most used by young people who rely on our service.' Another Irish Traveller, named Tina Purcell, was living on a site in London. Her daughter, she said, had been bullied after the debut of the 'Bigger. Fatter. Gypsier' advertising campaign. 'My daughter loved attending school but now she wants to stay at home. As soon as the poster went up outside her school her school friends were constantly asking her questions ... "Is that your relatives on that poster?" "Don't you wash?" "Why are you at school? You're supposed to be at home scrubbing," "Shouldn't you be married by now? Traveller girls get married at fourteen and stay at home don't they?"'[39]

Although Channel 4 has announced the series will not be renewed, many feel that the series has damaged their public reputation, perhaps permanently. Further spin-offs have not been ruled out, either, and rights have been sold in other countries, including the US, which saw *My Big Fat American Gypsy Wedding.* A handful of weddings captured on an often judgemental reality TV camera were being dressed up as representing the entire community.

Dale Farm, of course, was another iconic example of the media coverage that Gypsies and Travellers have come to expect. The coverage had loosely divided into the two media camps, left and right, but the online comment boards for newspapers on both sides were, almost without exception, filled with vitriol and hostility towards Gypsies and Travellers – not just those at Dale Farm, but those anywhere in the UK. One online comment called for Travellers there to be gassed to death. On the day of the eviction the *Daily Mail* comments thread went wild. 'A pox on these foul creatures. I just wish they and their like would disappear before it costs even more tax-payers money' and 'acting like feral humans' and 'I wonder if scrap metal thefts will go down in Essex ... Get the taxman in to see how they can maintain there [sic] lifestyle' and 'Get out the slurry spreaders! It is a green belt after all, and we are obliged to look after our countryside! Then again, slurry might encourage them to grow!' were among the sentiments given voice. Even a sympathetic piece in the *Observer* attracted abuse. Of five hundred comments posted, 150 were arguably racist, according to an analysis by the Irish Traveller Movement.

Yet, as the Irish Traveller Movement has pointed out, despite the fact that they infringe the Code of Practice of the Press Complaints Commission, it is difficult to lodge a successful complaint, because such comments are usually aimed at groups rather than at an individual. Third-party complaints, on behalf of groups, are hardly, if ever, heard. In his report on the inquiry into the media, Lord Leveson suggested that this should change – to an outcry from nervous editors. One MP even suggested that third-party complaints were actually hijacked by 'sinister' pressure groups, not realising, it seems, that if 'sinister' elements had infiltrated anywhere, it was on the message boards.[40]

What could be so sinister about a woman in a spectacular wedding dress, or a huddle of homeless families on a field plot? In *The Road to God Knows Where*, Sean Maher, an Irish Traveller who was raised roadside, wrote: 'Well, the road was my home and cradle, as it was for my ancestors. I know it has a great and ancient history, passed down by word of mouth true and faithfully, completely unknown to the buffer and lost or ignored in the annals of Irish history.'[41] His ode expressed the feelings of many Gypsies and Travellers about their way of life.

Still, the old ideas about vagabondage refuse to fade away, and any example that marks a Gypsy or Traveller as 'abnormal' or 'criminal' is seized upon, since the 'unsettled' threaten the control freakery of the modern nation state, in a paraphrase of the University of Leeds sociologist Zygmunt Baumann. 'Each place is for the vagabond a stop-over, but he never knows how long he will stay in any of them,' said Baumann. 'To control the wayward and erratic vagabond is ... a daunting task.'[42]

While the denigration of the nomadic lifestyle is not distinct to the Irish Traveller experience, it has become something of a 'national obsession in Ireland', in the words of scholar Jim MacLaughlin. Most people in the settled community in the country do not understand nomadism – travelling in the summer, stopping or settling in the winter – he found. Most didn't want Traveller sites anywhere near them. 'One local councillor recently suggested that "if Irish Travellers wanted their ethnicity, they should go and do it somewhere else,"' MacLaughlin reported.[43]

Odd this, since nomadism has been the fundamental human condition for some 500,000 years (and then some), as the veteran New Traveller Tony Thomson has argued. Stopping-places were used for hundreds of years until they were enclosed by various acts of law, he has explained. 'The traditionally used camping places ... have witnessed nomadic dwelling for millennia. That they remain amongst the most beautiful places in the landscape surely offers us some lessons in the nature of sustainable development.' Why then, he asked, is it the case that '[n]omadism is preconceived as something criminal or extraordinary', when in fact it is 'an instinctive response to environmental and social stress'?[44]

Indeed, sustainable nomadic living has qualities that the settled community could learn from. 'Nomadic dwelling demonstrates an alternative relationship to land, and we live at a time when a re-evaluation of our relationship with land through the resources we consume and the lifestyle we lead is vital if human life is to continue.' He goes on to make the point that the establishment response to nomadic communities − often calling them 'hippies' − reveals an 'ideological dimension of the hostility' towards nomadism. Caravans and other structures suitable for travelling, he argues, could provide cheap, sustainable homes in localities where people want to be, with a small footprint on the environment. Travelling is not an anachronism, but a pertinent response to the crisis of climate change. Seasonal work, and seasonal conditions, are well suited to life on the road, interspersed with months in one place.

So why do people distrust nomads so much? In his research on the inherent distrust of English Gypsies and Irish Travellers, Anthony Drummond set out a framework for understanding the problem. He argued that sedentary living − the 'norm' for most people in modern society − was not just favoured, but guarded, *defended*. To that end, the settled community would often pursue 'active and intentional incitement of fear and hatred of nomads'.[45] He could have been providing a case history of Meriden.

11
GYPSY WAR IN MERIDEN

The build-up to and aftermath of Dale Farm had repercussions elsewhere too. Dale Farm had become a useful rallying call for other communities that felt 'threatened' by a proposed Gypsy or Traveller site. Here was the perfect cautionary tale – of what could happen if Gypsies or Travellers were allowed to 'invade' a community. Many local councils saw that they could come down harder, and faster, on unauthorised developments – and they did.

The most infamous example came in Meriden, a village some eight miles from Birmingham International airport, where a small number of English and Scotch Gypsy families had decided to move – without planning permission to do so – in April 2010. The owner of the field was Noah Burton. He had previously lived with his wife and her family on a stud farm for pedigree horses at nearby Balsall Common.

Noah comes from a well-liked and respected Romani Gypsy family, with roots in Wales, Scotland and the Midlands. One particularly famous member of the family, the legendary bare-knuckle fighter Uriah 'Big Just' Burton, had 'kidnapped' around seventy-five men in November 1963, in order to have their help in building a monument to his father up on a remote Welsh mountain. He freely admitted to his misdeed, saying that all of the men had promised to help him but some of them needed to be cuffed to honour their promises.[1] (The real story is perhaps a little more prosaic; they were all well paid for their work and went mostly willingly, after a little grumbling.) Big Just Burton was much respected for his long fight to open up a private site in Wales in which many homeless people had sought sanctuary.[2] He was also thought to be one of the few British Romanies to have operated any sort of *kris*, or Gypsy law – according to Noah, he was known to fine Romanies for misdeeds, then throw a party twice a year for all-comers (including the wrong-doers) off the proceeds.

Noah's life, too, was more prosaic than that painted in the tabloids, where he was portrayed as the 'Bin Laden of Meriden'. Noah took on primary responsibility for looking after his mother and siblings when he was just a teenager. He became a highly skilled restorer of antique cars and caravans, and travelled throughout Europe – sometimes going as far afield as Australia and the US – following work. He then returned to the Midlands, where he married Joanna, the daughter of Nelson Smith, of one of the most prominent English Gypsy families, and settled down to raise a close-knit family, of whom he is clearly proud. But when his twenty-year marriage broke up, with an elderly mother to care for and no home to go to, he took the fateful decision to occupy a field that he owned, but on which he had no planning permission to live. It was 30 April 2010, the Friday before the early May bank holiday weekend.

He never anticipated exactly how the decision to occupy the field would turn out. Looking back, he described the situation: 'It's been like World War Three here … I never ever realised how much hatred there is towards me.'[3] He and the other families that moved with him onto the site claimed that they had been subjected to a number of incidents since they moved there: threats and intimidation wrapped up in a broiling dispute between some Meriden residents and the Gypsy families living on Noah's field.

A group of villagers, led by David McGrath, a former Birmingham City councillor, and Doug Bacon, a former local police officer, were incensed that the Gypsies had occupied the site without planning permission. On camera they explained over and over that the site was part of the so-called Meriden Gap, a green-belt lung between the conurbations of nearby Solihull and Coventry. Many of the local protestors (plus some well-wishers, who travelled to support them from hundreds of miles away) were clearly fervent countryside lovers, and were deeply upset that the peace of the green belt had been disturbed in this way. Those sentiments were absolutely understandable – even to the families who had occupied the field and acknowledged that they had broken planning law. But it was the model of protest adopted by the residents that came into question.

It all started with the erection of two small camps, named 'Nancy' and 'Barbara' (after the owners of the land), which were set up to picket the site, night and day. Officially, the people at the sites were members of the Meriden Residents Against Inappropriate Development (RAID). RAID committed itself, according to its own website to 'a twenty-four-hour, seven-days-a-week protest camp' – the home page even included a 'count-up' of the camps' time logged, to the day, hour and minute.[4] In another entry on the website, campaigners pledged that they would continue what they called their 'vigil' to 'monitor for illegal activity'.[5] This constant and unprecedented surveillance both irritated and frightened the small number of Gypsies at Meriden, some of whom were children, older people and disabled women – among the most vulnerable.

At a planning meeting of Solihull Metropolitan Borough Council in February 2012, RAID's ceaseless monitoring came up – somewhat inadvertently – for discussion. The meeting's ostensible aim was to decide whether the council would take enforcement action against the RAID encampment, which, like the Gypsy camp, was flouting green-belt rules. David McGrath, RAID's chair, explained to the planning meeting that he had handed over their photos of Noah's field to the council.

David Bell, one of the councillors, said that the monitoring had been a help. He claimed that the 'RAID camp has been the eyes and ears of the council', going on to say that the organisation was 'helping our officers to defend our green belt'. He went on to praise RAID members. 'How would the council monitor that land twenty-four hours a day? Residents are doing the job of the council,' he said. 'If the decision went against the applicant [RAID], if they don't monitor the site, what's the outcome? ... How do we support the residents to monitor the site to make sure that no further illegal acts take place?'[6]

Council officials appeared somewhat discomfited by the notion, so eloquently expressed by Councillor Bell, that local residents could monitor other residents. Later, the director of public communications explained that councillors expressed their own views, rather than council policy.[7] Indeed, the council's lawyer made it clear that the council itself had the authority to collect evidence through its own monitoring. Councillor Ryan expressed what many of the settled community were thinking: 'We talk about the "Big Society", so why can't we engage local people in monitoring? ... They [the RAID members] have been good citizens ... They are trying to defend against illegal actions.'

The planning meeting voted, reluctantly, to expel the RAID camp, but the 'localists' were the winners of the argument that day. One set of residents – the 'legitimate' – were permitted, even encouraged, to police unwanted groups, just so long as they had permission to be on the plot from which they were doing their monitoring. It wasn't the surveillance that was a problem; it was the encampment on green-belt land.

The RAID group was considered by many local people as heroes campaigning against criminals; the real picture was far from simple. The Gypsies at Meriden do not have criminal records. They pay tax like other local people too. But their very identity was seen by some as suspect, with or without evidence against them. This didn't seem right to those living in Noah's field. When Senga Townsley watched TV footage taken from inside the RAID encampment, she saw what appeared to be TV monitors trained on the site and complained to the Information Commissioner. They felt that their right to privacy, which is enshrined for all citizens in Article 8 of the Human Rights Act and the European Convention on Human Rights, was under risk of infringement.

In fact, the RAID camp was enjoying a lot of positive publicity – not least from the Conservative *Express*, *Sun* and *Daily Mail*, which regularly sent their correspondents up to camps Nancy and Barbara to keep tabs on progress. It was the *Daily Mail* that dubbed Noah Burton the 'Bin Laden of Meriden', in two separate headlines. The *Telegraph* called him the 'Gypsy King' of Meriden; *The Times*, a 'Gypsy fixer'.

In some ways these were just more in a long line of unfriendly depictions of Gypsies to add to the history books. But the residents of Meriden – on all sides – were only at the beginning of their suffering.

The real story was much grimmer for the Romani Gypsies on the site. And RAID was also attracting its fair share of criticism – not least from some former members.

One prominent former member, who did not wish to be named, had been much involved in setting up the RAID group and was initially supportive of their stated desire to protect the green belt.[8] But the person soon became disenchanted with the results. The atmosphere in Meriden had darkened, the former member said, as villagers took up positions on either side of the fence. There was absolutely no evidence to suggest that RAID members themselves were responsible for any of the racist incidents that then followed, the person was at pains to state, but follow they did. Racist graffiti with the words 'Fuck off gipsie [sic] scum' appeared on a railway bridge not far from Noah's field; the perpetrators were never found.

The Gypsies were also threatened on Facebook, with one local teenager posting: 'Sixty farmers with shotguns will sort this lot out.' The Gypsies at Meriden were worried and referred the matter to West Midlands Police, which confirmed that the threats had been published on Facebook. The police then asked the Gypsy families to accept an apology rather than take any formal action against the teenagers who had been involved. The Gypsies agreed to the plan – an 'olive branch', as Noah Burton put it, somewhat wryly, before adding, 'It didn't work.'

Racism is particularly problematic in the nation's rural areas, and Gypsies and Travellers come in for more than their fair share of prejudice. It is often denied to be happening, because both English

Gypsies and Irish Travellers are white (and therefore often invisible) victims of this racism. 'We are easy targets,' said Noah. 'Who stands up and talks for us? By nature we hide ourselves, we go through life not telling people who we are, because then we don't get work, but because we hide ourselves we don't have a voice.'

Noah and the other Meriden Gypsies call RAID a 'vigilante group, harassing people looking for homes. They can bang on about the green belt, they are not even considering the sites, they are not asking if it is suitable, ah, it's been proposed, how do we stop it? Encouraging them out there, keep encouraging them to string it along, to let that momentum build up.'

It seemed patently unfair to the Romani Gypsy community that no prosecutions had been filed in the racist attacks that they had reported to West Midlands Police. The hate crime prosecutor for the West Midlands, Rosemary Thompson (who has since retired), said there was a rationale behind the authorities' response. 'I have no doubt … that the communities have been subject to harassment. I am, however, concerned that we might end up concentrating on the issues around planning and the civil law context of this agenda which the [Crown Prosecution Service] would not get involved with. It is difficult, as we certainly want to give the community the confidence to report hate crime and also the confidence in our organisation to treat their cultural differences sensitively. I have given this some thought. In terms of race hate crime, it is easy to prove when a criminal offence such as assault has been committed and in the process of which the person is called a derogatory term in relation to their ethnicity. However … the criminal offence of harassment is much more difficult and very often it is one person's word against another. There is certainly not an easy solution.'

In 2007 Neil Chakraborti and Jon Garland compared the levels of rural racism in three counties, including Warwickshire, through a series of focus groups conducted over a four-year period. (Before 1974, when it became part of the metropolitan borough of Solihull, Meriden had been situated in the county, so it was an apt point of comparison.) Chakraborti and Garland found that the rural 'village' was a romanticised concept, considered by many to be a close-knit community. 'The key components of that notion [were] familial ties, long-term residency (including the ability to trace one's ancestral roots back several generations) and a low turnover of population.'[9] People reported feeling guarded towards 'established minority ethnic groups', but their sentiments were much more open when it came to Gypsies and Travellers. It 'was acceptable to express hostility and to use inflammatory language towards Travellers and Gypsies; indeed it appeared that these groups were regarded as "fair game" for vitriolic abuse, in much the same way that asylum seekers have also been scapegoated by sections of the public and tabloid press in the last decade'.[10] Villagers said they felt a *need* to fit in; those who didn't were marginalised.

This chimes with the experience of Barbara Cookes, a retired farmer, and others in Meriden who decided that they were happy to accept the Gypsies as their neighbours and are now ostracised by some in the community. A former RAID member, Barbara had initially allowed group members to use her land as one of the first locations for a protest camp (the eponymous Camp Barbara), but as she got to know the Gypsies – many of whom had lived locally for several generations – she changed her mind about which side she was on.

Her first reaction to the 'Gypsy invasion' had been one of hostility. She recalled: 'On the last day of April, I saw Noah and the others going past on their homes on wheels. I was a little bit put out; after all, I can't get planning permission for my two log cabins. The farmers were there in half an hour, saying they would stop it at all costs.'[11] Soon the protestors were encamped on her land, near the illegal site, and her feelings about both sides in the dispute started to shift. 'We had Camp Barbara here, we had three gazebos, it got on my nerves a bit. People bought food and drinks and it became quite a campsite, but I had an ill neighbour; the camp was here for eleven weeks.' She insisted that they go, finding the noise of the protestors, some of whom liked a drink and a bit of a party, excessive.

As she came to know her Gypsy neighbours, her attitude towards them changed too. 'I find them very friendly, really, I can't knock them; if I wanted a good turn doing they would do it ... I was down the lane with my dogs, and along came Noah in his pick-up truck. I introduced myself, "I'm old Barb from the barn," and he said, "Yes, the only smiling face around here." People at the camp asked me why I spoke to him, but I was always taught to speak to everybody – everybody has a heart. They thought I was being too friendly to them, but I wanted to get to know him and his relatives.'

Seeing the human side of the Gypsy families had cost her dear. In the summer of 2012, the Townsley girls, Dana and Susie, had washed up for hours and helped her make tea at a village Open Gardens day in aid of Cancer Research UK. Some in the village liked the girls – but not all approved of Barbara's choice in helpers. Over the past year, she said, 'People we have known for many years will try and get past me now without a wave, they go straight by.' Recently she had been plagued by silent nuisance phone calls but this had not shaken her conviction that she had done the right thing in seeing the Gypsies as human beings, as neighbours – even as friends.

The graffiti, the Facebook threats ... one prominent former member felt that RAID's presence was inflaming a tense situation, though that person continued to stress that there was absolutely no evidence that RAID members were responsible for the attacks. Looking back over the first two years of the campaign, the former member said, 'It was like a *Wallace and Gromit* angry mob here; there was a lot of passion.' Some people in the village, he was sure, had started to resort to dirty tricks. 'For a fact I know that there were four occasions when rubbish was dumped around the village. I was well against that. It was blamed on the Gypsies. There were things some people were trying to do, make the Gypsies responsible for.'

Information obtained through Freedom of Information requests to Solihull Council seems to bear out his allegation. One email, sent by Keith Portman, the police officer responsible for keeping the peace between the two groups in Meriden, to officials at the council, states: 'I am receiving numerous phone calls from the Gypsy's [sic] and various support networks regarding alleged racist abuse and threats; residents obstructing the entrance to the site, fly-tipping house bricks ... there are clearly increased tensions in both communities. There are a pile of house bricks dumped at the side of the road under the road bridge in Eaves Green Lane, where the racist graffiti was written. Not sure who dumped them but suspect it was a resident with the intent to either blame the Gypsy's [sic], hence the racist graffiti, or to be used as a road block in the event of work on the site.'[12]

David McGrath, the former Birmingham city councillor who had become a leader among the villagers in their struggle against the site, countered such suggestions. In an emailed statement, he said: 'In the email to which you refer, Inspector Portman states he is "unsure as to who dumped the bricks" and then gives a view as to who may have done so. Meriden, like many rural areas, is subject to fly tipping and had the Insp[ector] had evidence to support his personal view, I have no doubt he would have acted upon it.'[13]

In 2010, Senga Townsley, a young disabled woman, also came to stay on the field with her Scotch Gypsy family. Her close-knit family had worked their way down from Scotland, with her father, William, trading antiques, and working in scrap and tarmacking, and her mother, Susan, keeping house. They had worked mostly in the north of England, but had sometimes travelled further afield, once as far as Canada, where Susan recalled, smiling, 'there were nae problems being Gypsies there, they called us barn painters'.[14]

But as laws governing travelling became stricter in both Scotland and England in the late 1980s, the life became more difficult for them. Noah and his family had been friends for decades, Senga explained, and his support and accommodation became more and more vital to them. 'When Noah got married to Joanne, we started to overwinter in Trevallion [the stud farm that Noah's father-in-law owned]. When he got separated, that affected way more people than just him. When Noah got separated, he already owned the land at Meriden but he had never thought of pulling on there.'

The Trevallion stud farm was no longer somewhere the Townsleys could stay over the winter, and the pitch they had in Doncaster had been rented out. Senga had to move into a house in Doncaster for six months with her sister, Susie, her main carer, but found living 'in bricks and mortar' difficult – not least because her physical disability meant it was hard for her to go up and down the stairs. The Townsleys were all but homeless, as was Noah's extended family – his elderly mother and his brothers, Jim, Pinkie and Dean.

Senga recalled that another friend without a site had said two years earlier, 'I'm going to "Gypsy war it,"' a phrase she had never heard before. She was then told that it meant moving onto a piece of land without planning permission. She had told her friend at that time: 'You don't want to do that, it causes real trouble.' Two years later the Burton and Townsley families were in the same position. 'Noah said, "I've got this land, this is what we have got to do, we have to pull on. We need to do it on the bank holiday." So for me to sit here and say we didn't know what we were doing would be a lie, but we didn't understand the ramifications of it. We just knew that is what people did – the mechanics of it, they said this is what we are going to do. I didn't have no clue about this. My dad knew, but we didn't really know.' They planned to do it on the early May bank holiday weekend, but her parents, fearing trouble, asked Senga and Susie to stay put in Doncaster.

Senga's mother, Susan, had never done anything like this in all her life as a Traveller. 'I was nervous, but we never thought it would be like this. We thought it would be like this – you just pull on, you get your electric, your sewer, the water sorted out and then you fight the council. No one ever mentioned fighting the residents,' said Susan.

It did not go as planned. Senga remembered that, 'Mum rang us up and she said, "You won't believe what it's like. We tried to pull on – some old man blocked us. It's really bad."' RAID chairman David McGrath was called back from his holiday in Torquay,

Devon, at a time when he was recuperating from a grave illness, exacerbated, he felt, by the stress of the situation at home. He said at the time: 'We had unpacked the suitcases and were about to go out for a meal. But when we heard what was happening we repacked the cases and came straight back.'[15]

It was a terrible time for everyone caught up in the Meriden encampment, on both sides. Local housed residents complained of sleepless nights brought on by worry over and conflict with their unwanted new neighbours. As for the Townsleys and the Burtons, the stress of the move and the fierce reaction among some of the local people had also made William Townsley, the father of the family, seriously ill. 'It was like the perfect storm,' his wife Susan recalled. 'First Noah and his marriage falling apart, then William falling sick, Senga and Susie stuck in Doncaster – all those things came together at the same time.'

When the day for their 'Gypsy War' arrived, Susan had called her daughters in Doncaster. 'We were only supposed to stay in Doncaster for a couple of nights till it got settled,' Senga said. 'But then I got a phone call from Mum saying, "Dad's in hospital. Don't panic, but he's got heart pains." We jumped straight in the car and drove down. If we had been planning to do this in any way, we would have known what we were doing! We didn't even know where we were going, but eventually we found the field, and saw all the people standing outside. They all had cameras. We asked the policemen where our father had been taken, but nobody knew. Eventually we found him in a hospital in Solihull, and after the visit we came back and stayed in the trailer with Mum. It was really scary as we were at the top end of the field, where they could take photos of us.'

They decided to stick it out during the furore, thinking it would last just a few days. 'We honestly thought, In a few days it will be over. The day after my dad got out of hospital, we had to drive back to Doncaster to get our stuff, and we heard on the radio that there were fears for our safety. But we decided that we would pick our stuff up and do it together: "we will have to commit to it". We thought the tide was turning. We thought it would calm down after a few days and then we can get on with our lives.' Two years later, the protest camp was still watching over them. 'It's been heightened sometimes [but] there have been months when we've barely noticed each other,' she said.

Life for Senga had been particularly hard, as she was targeted both for her disability and because she is a Gypsy. 'I was called a cripple once, when there was a problem with pizza being delivered and RAID wanted to stop the delivery. Someone shouted, "You pikey cripple," and I was really upset. The police were nice, but there was nothing they can do, as it's our word against theirs. They have also been saying that I put on show for court, and that I'm putting on my disability, they say I'm making it all up.' Senga's situation was very real, however. She was diagnosed with cerebral palsy when she was just a few years old. Sometimes she walks with sticks and sometimes she uses a wheelchair, depending on her level of pain, or how far she must walk. And she had moved to Noah's field specifically because the Doncaster house had proved impossible. Still, some residents claimed that she was taken to court merely to curry sympathy.

At the encampment, life was easier for Senga in some ways. Her family were able to build an accessible utility room where she could shower and wash in privacy. But trying to get on and off the muddy site with walking sticks made it difficult on occasion for Senga to get to work, particularly in the winter, when her sticks would sink several inches down in the muck. Sometimes she had to be supported by another person to get to and from the car in order to get to her job. The local council had denied permission to put down any hardcore for paths.[16]

But settling in Meriden was better than being homeless, she said. 'If you are in one place it makes things like getting exercise easier, it keeps weight down. But walking here is difficult because it's muddy and walking sticks and mud don't mix.' She knew that if she could settle in one place, she could manage her condition much better. 'It would be easier if we could just get settled. I'm not saying I would never travel, but to have a permanent base and then be able to get pain management and physiotherapy, that would make day-to-day living easier for me. Disabled people can have a good quality of life, and I could improve mine if we stayed. As it is, I don't really know how to manage my condition; I don't know if I am doing good or bad.'

The insults she had endured hurt a great deal because of her deeply seated veneration for the older generation, a traditional custom among the Romani Gypsies. 'It hurts more here because the people who are doing it are older. When we have suffered abuse before – I have been called "dirty pikey" loads – you genuinely don't take any notice. But it seems worse because the people you are dealing with are older and more educated; you feel that people of a certain age should not do that. It shouldn't become personal [to them]; elderly people don't normally react like that. It's like being hit by a brick. You don't know what to respond, we don't know what to respond – we need to get on with people, we need to integrate.'

Somehow, though, life has slowly improved for the Gypsies in Meriden as they have made more contacts, including with neighbours like Barbara. 'Some of the people in the village are really nice,' said Senga. 'In the beginning it felt horrible going anywhere in the village, you didn't want to make eye contact, but now you feel so comfortable except when you drive by that one bit. The local shops are friendly, it's such a shame … The minority has got smaller and smaller, even some of them at the protest camp are friendly' – with Doug Bacon singled out for praise by the Townsley family for trying hard, both in public and behind the scenes, not to make the campaign against them personal. 'It is a very small minority who want to make it an attack: if they discredit us, make us look bad, they will get rid of us quicker … They want to poke you so much you will react, but it takes a lot to make us react.'

'People say stuff like "it's no smoke without fire", but why did people hate black people?' she asked. 'We have a lot to be blamed for – we have isolated ourselves. The only thing that makes the news is if we pull on somewhere. Everyone thinks we don't pay taxes, for the large majority, it's not true. It is a fact that property values drop, they work hard for their mortgages, I get that, I feel bad for that, [but] it's not our fault and it's not their fault ... It doesn't have to get personal. We do pay taxes. I work for a living – everywhere I have been settled I try to work. I always work when I can. We don't even have a speeding ticket! People print that we are thieves, not citizens – this is our country and ... we have a right to have somewhere to live; that's what has to change. People don't want you to exist: the Gypsy problem should just go away; we should just live in a house. Cultural exceptions are made for other people. We just want a chance to live somewhere. We just want a fair chance ... We need somewhere to live, so our children can go to school, go to the doctor. No one has ever monitored my condition. That's all we are asking.'

Members of Meriden RAID insisted that their campaign was not against Noah Burton, Senga Townsley and the families on the site. They were simply trying to defend the green belt. In the beginning they were successful. Solihull Council turned down a planning application made by the Gypsies for eight pitches on the field in July. But the Gypsies appealed against the decision, and tensions in the village remained high.

In September 2010 RAID members travelled with their local MEP, Nikki Sinclaire, to the European Parliament and to the European Court of Human Rights on a 'protest coach trip' in hope of securing support and funding. Sinclaire, a great supporter of Meridan RAID's campaigning, was quoted on the group's website: 'there seems to be no balance regarding the rights of the long-term local residents affected by the development. It is obvious to everyone that in this instance the settled community of Meriden has had its right to a private and family life fundamentally breached by this unethical attempt at development. Not only that, but the planning system and laws put in place – many of them influenced by Europe – leave people feeling powerless and frustrated – and actually encourage this type of thing.'

David McGrath also noted the importance of the trip. 'This is a big thing for us – we have worked very hard to organise this and we feel passionate that every decision-maker in the country will hear about how places like Meriden have been the victims of bulldozers and barristers – aided and abetted by a crazy planning system that gives special rights to some and not others,' he said in a statement published on the RAID website. He continued: 'This is an attack on our rural way of life and we will fight to change things at every court in the land. It is also a breach of Article 8 of the European Convention of Human Rights (a right to a private and family way of life). Gypsies and travellers are given a bad name by a few who refuse to come to the table, engage with communities and play by the same rules as the rest of all of us'.[17]

The RAID contingent picketed the European Parliament with banners proclaiming 'We have human rights too' and 'Protect the Meriden Gap'. They were dismayed to find that not everyone agreed with their point of view – and, indeed, some forces were unwelcoming of their bid to have their case heard. French riot police and parliamentary security staff asked them to remove their campaign T-shirts and tracked their movements inside the Parliament building.[18]

The following March, Solihull council started a full planning inquiry into the proposed site, although Secretary of State for Communities and Local Government Eric Pickles reserved the right to step in and overturn any decision made by the planning inspector if he did not agree with it.[19] RAID campaigners gave evidence, saying that the site had caused a rise in traffic accidents and that it was 'inappropriate' for the families to be on green-belt land. Johnny Howorth, the *Guardian* film-maker, recalled giving evidence at the public inquiry. 'I will always remember a few pensioners, who were vehemently opposed to the Gypsy families staying at Meriden, mouthing swear words at me when I was giving evidence. I have never experienced anything like that. The Gypsies were always keen for me to hear both sides of the story – but some people in Meriden RAID immediately thought I would take the Gypsy side if I talked to them.' He was partly motivated to give evidence by an incident that had occurred outside the council planning meeting in July 2010, when the Gypsies were having their application heard. One RAID member, who appeared to realise he was on Howorth's screen during filming, accused

Howorth of 'being with the "Gyppos"' and then tried to bat his camera away.[20] The planning inspector, Phillip Ware, upheld the denial of the planning permission.

On 25 October Pickles upheld Ware's decision. He also refused permission for the Gypsies to stay at the site temporarily, saying 'the harm is too great'. He cited a 'serious loss of openness in the Green Belt which would be exacerbated if other elements of the proposal were undertaken' and the danger to highway safety and to trees. He also cited the 'limited likelihood of peaceful and integrated co-existence' in Meriden – something that both sides, at this point, could agree on, at least. Pickles insisted that he had given 'some weight' to the immediate need for Traveller sites in the district, the lack of a suitable alternative site, general health needs and continuity of education for the Gypsies, 'but added that such considerations did not outweigh the harms'.[21]

In the winter and spring of 2012, most members of Meriden RAID became wary of taking much of a stand in public. Requests for interviews were routinely referred up their hierarchy to vice-chair Doug Bacon or chairman David McGrath. This meant it was all but impossible to ask ordinary members of Meriden RAID for their views about the controversy. McGrath and Bacon, in turn, made appointments (with regard to me, working at this time for the *Guardian* and for this book) on a number of occasions, then abruptly cancelled them. They gave reasons for their new shyness: one was Johnny Howorth's evidence at the public inquiry; others included the pressure of work and the perceived bias of any media team that thought it important to talk to both sides in the story; another was, ostensibly, and at very short notice, to avoid 'prejudicing'* any court appearances (although in Basildon

---

*   The concern about court appearances being 'prejudiced' by these interviews was raised by David McGrath in a written response to questions that he provided on 6 March 2012, after several interviews were cancelled. He requested that this statement be reprinted in full, without editing of his responses. The statement is reprinted on pp. 321–9.

all sides freely gave interviews in the run-up, during and after court appearances).[22]

They did not always cancel their conversations with the press, however. After planning permission for RAID's makeshift shelter was refused on 1 February 2012, David McGrath insisted to me that his vision was one of 'ethical localism', whereby local residents can resist 'inappropriate development'. He was encouraged by the success that RAID had made in creating a localism movement, which he said now numbered around 'forty or fifty' groups. These local organisations would be 'professionalising' similar protests around the country.[23] But the roll-out of the RAID model, and its potential commercialisation, alarmed other people in Meriden.

A few miles from the village, in Hockley Heath, Solihull Council identified a possible site for development for Gypsies and Travellers. The local residents' association hastily constituted a group, called Hockley Heath Residents Against Inappropriate Development, and approached Meriden RAID for help. This help, according to the association's website, came at a price – the association said that it had engaged McGrath and Doug Bacon as 'consultants' who would assist them in their campaign against the site going forward as development. The website asked for funds for local residents to meet the bill of the two consultants, saying that £4,560 had been raised already, 'just over half the bill'.

In a written statement, McGrath explained: 'This money will be paid to my company and from this will be deducted the services of a planning consultant, researcher and ecologist. Residents in Hockley were concerned that they should have a professionally prepared response evaluate [sic] a proposal to locate a traveller site in Hockley Heath. The reports identified clear planning reasons why the site would be inappropriate. Solihull Council also carried out its own independent survey and also concluded that the site was inappropriate.' He added: 'Meriden RAID raised and spent over £67,000 engaging the services of planning consultant, highways consultant, ecologist etc. Meriden RAID cannot pay for other groups. Local groups must raise funds in the same way and pay for the expert analysis.'[24]

The Hockley Heath group also approached the local parish council for funding to help pay the bill. The council decided to meet over £6,500 of the costs run up by the residents to oppose the proposed Gypsy and Traveller site. The decision to meet the bill was problematic. According to Barbara Cohen, a lawyer specialising in equality issues and former head of legal policy for the Commission for Racial Equality: 'Under Section 149 of the Equality Act 2010, parish councils, which are listed as public bodies, have to have due regard to the need to foster good relations between people who have a protected characteristic (in this case Gypsy/ Traveller) and those who do not. The parish council must take equality issues into account. So if a parish council has made a grant to a community group which might exacerbate poor relations between Gypsies and Travellers and others it is arguably that they have failed to comply with its equality duty under the Act.'[25]

After being challenged about the legality of this funding decision, Hockley Heath parish council asked Warwickshire county solicitors for advice. It soon issued the following statement: 'Hockley Heath Parish Council is aware of its obligations under the Local Government Act 1972 and the Equality Act 2010 and believes that it has acted in accordance with its legal obligations at all times. Hockley Heath Parish Council does not have any further statement to make at this time.'[26]

With the story out in the community, residents in nearby areas began reporting payments made by other parish councils to Meriden RAID. In nearby Berkswell, people had also turned to Meriden RAID for 'consultancy' when Solihull Metropolitan Borough Council had threatened the community with a proposed site. As in Hockley Heath, they too had been persuaded that the parish council needed to cough up. It pledged a hefty £10,000 towards a 'fighting fund' to keep out the Gypsies; in the end it had only paid £3,600 as of 21 June 2012. Part of the fee covered a 'survey' conducted by members of Meriden RAID of land that was being considered for a site. The owner of the land in question was at first involved with the fledgling residents' committee, but was cut out of the loop around the time that Meriden RAID became involved. The parish council never asked her about her own plan for the land – which was to withdraw it from discussion. After the site had been withdrawn, the survey's results were still lodged with the borough council. Yet the report had not been shared with the land's owner, despite her repeated requests – and Meriden RAID or other 'consultants', she claimed, may well have trespassed on her land without permission to carry out the survey. She decided to lodge a formal complaint with Solihull Council about the situation.

But Berkswell was not the only community looking to RAID for advice. Residents in nearby Balsall Common also solicited funding from their parish council to oppose the site.

Parish councils had once represented the cuddly side of politics – paying for street lamps, mowing the village green and providing floral displays for events like the Queen's Jubilee. Many still devote their energies to such worthy projects. But now they had been co-opted as the front guard of localism, the push to devolve power down to the lowest level – and some councils had started to make increasingly questionable political and legal decisions. The money paid by Hockley Heath parish council for 'consultancy' work to defend the village against the Gypsy site risked running foul of the Equality Act 2010, under which councils were required to foster 'good relations' between different ethnic groups.

The issue of parish councils shelling out for these activities was brought up at the Solihull Metropolitan Borough Council's cabinet meeting in November 2011, but no action was decided. The money for Hockley Heath's 'consultancy' was paid directly to David McGrath's company, Mr McGrath confirmed.

Funding is important, of course, but so is the proliferation of the groups throughout the country. One group, in Yorkshire, attracted much local interest as its chair, Neil Whitelam, stood in the general election of 2010 as a British National Party candidate for the Holderness constituency. Since then, he has said that he holds no political affiliation to the BNP, but the RAID website in Holderness talks of 'nationalist' members of the community fighting against a 'fully fledged Gypsy site' in the area.[27] Such language alarms many Gypsies and Travellers. As for Meriden RAID, David McGrath said in a statement that the group 'utterly rejects racism and we have consistently made our view on this matter clear'.[28] Both he and Doug Bacon have made strenuous efforts throughout their campaign at Meriden to make it clear that they completely repudiate racism against Gypsies and Travellers. They also state unequivocally that they believe Gypsies and Travellers have a right to appropriate accommodation.

Solihull Metropolitan Borough Council asked the residents supporting Meriden RAID to take down their encampment by the end of April 2012. Instead, they remained, and even fortified their presence. By the end the RAID encampment looked rather like a bunker from the Second World War. The Burton and Townsley families were supposed to leave Noah's field at the end of March 2013. They had been under the kind of pressure and, on occasion, subject to racism that would break many people – and on many occasions they responded with a degree of empathy towards those who stood against them. On some occasions they had to admit that harsh words had been exchanged, words that some of the families on the site said they now regret. And sometimes this empathy has been reciprocated by members of RAID, raising the hope that perhaps, if the Townsleys and the Burtons could find a home nearby, there could be some form of reconciliation in the future.

Still, as of that decisive March, they had only secured a home for something short of three years. In early April 2013 they started to sell their belongings and move off, a small community splintered for the lack of accommodation. At the time of writing, one of their group had already been moved on by the police twice from stopping places. None of them – women, children, older people and disabled people among them – had anywhere secure to go to.

The battle in Meriden would soon be over. But the model was spreading, nonetheless. Local people were learning how to put up an active resistance to new Gypsy and Traveller sites, using as many legal loopholes as they could find to the sites being taking a foothold. The battle at Meriden may be over, but the war had only just begun.

The Meriden group became a standard-bearer for localism, organising a conference in January 2011 of similarly minded people from around the UK that 'attracted some seventy-five delegates', according to an article for the Institute for Race Relations by Ryan Erfani-Ghettani. 'Using the Localism Act, local "residents'" groups are emerging to fight, usually successfully, against Traveller and Gypsy attempts to establish legal sites – and all this despite the fact that local authorities have failed to provide the necessary statutory pitches ... Groups have been writing to each other to offer campaigning strategies, sharing tactics and forging coalitions. A legal infrastructure appears to have developed, and action groups are claiming to have access to a shared network of planning and legal experts ... Localism has put the power back into communities in one sense – the power to buy expertise.'[29]

Since the war over the green-belt land in Meriden began, many residents' groups battling such sites, and aping Meriden RAID's tactics, have appeared, including in Leicester; Crewe and Pickmere in Cheshire; Attleborough in Norfolk; Newent in Gloucestershire; Stanton Wick in Somerset; Stanley, Wakefield; Penderry in Swansea; Flackwell Heath, Buckinghamshire; Tonbridge, Kent; Windsor in Berkshire; and Aldebury in Wiltshire. Though some councils try to do the right thing, they are often opposed by and prevented from doing so by local people – more and more often, doing so using tax-payers' money. Local district and metropolitan boroughs pay up, as is their duty, to identify sites for homeless Gypsies and Travellers, using tax-payers' money. Then parish councils (which are funded with a precept through local councils) are being systematically used by local residents' groups for funding to oppose such sites – the efforts, all funded by tax-payers' money, often cancelling each other out.

This is, to some extent, understandable. Many residents' associations, as in Meriden, have raised tens of thousands of pounds from their own members in order to oppose Gypsy and Traveller sites that they fear will have an impact on their local area and that they feel are being imposed on them from above with little consultation. It is not surprising that they are trying to find someone else to pay for that, after they've spent so much themselves. The planning system is pitting local settled people against local Gypsies and Travellers – devolving conflict down to the local level, between putative neighbours, where it has the potential to become personal, even bitter. But the system is, if anything, even less fair to Gypsies and Travellers, who – whether homeless or housed – are often paying taxes that go to fund 'consultants' who come up with reasons why the Gypsies and Travellers shouldn't have anywhere to live in their parish.

Eric Pickles and other champions of the localism agenda may not have meant this to happen, but Gypsy and Traveller families have been set against their neighbours, who are, all too often, banding together to deprive them of a legal place to live. Meriden has become a template of how residents' groups can use planning, the legal system, public opinion and the media to fight against Gypsies and Travellers, with the effect that these nomads are left with nowhere – legal or illegal – to live.

Noah Burton and the other Gypsy families at Meriden had almost exhausted their funds to fight for the right to a home. The local residents had also been fundraising continuously to wage their expensive legal battle to keep the Gypsies out of their back yard. Meriden RAID were also in breach of planning law for many months in their makeshift shelter – and when the Gypsies eventually moved off, they still had nowhere legal to live. Localism has not solved the problem for either side.[30]

As former Deputy Prime Minister John Prescott said, in a clear critique of the policy of localism: 'It panders to the worst kind of Nimbyism, and the worst kind of prejudices that people can have. This is a housing problem, after all, and it needs sorting out.'[31]

12
TARGETED

Noah Burton was surprised to find how much he was hated once the Meriden story became nationally prominent. For years, he said, he had 'passed' in public as a white British man, with few people realising that he is a Gypsy unless he told them. 'You go through life in a disguise. If you pull into the garage and there's an article in the paper, and you're paying at the pump, the garage man is saying, "Look what the dirty Gypsies have done," and you say, "All right mate, best thing for them," you laugh about it with them, you don't want to tell them. They call us a load of thieves, but our skin is pretty thick to it.'

But as Meriden became a national story, his face and ethnic identity became widely known. He was recognised for being who he was, and couldn't disguise himself any more. His work – restoring antique cars and caravans – fell off a cliff. He was, quite simply, no longer trusted. While his home – his caravan – had been attacked previously because it advertised its 'Gypsyness', he was not used to being seen as such personally. The reaction he received shocked him. 'I've been brought up with prejudice, racial prejudice against me; we've stopped on waste ground and had the caravans stoned at night. We've been brought up with it – it's nothing new to none of us. That's why we go through life disguising ourselves, it's the only way we can get through life. Before I took off the disguise I never ever realised how much hatred there is towards me. But then we came here, and we have this lot outside the gate, and if you look at them, they are all a certain age, they are a different generation. For them it's a social gathering, we are a pretty easy target, and they can bully us and hide behind a big green-belt banner.'

But, in some ways, Noah said, after Meriden, it was a relief to take off the mask. He reflected on the civil rights struggle of blacks and Asians in the 1960s and 1970s: 'They couldn't pretend, they couldn't pass. Maybe if we had been in that situation we would fight harder against racism against us. *They* didn't have an easy way out.'

What Noah said had been illustrated vividly in an incident in a café near Birmingham Crown Court on the day that the Meriden families heard that they had just one year to stay. Noah's brother Jim and a friend of theirs who lives on the same site, Joe, had joined Noah for lunch. They were talking about hiding their identities so that they could get work. Joe mainly worked as a barn painter, and he never revealed his ethnicity to the farmers who hired him, because he feared that if he did, he would never find jobs. Jim agreed; being a Gypsy was a distinct disadvantage in the workplace, much as he was proud of his identity. Then it was time to go back to the Court to hear the verdict on their leave to remain at Meriden. With a well-practised gesture, both Jim and Joe tugged their jackets over their heads, to obscure their faces from the cameras.

Officially, Gypsies and Irish Travellers (though not New Travellers) are protected under race relations law in the UK. The truth is that many face discrimination, abuse and prejudice, some on a daily basis. It's nearly impossible to meet a member of the community who has not faced verbal or even physical abuse, or had their property attacked. Such incidents are often mentioned casually, with few reporting attacks or discrimination to the police. When they do, they believe they are highly unlikely to get justice – and the facts prove them right in this assumption. They are, unfortunately, used to being the scapegoats.

Throughout history Gypsies and Travellers have been scapegoated – the usual fate of outsiders. In his book *Folk Devils and*

Moral Panics, the sociologist Stanley Cohen explained how outsiders are blamed during unsettled times, using the Mods and Rockers of the 1960s as an example.[1] These ideas have been developed by other writers, such as Abram de Swaan, who applied them to the treatment of the Tutsi population in Rwanda during the 1995 genocide. In that horror, de Swaan says, the settled community increasingly pitted itself against the nomads and outsiders – the Tutsis – who were branded as threats. 'In the villages new identifications developed, uniting neighbours against outsiders; against landless vagrants but also against the peasants of adjacent villages, pilferers of the common woods, cattle rustlers or upstream pollutants.' The outsiders here are seen as not just evil, but polluting – a recurring theme in the depictions of Gypsies and Travellers across history. This supports an argument put forth by Ryan Powell: 'Notions of a lack of morals, dirt, violence, deviance, laziness, illiteracy and racial purity ("real" Gypsies) have all been used to justify discriminatory responses to Gypsies and Travellers and explain their continual stigmatisation.'[2]

The notion of the 'other', first put forward by Edward Said in 1978, is central to academic Joanna Richardson's 2006 paper, *Can Discourse Control?*, which looks at how Gypsies and Travellers in Britain are stigmatised and set apart from mainstream society, much more so than other groups. She clearly demonstrates that the media and other institutions, including Parliament, play their part in both 'othering' Gypsies and Travellers by making them into scapegoats.[3] She describes how suspect groups are subject to surveillance, in order to control them. Intelligence is collected and then interpreted – something that was in force at Dale Farm and Meriden, but was not only used in those hot spots.

In fact, close surveillance of Gypsies and Travellers had been developed in relation to an inter-agency model of site management used in Milton Keynes and in Oxford.[4] According to a report from the Equality and Human Rights Commission, 'Activity on the sites was monitored by CCTV cameras. The residents of all the Oxford sites protested at the police role in accommodation management, a model that is not practised in relation to housed tenancies. The arrangement was discontinued in Oxford, and the police role in the Milton Keynes multi-agency group was reduced. This high-profile example highlighted for Gypsies and Travellers the continuing, if not always so, clearly direct policing of their lifestyle.'[5]

Another study, carried out by the criminologist Zoe James, looked at the police management of New Travellers in Devon. The EHRC reported that the authorities had 'forced them to camp in even more marginal locations. [James] described a range of ways in which Travellers were harassed by the police, including the use of helicopters. Because of the power to remove and destroy vehicles (living accommodation) if directions to leave are not followed.'[6] James argued that by these methods: 'groups of people are controlled in society by methods that are not visible and therefore unaccountable'.[7]

The EHRC concluded, 'the police primarily engaged with the communities through enforcement practices. At the same time, Gypsies and Travellers rarely felt able to report crimes against themselves to the police, so they experienced a high rate of surveillance but under-protection.'[8]

The nineteenth-century Italian criminologist Cesare Lombroso is partly to blame for the notion that Gypsies, Roma and Travellers are 'criminal by nature'. 'Gypsies epitomise a thoroughly criminal race, with all its passions and vices ... they prefer to suffer hunger and misery rather than subject themselves to any sort of continuous work ... [and] have the same lack of foresight as savages and criminals,' he wrote.[9]

This stigma holds true today, despite all lack of evidence. As the Equality and Human Rights Commission states: 'This is expressed through public and media allegations of rises in crime when Travellers enter a neighbourhood, despite evidence to the contrary, both locally and nationally. This is contrary to what the Association of Chief Police Officers, and local studies of crime have actually found. ACPO, for example, says that there is no evidence that the communities are disproportionately involved in criminal acts.[10] The independent scholar Robert Dawson has documented similar levels of criminal activity in the Traveller and non-Traveller populations.[11] However, the suspicion with which Travellers are regarded means they are more likely to be reported by neighbours or targeted unfairly by the police.

A particularly nasty flurry of recriminations took place in a rural county of England as the county was carrying out its needs assessment for new Gypsy and Traveller sites in 2012.* 'As you can imagine, this is rather an emotive topic, and the vast majority of the local people cannot understand why we are wasting public money in finding sites for this much-maligned sector of society,' the policy and planning officer for the area said. 'I am the lead officer of the project-management group overseeing the plan on behalf of the council, and in that capacity I have had a number of telephone conversations with [local news editors] about the tone of their coverage, and the awful postings they have allowed on the website. I have managed to get a number of the worst comments … removed, but [some newspapers] basically allow anyone to post what they want and they are only taken down if someone complains. My view, for what it's worth, is that [the local press] has made this sensitive issue more inflammatory by allowing offensive comments to be posted, and by the sensationalist tone of their reporting – including inaccurate stories very loosely based on press releases from the local authorities concerned.' Council officers even referred a number of the comments – for, example, a suggestion to build a high fence with gun turrets around any new sites – for investigation by hate-crime officers. None of the referred comments were taken forward for prosecution, a common problem.

Deputy Chief Constable Janette McCormick reiterated that there is no proven link between Gypsies and Travellers and increased crime rates. In fact, because until 2011 Gypsies and Travellers were not recorded separately on the Census (they were forced to tick the 'White – Other' box), she believed it would be impossible to say whether or not they are over-represented in the crime statistics, whether as perpetrators or victims. Further, the British Crime Survey (recently renamed the Crime Survey for

---

* Not named at the request of the county and its planning officers.

England and Wales), which interviews a representative sample of households each year about their experience of crime, does not visit any Gypsy or Traveller sites. A researcher for the survey said that they were such a small community that the results would be numerically insignificant, in any case.[12]

A few police forces (including McCormick's own in Cheshire), are now flagging cases where Gypsies or Travellers are victims, but the data is not yet good enough or available in such volume for its results to be analysed. However, some limited research by individual police forces suggests, conversely to public opinion, that there is sometimes a drop in local crime rates in areas surrounding small, well-managed sites. During the Stow Horse Fair, for example, the local crime rate often goes down, despite the public perception that it soars during fair days. The assumptions were plain enough in the town's small supermarket in the spring of 2012, with the fair in full swing. As soon as English Romani Gypsy and Irish Traveller young people entered the shop, all eyes were upon them; security staff hovered around. They paid for their simple purchases, thanked the cashiers, and left quietly.[13] Such prejudice is particularly hurtful considering that Gypsies and Travellers *are* often victims, not perpetrators, of crime.

They are especially at risk of experiencing theft or harassment when they stop at unauthorised sites.[14] Yet, even when they are the victims of a crime, they are unlikely to bother reporting it to the police, because they believe they are unlikely to receive justice if they do so. Indeed, in a 'Needs Assessment' of Devon covering various nomadic groups, including New Travellers, Showpeople, Irish Travellers and Romani Gypsies, Zoe James heard that twenty-three per cent had been victims of crime – about the same as the national averages – but only seventeen per cent of these individuals had reported the alleged crimes to the police. Most shockingly, the reporting rate was even lower when a racist offence was involved.[15] Similarly, the academic Margaret Greenfields found significant under-reporting of racist offences in similar needs assessments in the West of England and Cambridgeshire.[16]

McCormick believed that it was the case that Gypsies and Travellers were targets for crime, though the evidence is limited. Three linked problems seemed to her to be at the root of their vulnerability: first, 'a general tolerance in society of racism against [Gypsy and Traveller] groups'; second, 'a lack of reporting' due to the distrust of police and the justice system more broadly; and third, 'a lack of recording' of the Gypsy or Traveller ethnicity of the victim by authorities involved. 'We have nothing to say that they are disproportionately affected as victims of crime,' McCormick admitted, but that was 'because there has never been any baseline, there has been no census information – no push to do that'.

Despite 'common sense ... that they are victims of racist crime', she still felt that it was a challenge to prosecute a case – mostly because, with all of the stereotypes hanging over Gypsy and Traveller communities, the victim is usually a pariah and the offender is sometimes viewed as a hero. This was especially true where the flashpoint for a racist crime came while a community was fighting to keep hold of a site, as at Meriden. 'Racist crime against the communities manifests itself particularly around planning applications,' she said. 'It is well documented and well articulated that society feels that it is appropriate and acceptable to be prejudiced against Gypsies and Travellers. I don't think people perceive it as a race issue. If that was any other race issue, that wouldn't happen but I don't think that connection is made.' The response of her constabulary has been to educate the local residents. 'We have a number of training packages with local authorities ... In areas where [planning applications have] been managed well, tensions are less ... Managing those key decision-makers and educating them really helps.'

But some local councillors, rather than managing tensions, inflame them instead. Deb Roberts, an independent councillor in South Cambridgeshire, declared that if she had cancer she would strap a bomb around herself and blow herself up among the Travellers in Cottenham. The Standards Board, an English public body that promoted high standards of conduct in local government, merely rapped her knuckles for the statement. Other Cambridgeshire councillors were documented saying equally offensive things about their local residents, with one suggesting that Travellers' sites should have minefields built around them. As punishment, he was ordered to attend equality training.[17] When the head of communications for South Cambridgeshire District Council was asked about the insults made by council members, he said: 'You have mentioned three councillors … but we have fifty-seven members. It seems to be out of context to call it "an institutional problem."'[18] No action was taken against them.

Roberts, for her part, did not seem to be chastened by the Standards Board; she later told a council officer that the Smithy Fen Travellers should 'stew in their own shit' during a row over sewage handling at the site. The Coalition government abolished the Standards Board on 31 March 2012, and now each council merely monitors members' behaviour, so it is unlikely that similar statements will meet a stronger answer in the future.

No criminal charges have been taken forward either. McCormick explained why they are so rare: 'The attitudes towards the communities are quite subtle, so often the crimes don't reach the criminal threshold. I think that is a huge confidence issue, if someone does report it, and it doesn't reach the threshold for prosecution, they have to take civil action and they feel disappointed with us. Often what is reported doesn't breach section 4 or 5 of the Public Order Act – and, if anything, it might be more difficult because the government is now think-ing of taking the word "insulting" out of [the] legislation … That small bit of leverage might go, because of the perceived need to protect the right to free speech. But that [change] might have a huge impact on a minority,' she said. She pointed to a recent example, involving an application for planning approval, where local residents were flashing 'No Gypsy' placards as part of their residents' association protest. 'You could say that is a criminal offence [under the hate crime law], but if we prosecute it then we would alienate the settled community. The other alternative is to manage that and look at informal mediation.' But official mediation upsets Gypsies and Travellers – it's just one more way in which the settled community attempts to enforce their norms.

At the same time, well-selected prosecutions are worth taking on – worth the risk of reporting to the authorities and sticking a neck out in front of the media. One successful action, according to the Irish Traveller Movement's Sean Risdale, involved an anti-Gypsy cartoon that had been printed in a magazine. 'I think one of the major current gaps is that Travellers don't often fit in to broader alliances of ethnic groupings. For example, I can't think of many instances of Racial Equality Councils taking up their issues. Essex Race Equality Council was a good exception, until its funding went. It sued *Viz* magazine in the 1990s when they published a cartoon called "Thieving Gypsy Bastards" and won. *Viz* had to pull the cartoon and printed an apology. It can be done.'[19] That was more than two decades ago, however. The pub chain JD Wetherspoon is currently being sued by the Irish Traveller Movement of Britain for barring a group of Irish Travellers (as well as a senior police officer, Mark Watson, and a senior partner at the law firm, Howe and Co., Martin Howe, who were with them) from entry to one of their establishments on the Holloway Road, North London, called the Coronet.[20]

The alleged incident at the Wetherspoon pub is not isolated. In Liverpool, Meriden, Dale Farm, Norfolk and Darlington, Gypsies and Travellers have reported cases of discrimination. They have claimed to have been barred from restaurants, wedding venues, leisure centres, clubs and pubs – purely because of their identity. But few thought it was worth reporting the discrimination; they did not think they would get justice. One English Gypsy, the much-respected Billy Welch, organiser of Appleby Fair, recently succeeded in taking a discrimination charge right through the legal system, only to be forced into mediation. The story was familiar: he had been refused admission by a pub. But despite persuading the EHRC to get involved, he had been denied a civil case in court. Experiences such as these only reinforce the belief among Gypsies and Travellers that their situation is hopeless.

A firm of lawyers, Howe and Company, has stepped up in response. Along with the Irish Traveller Movement, they are developing plans for a crime hotline, where Gypsies and Travellers may leave messages about their experience of crime. Where possible, the lawyers will take legal action – using all civil and criminal means possible.

There is so little confidence in the police as neutral law enforcers that many Romani communities, as well as Irish Travellers, choose to police themselves. Academic Thomas Acton has analysed the alternative justice system created by different Traveller cultures. 'Whereas the Kalderash Roma have developed a form of criminal law, English Romanichal Gypsies practice only civil law among themselves,' he said, explaining that 'such a system is therefore better termed "justice by avoidance" than "justice by feuding"'.[21] For example, some sites in the UK are avoided by certain families, even if they are in desperate need of accommodation, because of ongoing quarrels with a family who have already pulled on there.

Occasionally feuds get fired up, nonetheless. One such came up for debate at a planning meeting for the Appleby Fair, one of the traditional Gypsy and Traveller gatherings, in June 2012. A large extended family had been 'spoken to' by police officers in order to dissuade them either from coming to the fair or from 'tooling up' if they did. On a previous year, the same family had been forced to discard weapons, including knives and machetes, before participating in the fair.

Acton recalled how, at a meeting of the Fifth World Romani Congress, the Swedish delegation of Drzara Romani (originally from Serbia) began shouting at one another. The then president of the UK Gypsy Council, Charles Smith, turned to Acton and remarked that if the words had been exchanged at a family wedding, 'there would be murder done'. Within some Romani

communities, conflicts are resolved through the *divano* (an informal meeting of clan leaders) and then, if no settlement can be
reached, a *kris* (or traditional court), which is convened to air
both sides and restore peace and mutual respect.[22] According to
Acton, the *kris* 'provides an environment within which individuals can speak very robustly, because there is a guarantee
of non-violence'.[23]

The *kris* is a long-standing tradition, but it is seldom used in
the UK. Other Romani lines maintain order through the threat
of feuds, and here, as in the Republic of Ireland, Irish Traveller
disputes are either settled with fisticuffs or with avoidance.
Elders in the Gypsy and Traveller communities in the UK are
often those who have shown that they can acquit themselves
well with their fists.

Damian Le Bas, an English Gypsy and the editor of the
Travellers' Times, is clearly ambivalent about this approach to
resolving conflicts, saying that the *kris* doesn't exist in the UK,
and that British Gypsy justice is quite male-centred. 'There are
influential people in our community – it's hard to say that there
is a leader, that's always been tied up with being able to use your
fists, and this is also true of Irish Travellers. But it is a non-Gypsy
notion, the "King of the Gypsies". Calling yourself that here means
you will be fought. The closest thing to it that I can think of was
my Granny's cousin, John Frankham, who was a Commonwealth
boxing champion.'[24]

Self-policing may maintain order, but it has problems too:
stronger families can very easily take advantage of weaker families.
At Dale Farm, there were persistent rumours that several of the
poorer families were reluctant to leave, because if they returned
to Ireland or moved to another site in England, they believed
they would be forced to pay protection money to the established
families. If they refused, they would be pushed out – perhaps
violently. They would not be welcome among their own kind,
unless they were willing to pay for the honour.

Any community that polices itself faces these sorts of issues.
The weakest suffer at the hands of the people who have wrested

control – the same was true in the East End when the Kray twins ruled the roost, or in Mafia-controlled Sicily. An outside, state-run police force provides a tool for picking off individuals who take advantage of others. Strong policing of criminal or exploitative elements may be the only way forward. But for that to be an attractive solution for the more vulnerable Gypsy and Traveller families, the criminal justice system needs to prove its commitment to fairness before the law as well as an ability to protect them if they report crimes. For now, the 'huge confidence issue' cited by Janette McCormick makes this impossible.

In the view of the Romani journalist and broadcaster, Jake Bowers, engagement with the police is the only way forward. Otherwise the weakest will always be pushed to the wall, especially when tensions between English Gypsies and Irish Travellers turn violent over that scarcest, most valuable of resources: accommodation. 'One of the big ones for conflict was a site in East Anglia, which was first settled by English Gypsy families,' Bowers recalled. 'But then an Irish Traveller family came along with guns and a bag of cash, saying, "Do you want to be bought out and leave, or get shot?" That kind of thing goes throughout the community. There is a lot of fear and paranoia that swirls around. For instance, a few years ago there was a rumour that Irish Travellers, backed by Bosnians, were kidnapping children for money from English Gypsies. There was said to be some evidence it happened in Kent ... So I ended up in Cumbria, hearing that [the group] was on the way. [I was] standing with a load of men with baseball bats outside a site. It became a bogeyman that was blown out of all proportion.'

He continued: 'If you work with the police in our community, you're seen as a grass. But if you don't talk to the police, the law of the jungle wins, the heavies win because they have got more muscle. You get really horrible behaviour – such as feuding, and suffering behind closed doors, domestic violence, protection rackets and the effects of all of that are really terrible.'

Because of the shortage of authorised sites, a rivalry has grown up between some Irish Traveller and English Gypsy families, and as a result some members of the two communities are often very reluctant to live side by side. So even if there are empty plots available on a site, they will not be used if the majority population on one site is of one group rather than the other. In the months after the clearance of Dale Farm, with the Sheridans and other families living by the roadside, the Basildon Council, for instance, had begun to explore a possible authorised site nearby, which, for equality reasons, would have to be offered equally to English Gypsies and Irish Travellers. The Dale Farm men said that they would not move onto it if there would be Gypsies there. According to one: 'The English are like the Mafia. They would come on, threaten us with guns, and then we would have to go.' When asked, English Gypsy families said the same thing of Irish Travellers. Neither side would ever consider involving the police in any ensuing dispute.

Gypsies and Travellers fear the police partly because of their sometimes (mostly historic) violent role in evictions. There have also been many well-documented cases of racism directed against them by individual police officers in the past. This leaves Gypsies and Travellers wary of the authorities, and less likely to report victimisation of any kind, whether from the settled community or from stronger families who have taken control of a site or area. It may even be that they are even less likely to report harassment and victimisation by fellow Gypsies and Travellers, following the code that policing should stay within the community. Even if they do report harassment, few, if any, cases are prosecuted. This reinforces the belief that Gypsies and Travellers need to sort out problems among themselves. It is a vicious circle. Until it can be broken, the public will continue to believe that Gypsies and Travellers as a whole prey on the settled community, but are rarely victims themselves.

As Damian Le Bas put it, 'There is a sense that we have more than our fair share of criminality – I am not going to attempt to justify that in my way ... What is essential is to comment on unjustifiable, brutal things, like slavery and honour killing. But to hint that it is running through our veins is unacceptable. These cultures are not macro; certain families transmit them.'

The instinct to self-police and the need to maintain trust within the community encourages other practices, including the tradition of facilitating introductions between young people, which often lead on to relationships and marriages, among Irish Traveller families. The media, seemingly ever keen to find a new accusation to throw at Gypsies and Travellers, ignited a furore in May 2012 by claiming that 'forced marriage' was endemic in the travelling community.

Forced marriage is a serious issue – sometimes leading to other crimes, including rape, robbery, domestic violence, child abduction, even honour killings and other murders. In 2011, the UK Forced Marriage Unit investigated more than a thousand referrals about suspect marriages. But thus far there is no evidence that the problem exists among Gypsies and Travellers. There was reference to one study cited in a single FMU research paper entitled 'Forced Marriage in the UK: A scoping study on the experience of women from Middle Eastern and North East African Communities', but otherwise, nothing.[25]

Whenever Irish Traveller families were asked about the subject, they reported that it was not a common practice – indeed, they responded with completely blank stares. Arranged marriages were not unusual, and marriage was certainly acceptable at a much younger age than in the mainstream population, but these customs were not the same as a forced marriage, they said. It was not an issue.

This ran directly counter to the public debate of the matter. In May 2012, the Chief Crown Prosecutor for the North-West, Nazir Afzal, was fresh from successfully prosecuting Asian grooming gangs, and announced that he was ready to tackle forced marriage among Travellers. 'There are some communities where we have feared to tread, and by "we" I mean every agency. I am hopeful that no longer exists. It no longer exists as far as I'm concerned, and the last bastion for me is the Traveller community,' he said in an interview with the *Independent*. 'I have become aware of massive issues of forced marriage in the Traveller community. It is widespread,' he stated unequivocally. The article went on to stated that Afzal was 'currently assisting representatives of the community who are working to raise awareness of forced marriage and women's rights, advising them on government strategy'.[26]

Social media networking sites and email discussion threads were flooded with responses from the Traveller community. Where had Afzal's information come from? Many people expressed bemusement that forced marriage was now considered to be a widespread problem in the community. Jess Smith, a Scottish Traveller who has written several best-selling books about the communities and has researched them for more than twenty years, said that she has never come across the problem of forced marriage.

It later emerged from senior sources within the criminal justice system and the Traveller community that Afzal's allegations seemed to be based on just one conversation with one worker and were not further substantiated.[27] One comment morphs into a supposed truth, which is then endlessly repeated, about not just one conversation, but an entire community.

While it is true that Irish Traveller women do experience domestic violence,[28] which is often linked to forced marriage in other communities, very few, if any, substantiated cases have actually ever been presented. Further, Mandy Sanghera, an expert in forced marriage, particularly in the South Asian communities, said that while she has seen evidence that Traveller families are keen to smooth the way for marriages with families they know and trust, she has only come across one case where a Traveller family did not immediately acknowledge the young person's right to choose a life partner.

Of course, under the UK's forced marriage laws, victims are required to file a protection order with authorities – the very authorities that are so distrusted. In the summer of 2012 the Coalition government suggested that forced marriage become a criminal offence, meaning that prosecutors would no longer be stuck charging a suspect with kidnapping or another crime – perhaps opening the door for arranged marriages to be yet another way in which Gypsies and Travellers are branded as criminals simply for practising their traditional lifestyle.

At the time of Afzal's press briefing, the Gypsy Message Board blog explored the historical and contemporary practice of marriage in the travelling community.[29] After demolishing Afzal's contention, the blog's author looked at arranged marriages among Gypsy and Traveller families: 'The main purpose behind arranged marriages amongst Travellers today is not to safeguard male interests so much as to safeguard the girl's by securing a man who wont [sic] mistreat her. Such men are most likely to be found amongst "friends" in the kindred.'

There is good evidence that domestic violence exists in the Gypsy and Traveller communities – but men, women and children from the community are campaigning openly against it, another form of self-policing, but also a clue that forced marriage is very rare. And, unfortunately, domestic violence is an issue.

In a 2009 analysis, the Equality and Human Rights Commission found that women from the Gypsy and Traveller communities who reported being the victim of domestic violence often have suffered abuse more severely and over a considerably longer period than women in the general population. Although there is no conclusive evidence about the prevalence of abuse (i.e. whether or not it is the same, higher or lower than the settled population), a small-scale study in Wrexham stated that between sixty-one and eighty-one per cent of married Gypsy and Traveller women reported that they had experienced abuse from a partner. Disturbingly, other studies have suggested that Gypsy and Traveller women are more likely to stay in a violent relationship, perhaps because only one refuge has been dedicated specifically for Irish Traveller women across the whole of the UK.[30] As yet, not one refuge appears to have been established in a site for caravans – mainly, domestic violence experts say, because news on such a refuge would spread very fast in the tight-knit community and would not be safe. Another reason for women's hesitation to leave abusive relationships may simply be that they don't have confidence in the criminal justice system to support them once they are on their own.[31]

In the East of England, a violence-reduction advice organisation called One Voice 4 Travellers has been set up for Travellers to try to fill this gap. Among the staff is the manager, Janie Codona, herself a Romani Gypsy, who often talks with women about their options when they are experiencing violence from a partner. She felt that providing culturally familiar alternatives, such as 'safe' trailers, would help. 'For those who have been living out in the open on a site all their lives, or if they're continuously nomadic, it can be too big a shock living with new people in a refuge or hostel. They can feel confined and isolated; anxiety and depression can set in. They risk leaving their life behind, so they stay in a violent situation for longer. Often, Travellers turn up at refuges with six kids in tow – there isn't always room to take in the whole family.'[32]

Bernie O'Roarke, a domestic violence specialist who works with Irish Traveller women for the charity Refuge, said she is gloomy about the possibility of combating the problem of domestic violence within the community. 'Once a woman is married to a man, that's her lot. The men can go and do what they want, [but] if she goes with another man she is a whore and a prostitute – that's the language used by the men. It is "stone age" in male attitude.' She said she has worked with several families in which three consecutive generations of women have suffered domestic violence. 'The young boys emulate their fathers, and the violence continues.' Breaking the cycle is nearly impossible. 'The men won't move out. The attitude is, "I own you, that's forever." It's like the Mafia: the only way out is to die.'[33] Because the women do not trust the police, they are left to fend for themselves and survive however they can.

The case of Bridget Joyce, an Irish Traveller woman, offers a harrowing example of how the justice system – both the traditional travelling model and the official authorities – fail in these circumstances. Bridget had been beaten by her husband, also a

Traveller, for some time, and, frightened for her safety, decided to leave him as well as her young son. She built a new life for herself in Manchester, finding happiness with a man named Michael Foy, who was a labourer. They were together for twenty years.

Then in 2006 Bridget's ex-husband, Michael Joyce Snr, by now in his mid-fifties, came calling for her. He had their twenty-five-year-old son, Michael Joyce Jnr, in tow. According to the prosecutor on the case, Howard Bentham, Bridget's ex confronted Foy: 'The best thing you could do would be to divorce Bridget and let her marry me again.' Foy replied: 'Over my dead body,' and Joyce retorted, 'That can be arranged.' Foy was beaten, stabbed and forced to drink his own blood, an attack carried out in front of Bridget. The judge determined that he had suffered 'a slow death', involving torture.[34]

Soon Bridget was bombed out of her house, apparently by Irish Travellers who, it was claimed by insiders, felt she had brought shame on the community. One domestic violence worker who supported her at this time remembers her well: 'She got to my heart. She told me that they spent a night murdering him, and took his heart out at the end of it, leaving it on top of the television.' Bridget remained a character, despite the awful events. 'She had fourteen patches down one harm, a nebuliser, a fag on and loved her vodka. She asked me to look at her letters and it was only then I realised she had been charged with the murder [a charge that was later dropped]. It was the June 2006 when it got to court, and she died in the March. She went out the day before and bought her laying-out clothes, her shoes, and a postal order for her Mammie in Ireland for £50.' The worker said that Bridget's experience was not singular among the cases heard.

If a community polices itself, it is, after all, the weakest who will suffer the most. Sites that are run by the fist and the gun – and they do exist, as do many very well-run private and local authority ones – are vivid proof that, somehow, the police must build better relationships with Gypsies and Travellers. Only then will people like Bridget Joyce feel – and be – safe.

13
LIFE ON THE MARGINS

In 2006 the Commission for Racial Equality concluded that Gypsies and Irish Travellers were the most excluded groups in modern Britain. Numbering at least an estimated 300,000 – as large as the Chinese and Bangledeshi population, if not more – they, of all the nation's citizens, were the worst off on various measures: they died earlier; their children were at higher risk of dying in infancy; they obtained fewer educational qualifications; they more frequently lived in sub-standard housing than the general population and often suffered mental health problems as a result; and they were more likely to commit suicide.

In the past decade, and especially since the start of the recession in 2009, their employment rates had collapsed, as many of their traditional trades had been regulated almost out of existence. Crime-reduction strategies, such as restrictions on 'cold calling' in the Consumer Protection from Unfair Trading Regulations (2008), had made it difficult for those used to securing work on the doorstep, as well as for women who went hawking. Regulations on scrap-metal dealing (a favoured profession) had been increasingly tightened since the Environmental Protection Act 1990, and from March 2013 all scrap-metal dealers were required to hold a licence and were no longer allowed to deal in cash.[1] Casual labouring work, a way of life for many Gypsy and Traveller men, has become harder to come by in the economic downturn. Their involvement in seasonal agricultural work had also been challenged by migrant labour from Central and Eastern Europe.

The nomadic way of life was increasingly threatened, and yet the alternatives – life on illegal and legal sites, as well as housing – were far from satisfactory. Their lives were lived on the margins of society.

After the clearance of the unauthorised pitches at Dale Farm, Nora Sheridan and her family had set up their tidy caravan on the roadside. In the summer of 2012 she walked over to the dusty old Dale Farm site, to see if she could find signs of the asbestos and oil-based contaminants that Candy Sheridan claimed to have seen when she appealed to the Environment Agency for an official inspection of the land. Nora was clad in sandals as she picked her way amongst the pitches. On almost every pitch she spotted pieces of asbestos – when she was a child her father had taught her to recognise it, so she could avoid it when they were travelling. Some of the asbestos was on land within fifty yards of the legal pitches at Dale Farm. As Nora's tally increased, she grew increasingly alarmed about the possible effects on the many Traveller children who frequently played up there, in what could only be seen as the modern equivalent of a bombsite.

In 2010 Basildon Council's Tony Ball had told a reporter that he hoped to create allotments for the residents of Crays Hill once the Traveller families were cleared off the site. Indeed, the council's waste-management plan for the clearance of the site stated that any soil or hard core removed from the site would be recycled because it was deemed to be 'clean'. That seemed laughable now. The Environment Agency was due to cordon off the site within the month so that a team could test for sources of potential toxicity – not just from the remnants of Ray Bocking's old scrap yard, but also from the illegal tipping that was a regular occurrence at the site. The worst contaminants appeared to have been churned up as a result of the eviction itself.

Constant and Co. bailiffs, under instruction from the council, had thrown up rough mounds of earth to bund the pitches in a bid to prevent the Travellers, including the handful with permission from the court to stay on site, from moving back. Nora had fallen into one of their trenches on her way to launder her children's school uniforms one night. In the digging, old car tyres, relics from Bocking's car-breaking business, had been unearthed. But the tyres were unlikely to be the source of the asbestos. It could have been an ingredient in hardcore dumped on the land, however. In his October 1995 witness statement over planning breaches, Bocking testified that council workers from its direct labour organisation routinely tipped loads of unwanted cement on his site.[2] Basildon Council stoutly denied it was responsible for tipping any hardcore on the site when Bocking owned it. More recently, he further maintained that the council stored old cars at his scrap yard. Bocking's theory was that the council served enforcement notices on him in 1994 in order to cover up its own involvement in creating an unofficial landfill at Dale Farm.[3]

Bocking's account was backed up by an improbable defender – the sainted Len Gridley, the local resident who had been fiercely opposed to the Travellers' presence on the back side of Windy Ridge, but in the year after the eviction had become their champion. The council, he claimed, 'knew [the site] was polluted since 1994, because they dumped a lot of [stuff] there. We are not clear whether it was legal or illegal'.

For decades, travelling families have stopped on the margins of cities and towns, where they hope they will not attract too much attention. But where they end up living is often contaminated, situated near landfills, electricity pylons and other blighted locations. A 1974 survey of sixty-five authorised sites by Sir John Cripps reported that twelve per cent were adjacent to rubbish dumping sites and twenty-eight per cent were located near to industrial development.[4] If anything, things had got worse since then. Researcher Pat Niner found in 2003 that fifty per cent of sites were based in dangerous areas, and in 2009 the EHRC confirmed the dire state of authorised sites: 'Although conditions vary, many publicly provided sites are of poor quality, with sites built on contaminated land, close to motorways, adjoining sewage works or on other poor quality land.'[5] A number of Gypsy Traveller assessments, the report said, 'have found bad conditions on some public sites, with significant failings in fire safety, contamination by vermin, chronically decayed sewage and water fittings, and poor-quality utility rooms'. The EHRC pointed out that the poor conditions on some of these sites were probably in breach of site licensing and health and safety legislation, but that 'sites owned and operated by local authorities are immune from prosecution even where clear hazards exist, as no obligation to repair or even adhere to fire authority guidance on fire safety exists, despite the existence of guidance from the Department for Communities and Local Government'.[6]

The conditions on some private sites were alleged to be worse. In theory the owners could be prosecuted for health and safety failures, but in practice there had been little sign of enforcement of the legislation – another way in which a well-founded distrust of authorities combined with self-policing created further hazards for Gypsies and Travellers.

The government insists that sites should not be located near to electricity pylons, heavy industry or landfill. In real terms at least half are – and those that are not are often not properly maintained. The guidance from the government, which states the need for sites to be situated in clean environments, was clearly not being honoured: 'It is essential to ensure that the location of a site will provide a safe environment for the residents. Sites should not be situated near refuse sites, industrial processes or other hazardous places, as this will obviously have a detrimental effect on the general health and well-being of the residents and pose particular safety risks for young children. All prospective site locations should be considered carefully before any decision is taken to proceed, to ensure that the health and safety of prospective residents are not at risk,' the government's guidance read.[7]

The report went on to say that the UK should emulate site location tactics pioneered in Ireland, where small sites on appropriate land had been proposed. Of course, small sites provide a limited number of pitches – not always enough to accommodate a large and often growing extended family, and typically not enough to foster a sense of a close-knit village among a group of families, as had been created at Dale Farm. Regardless, the government warned that unless more pleasant, safer sites were identified, it would 'have a negative impact on Gypsies and Travellers' health and access to services'. Living on polluted or dangerous sites had 'a profound impact on how [Gypsies and Travellers] feel they are perceived and treated by the wider community' said the report. 'Likewise such locations reinforce the prejudiced perceptions that many in the settled community have of Gypsies and Travellers, such locations are therefore a major impediment to the social inclusion of Gypsies and Travellers.'

Dale Farm sat on contaminated land, with a huge electricity pylon towering over the families, but it was not surprising that the families had chosen to live there: authorised sites had proved to be hazardous too. One site, located underneath the Westway elevated road, the A40, in London, had been tested and found to have raised levels of lead in the soil. In the past few years a lorry had actually fallen off the elevated road and crashed onto the site, and another had shed its load. A site in Neasden, in North-West London, had been established next to a cement yard. Another, near Glastonbury, was on the site of a former tannery, and chemicals used in the tanning process – including toxic arsenic – had been discovered in the dirt. The local council had asked the families to move on for their own safety, but admitted that there was nowhere else for them to go. It cannot be a coincidence that so many Gypsies and Travellers have breathing difficulties, and die earlier than their peers in the settled community, because of these appalling living conditions. They have been forced to live on land that most people have refused, as more and more of the country has been transformed into suburbia or cordoned off as green belt.

Pushed by Candy Sheridan, the Environment Agency (EA) visited Dale Farm in August 2012. Their workers wore reflective tabards as they tested for contamination all over the old site – a disturbing sight for the Travellers, who were living so close by. Candy broke off her holiday to fly back to Essex and sign for two thousand soil samples, sixteen water samples and two possible asbestos samples from one yard alone. In late August an EA official wrote to Candy, reporting that the agency had identified asbestos at the site and advising her to tell the residents not to allow their children onto it. The EA returned in September to take several more samples, but the Travellers had not been told what else had been found.

Nora Sheridan had moved to Dale Farm so that her children could get a decent education. Her eldest son, who was then twelve, was no longer in school because of fears of bullying; he was now home-schooled, as she mainly was, as she lived on the road. But she beamed as her seven-year-old, Jimmy Tom, read out from a picture book. She explained that he had been identified as being gifted in both English and maths, and she wanted him to 'go all the way, even to college'. For her that meant they had to stay put, in awful conditions, at the side of the road at Dale Farm — showering in the local leisure centre, begging the residents of the legal site nearby for water and spending almost all her money on heating and light.

Her pride in her children, and her wish to better their lives through education, was obvious. She was also right to push for these opportunities when they presented themselves. Although individual pupils can and do achieve very well, Gypsy and Traveller pupils are among the lowest-achieving groups at every stage of education, and the least likely minority ethnic group to attend school. They have lower attendance figures, with many older Traveller children leaving school after primary education — just as Nora's eldest son had, because of bullying or the fear of it. They also have the highest levels of permanent and fixed-term exclusions when compared to other minority ethnic groups, and the highest levels of pupils — some 43.2% of Travellers in primary schools and 45.3% in secondary schools — entitled to free school meals. There were cultural obstacles too. Sex education is frowned on, and many expect their girls to marry young and leave school;

their boys are often expected to learn a trade for which, traditionally, there are no formal qualifications.

These various factors mix to form a bleak picture. In 2011,
only twelve per cent of Gypsy and Traveller pupils achieved five
or more good GCSEs, including English and Maths, compared
with 58.2% of all pupils in the UK.

Underachievement at school is associated with living in poverty. Starting in April 2011, the Coalition government said that
poor pupils would benefit directly from a new initiative, called
the Pupil Premium, which provides an additional £430 per pupil,
paid to their school, to help raise the attainment of disadvantaged
children. These pupils might also benefit from a recently established £125 million Education Endowment Fund, set up to fund
innovative approaches to improving the educational performance
of disadvantaged children in underperforming schools.[8] However,
such programmes seem destined to have a limited reach into the
Gypsy and Traveller communities, given the number of their
children who leave school under sixteen.

The Coalition has recently begun to review the existing legislation protecting mobile Gypsy and Traveller families from prosecution if their children truant from school. Under the 1996 Education
Act, if parents can prove that their families are nomadic, their
children are required to attend school for at least two hundred
half-day sessions in a year – an exemption that the Coalition is
considering for repeal. The Coalition 'believes that this concession has come to be seen by some schools – and by Gypsy and
Traveller families themselves – as giving tacit consent for mobile
pupils to benefit only from a significantly shortened school year'.
Cuts to local authority funding under the Coalition's austerity
plan have also hit the Traveller Education Services – dedicated
teachers, trained in working with Travellers, are losing their jobs,
their expertise lost for good.

These developments are particularly tragic in the view of a
generation of parents like Nora Sheridan, who are dedicated to
educating their children while preserving their travelling culture. More families are starting to acknowledge that poor literacy

skills are holding young people back in a qualifications-based job market. A small number of teaching assistants and teachers now come from the communities too. But change is slow, and not everyone values higher levels of educational attainment for Gypsy and Traveller children. Academics Margaret Greenfields and David Smith, for instance, identified a strong element of conservatism, especially among Gypsy and Traveller boys, who tended to opt for family-based self-employment, which did not require much in the way of formal education. Many of the boys they interviewed couldn't even conceive of alternative employment – what the researchers called 'aspirations outside the norm'. Their teachers often found that frustrating, but felt they had little opportunity to change the boys' attitude towards schooling.

Damian Le Bas Jnr, the editor of the *Travellers' Times* and a talented writer and actor to boot, gained the highest first in his year at Oxford University as a theology student. Yet he has always felt that his academic achievement was not prized in his community. He believed this was due to the importance placed on entrepreneurial success. 'I stayed in school, but not for business reasons. If I hadn't gone to Oxford, I would be making more money, so I can't make that argument, because Travellers like to make money. Money talks. People would listen to me if I had a flashier car (I have a Peugeot 206). If I had a custom long-wheelbase transit, fully chromed out, things would be different. I have a chip on my shoulder that the talents I have are not the ones that Gypsies value, like making money and fighting … My family were very proud of me but would also have been proud of me if I had made loads of money.' But he also made the point that valuing education would further most Gypsy and Traveller parents' goals for their children. 'I think a lot of time in education is wasted, but it is hard to pass chainsaw certification if you aren't in school.'

Many Gypsy and Traveller families allow their teenage children to leave school, but many also go on to college to gain vocational qualifications. Delaine Le Bas, Damian's mother and an internationally renowned artist, runs art workshops in schools. She acknowledged the difficulties. 'Education in a school environment fails lots of children anyway. For a community that doesn't like sending its children to school, it's even more problematic. Finding other ways to encourage people to do what they want to do – but how do you make that happen?'[9]

And pursuing an education when you have nowhere to study at home is difficult. Nora, for instance, does her best to give equal time to all three of her children in her efforts to promote their learning. But living in a cramped caravan, without access to running water or utilities, inevitably means most of their time is spent surviving. There is little time for getting ahead.

Whether or not their site was contaminated, the Irish Travellers at Dale Farm wanted to stick together. Yet, nomadism, living by the roadside, was also their choice for how to do that. Was it their right to keep travelling, to keep living in caravans, to continue living on the outskirts of society while at the same time taking advantage of the settled community when it suited them?

After the eviction, not everyone moved out onto Oak Lane. Michelle Sheridan and her family, including Tom, who was by then just over two, went on the road again in the early months of 2012, leaving her sister Nora behind in Essex. 'I couldn't handle it. I know it was bad to leave but when I went up to our old pitch I would just cry, I couldn't take it any more,' said Michelle. They set off for the Midlands, and from to time would join up and travel in convoy with a small number of other families who had left Dale Farm. And, as it was in the late 1960s and early 1970s, when Irish Travellers came to the Midlands to escape recession and the Troubles, they found themselves being moved on count-lessly, sometimes on a daily basis.

Michelle could tick off the places from which they had been evicted. 'We used to move every few days unless there were more than six caravans. Then they would use Section 66 [of the Criminal Justice Act] and move us on within a day. We've been moved on from all round Birmingham, Solihull, Bilston, Wolverhampton, Bolton, Balsall Heath ... On one side of Birmingham, by Balsall

Heath, they wouldn't use Section 66, but on the other side, near the Children's Hospital, they would, so we stuck to [the Balsall Heath] side.' By chance or by fate, Balsall Heath had been the site of a notorious eviction of Irish Travellers back in 1968.

While she was stopping in the Midlands, she decided to drive to Meriden, so that she could meet the Gypsy families there who had also come under such heavy scrutiny. None of them were in on the day she visited. She recalled: 'We went out there and it's just a field with just a few tourers in it. So when we got there, we couldn't drive in, as it was muck knee-high, and we were afraid to walk in, and the gates were locked. I didn't know the families but thought we would say hello. We beeped but nobody came out.' Meriden RAID were there that day, however. 'We went a little further up the lane and we saw this little bunker and we was shocked – it looks like a war-time bunker. So I stopped up and said hello, and I said, "I thought you were evicted from here." One of the residents replied, "We're waiting for the High Court," and I said, "Do you really have nothing better to do with your time?"' At this point, the member of residents' association got curious. 'She asked who I was, and I said, "We are the Dale Farm Travellers, and we could come on here; the whole eighty-six families from Dale Farm is pitching up …" And she was getting whiter and whiter.' Michelle finally left, but not before offering to sell the residents some mattresses so that they could be a little more comfortable in their 'bunker'. Her offer was not accepted.

Having tried to travel, she was back at Dale Farm for Christmas that year. She didn't know where the family would go or what they would do next. But one thing she was sure about: she wasn't going to move into brick and mortar housing.

Fifty-three out of the eighty-six evicted families had been offered council housing. None of them accepted it. Tony Ball believed that some of them came under pressure from other families not to take it. How could they complain about not having running water on Oak Lane if they'd had a chance to live in council housing? What was the attraction of being nomads?

Their friend Ann Kobayashi tried to offer an explanation. 'The clans aren't unique to Gypsies and Travellers. [They] used to be a feature of some old villages that were settled and the old East End ... I think when you get a beleaguered community which encounters hostility and discrimination on a very regular basis, grouping together is one safety device. And the other is, in a sense, you don't give up what you've got unless you are absolutely sure that what you are giving it up for is worth it, and is going to help you as a group,' she said. 'And they are not sure of that.'

It is estimated that around two-thirds of the Gypsy and Traveller communities are today housed in bricks and mortar, rather than in caravans and other travelling homes. There is scant research on their experiences, but what exists suggests that the transition has not been an easy one. In one study of several locations in southern England, Margaret Greenfields and David Smith found that while many had successfully adapted their self-employment to living in an urban context, they remained highly excluded from the settled community.[10] When they moved to bricks and mortar, they were usually placed in social housing with other deprived and marginalised groups – eighty per cent of those they interviewed were in council housing. Most of the time, they moved there for reasons beyond their control. The most common reason given for new settlement was 'a lack of spaces on local authority caravan sites; a shortage of temporary transit sites; or a failure to gain planning permission on privately owned land'.[11] According to the government's own figures, at least twenty-five per cent of the Traveller population is technically homeless,[12] and housing was predominantly the choice of last resort for them.

This has, unfortunately, heightened tensions when Gypsy and Traveller families join the settled community, according to Greenfields. 'While there are often areas of conflict between housed Gypsies and Travellers and the sedentary populations amongst which they live, this most often occurs where Gypsies and Travellers have been forcibly settled as a result of a lack of appropriate accommodation,' she observed, based on her interviews and other research. 'They are often placed on run-down housing estates, where there is a lack of cultural knowledge going both ways, leading to fear, hostility and cultural clashes. For example, we have plentiful evidence of Gypsies and Travellers being offered accommodation by councils where their neighbours have grown up on a diet of anti-Traveller media reports. When they hear who their new neighbours will be, there may be demonstrations, vandalism or an abusive reception awaiting the new tenants. I have personally interviewed families who report experiencing dog faeces pushed through their letter boxes, windows being broken in their houses and caravans parked outside ... and, on two occasions, families who have had their homes fire-bombed.'[13]

When Ann Kobayashi spoke to some of the families at Dale Farm about their desire to stay, despite the dire situation, she learned that some had tried to live in housing in the past, and believed it was not a workable option for them. 'Some have lived in bricks and mortar and have had very bad experiences,' she said. But more than that, living in a house was for many, particularly among the older people, 'quite an uncomfortable feeling'. Ann continued: 'I had never realised that before, until some of the older couples ... they used to say, "Sure, isn't it grand, Ann, we can see whoever is passing, we know who is coming, we can hail them through the windows, this is what we like about living surrounded by windows. We can see everyone, even if we can't walk out," as both had disabilities ... They can see everyone and wave and they say, "Isn't that better than a house?" Their view of a house is that it was a prison, it was dark.'

The issue of keeping the community together came up time and time again. The housing on offer was often piecemeal, part of larger council developments, with no guarantee that other families from Dale Farm, or other Irish Travellers, would be living nearby to provide a sense of security. 'They were isolated, separate units with no assurance that the next one to fall vacant in that block would be offered to a Traveller, so they didn't know if they would have help; they like help on hand,' Ann recalled. The questions were always on the tip of their tongues. What if '"so and so has gone into labour, or he is poorly, can anyone drive?" ... that assurance that somebody would respond, do something' was an issue.

'There's also the business of it always being possible to travel if you want to,' she said. 'You can lock up your yard and you can take off for a few weeks or months ... If you are in a house, there is no accommodation for a caravan and you won't be in the thick of it ... At Dale Farm there is a constant movement of news and stories and dramas all the time, incredibly active as a community, and they feel when they look down some suburban streets that it is dead, there is nobody on the street, nobody leaning at the window talking. It's an uneasy community ... they see that closed-door, closed-in feeling.'

Ann learned too that the dread of facing discrimination loomed whenever the idea of housing was raised. 'Taking them to view housing offers, they would say, "Some people go through this process in the hope of getting bricks and mortar. We are going through it and we know they won't offer what we want, and we can't accept what they will offer, so what is the point?"' Still, they persisted, knowing that it would be important in the legal case to show that they were looking for alternative housing. 'The business of, "Keep your name in there, so we can say in a legal case, here they are," that was difficult.'

Some Gypsies and Travellers had managed to make a successful transition to housing on terms that were acceptable both to them and to the surrounding residents. One of the most striking examples had been established in Southampton, in what is known as 'The Bay' – along Botany Bay Road, a residential street where Gypsies set up home so long ago that no one could remember when they had first arrived, perhaps as early as the late eighteenth century. The road was unusual in that it hosted a mixture of accommodation, ranging from caravans, static mobile homes and chalets to residential housing and bungalows, all side by side.[14]

There are just a handful of such developments around the country, according to Donald Kenrick, who has been fighting for

Gypsy and Traveller rights for almost fifty years. Yet, he pointed to
The Bay and its fellow sites as an essential part of any solution to
the housing shortage in the community. 'There is a Gypsy colony
in Gravesend, where a site used to be. You would think you were
in a caravan site – lorries decorated in Gypsy symbols, horses
wandering around. There are a few other places like that around
England, enclaves where people still speak Romani.' Indeed, he
said, most Gypsy and Traveller families were, for all intents, settled – pulled up onto a site year-round. 'My estimate is that there
are only thirty families travelling all the time now; it's very low
numbers. And this is probably the last generation where we will
see families doing that. The future for individual families is fine,
but there will probably be less travelling.'

It is quite possible for the travelling and settled communities
to live together, as Margaret Greenfields's research has indicated.
'We have a growing body of evidence which indicates the closely
entwined nature of Gypsy Traveller and white, working-class
communities, over decades, and in some cases centuries in certain
predominantly urban locales,' she said. 'Thus in certain areas of
London we know that Gypsies and Travellers moved into housing
as early as the middle of the nineteenth century' – for example,
in areas such as Notting Hill, Sutton, Merton and North London.
'There is abundant evidence from East London as late as the 1950s
of Gypsies and Travellers living in London and in Kent, working
alongside Cockneys. In our latest work we have collected numerous narratives of intermarried families and indeed a growth of
"hybridised" identities. Their descendants still remain in the local
area, retaining a clear knowledge of their identity, some cultural
practices and yet who live alongside and are closely related to
long-established *gorgia* families.'

The trend of hybridised identities will only continue with
the growing numbers of Roma arriving from Central and Eastern
Europe, many of whom have been housed for generations and are
beginning to intermarry with British Gypsies and Irish Travellers.
Nomadism may not remain the primary way in which everyone
from these peoples identify themselves – and it is important to

remember that many Roma, Gypsies and Travellers were forced to travel because of discrimination and hatred, not because they actively chose travelling as a cultural emblem. Indeed, as the Romani scholar and academic Ian Hancock, put it: 'Most Travellers don't travel and haven't done so for a very long time. Certainly the slaves in Eastern Europe weren't travelling anywhere, and those here in the UK have been kept on the move because of legislation, history, rather than anything else. If you are forced to keep moving you have to develop means of livelihood [so] that even if the cops come, you have skills that you can't leave behind. We are not pastoral nomads. We are itinerant because of legislation.'[15]

Some Gypsies and Travellers will never want to settle in bricks and mortar, however. One way forward (with the right safeguards) is for Gypsies and Travellers to run their own sites, which they can do through Community Land Trusts (CLT). The first trial was taken up in March 2010 by the Tory-led Mendip District Council, in Somerset, which was staring down a shortfall of fifty-seven pitches in its area at the time.

Mendip's pilot scheme was an attempt to rethink how sites are planned. Few councils want to propose sites these days, such is the immediate opposition to them when any consultation has been announced – so much so that, of the £60 million available in Homes and Communities Agency funding through the year 2013, £14 million remains up for grabs. Some of the areas with the greatest need for sites did not even put in a bid. The most notorious among them was of course Essex, but Cambridgeshire (where Smithy Fen was meeting determined opposition), Kent, Hertfordshire and Surrey also passed. The five counties boasting the most Travellers and twenty-five per cent of the caravans only took four per cent of the agency's money to improve conditions.

In some cases, housing associations had stepped into the breach. According to the *Guardian*, in Worcestershire, Rooftop Housing was given the ownership of a site on Houndsfield Lane by Bromsgrove District Council and Bromsgrove District Housing

Trust, refurbishing the site with HCA funding.[16] The amenities included brand-new utility pods containing kitchen, bathroom and living space, five of which would have disability access – all too essential, given the ageing and often sick population; the architect had consulted local community members before building the pods, which is unusual. Rooftop planned to bid for additional sites in different parts of the country. Another housing association, Knightstone, had set up an advice centre for Gypsies and Travellers on two sites in South Gloucestershire. Broadlands Housing Association took over management of the Brooks Green site, which it runs with South Norfolk District Council (the council kept charge of deciding who gets a pitch on the site). The site was leased from its owner, Barry Brooks, for a nominal rent, and managed like any other council housing, according to neighbourhood officer Sarah Lovelock. 'They shouldn't be singled out,' she said, of the eight Romani families who had moved in.[17]

Candy Sheridan, for her part, was developing a new scheme along similar lines – but with self-empowerment as a key theme. In January 2013, after years of hard work, her Traveller Pitch Funding Grant was given the green light from the Homes and Communities Agency to carry out a small number of pilot sites. 'We have developed a Gypsy Co-op model that will be rolled out in the East by the end of this year … The pilot will, I think, become the blueprint of the future, for private and public sites alike. It involves the residents on each site becoming equal members, becoming workers' co-operatives, be[ing] in equal control of the site … without the "employment" of either a Gypsy or non-Gypsy warden. It ensures that each site has public liability and that sites are kept up to the Better Homes Standards.'

She had been working alongside her long-time ally, planning expert Stuart Carruthers, and an English Gypsy landlord named Levi Gumble, who owns a neat, somewhat under-occupied site on the edge of Stowmarket, a pretty town in Suffolk. A former boxer who now sells carpets to many local authorities, Levi had been caught in a long-running dispute with his local council, which wanted to force him to sell the site so that the council could run it themselves. He had refused, insisting that he keep control of the property. After the Dale Farm eviction, he had offered pitches to the displaced Irish Travellers, appealing directly to Tony Ball of Basildon District Council – one of only two site owners in the country to do so. Sadly, none of the families accepted, most preferring to stay together in the community they had built. Since then the site, along with another in East Anglia, have been proposed to serve as pilots in the Gypsy Co-op bid.

The Gypsy Co-op plan envisioned a future where Gypsies and Travellers are granted the power to run their own sites, free from local authority intervention and without one strong family running roughshod over others on the site. Still, it was early days for the initiative, although by February 2013 Candy had already persuaded a small number of families from Dale Farm to form two small co-ops, ready to take advantage of any planning permission opportunities that might arise.

Some Gypsies and Travellers who found a pitch on a local authority site, or in bricks and mortar, said that it was sometimes hard to keep to their tenancy agreements, especially while carrying out traditional Gypsy and Traveller employment. For instance, many sites prohibited them from the keeping certain animals, or from storing scrap metal.

Seasonal agricultural work had become a challenge to secure, as migrant labour from Central and Eastern Europe has increasingly competed with them for jobs. The Traveller Economic Inclusion Project (TEIP) interviewed ninety-five Gypsies and Travellers, with some eighty per cent reporting that their parents had worked on farms; only one of the people interviewed did so today. 'A strong sense of nostalgia for field work and a sense of sadness at its passing were apparent in many interviews. An unintended consequence of the decline in agricultural employment is the reduction of social contact with non-Gypsy labour now they no longer work together in the fields, resulting in greater social distance and a worsening of relations between the groups,' the report concluded.[18]

The formalisation of employment, although intended to protect more vulnerable groups, had in many ways created barriers to employment – especially for those who could not read, let alone fill out forms. David Smith and Margaret Greenfields reported that their research 'suggests that unemployment is high among Gypsies and Travellers and, on several indicators, they are among the most deprived groups in the population ... Adult literacy rates are well below the national average, with research indicating that twenty-one per cent of male Gypsies and nine per cent of females sampled could not read, while one-third could only write their own name'. Other travelling jobs had been essentially abolished with the introduction in 2008 of crime-reduction strategies, such as restrictions on 'cold calling', reducing the availability of casual work like paving and fencing for men and hawking for women. A third of those interviewed by the TEIP project voiced concern about the onslaught of new regulations.

Looking for a job in town wasn't always the answer. Giving a Gypsy site as an address to a prospective employer often carried a stigma. Some people hunting for employment would end up concealing their identity in order to gain it.

Moving into bricks and mortar wasn't a panacea either. 'In other families, living on estates where there were high levels of racism and frequent conflict with neighbours, males were reluctant to leave their homes to follow previous lines of work that involved long periods of travelling,' again according to Smith and Greenfields. 'Two-thirds of participants reported that their economic situation had deteriorated since moving into housing. For many, a combination of higher housing costs, fewer opportunities for casual work and restrictions on conducting work-related activities at home means that settlement has led to a decline in employment and a rise in welfare dependency and long-term unemployment. In a study of 158 Gypsy and Traveller households conducted by one of the authors, forty-four per cent of housed males of working age were unemployed and ten per cent economically inactive due to poor health.'[19]

But some families and individuals were succeeding against the odds, said Greenfields. A number of women were going into higher education as mature students and men were adapting traditional pursuits to modern demands. 'Women seem more alert to the transformation of work that is occurring, but we are also seeing some men keeping their traditional modes of employment but modifying them. So men are getting the qualifications they need to work as tree surgeons, for example, especially on private sites where they can keep equipment.' But, she warned, those on public sites or in housing have not got the networks they need to survive. 'They don't have the same cultural capital to find work; their networks are disrupted. They are often more marginalised. Some parents are identifying the need for their children to attain qualifications, but it is often related to fairly traditional work and it is highly gendered. There is still a preference for girls to undertake hairdressing, beauty, fit in round their childcare responsibilities; they are told that family comes first. But I'm starting to see women saying they want a fall-back, and that they want to study in case their marriage fails.' There is a growing divergence between those Gypsies and Travellers who are engaging with the outside world, and those who are not.

Smith and Greenfields's research had thrown up yet one more reason for the communities' struggles: 'They have the worst health profile of any group, dying younger and experiencing higher levels of physical and mental illness.'

At Dale Farm, health concerns were piling up. When representatives of an All-Party Parliamentary Group, the Red Cross, the Irish Traveller Movement in Britain and the Irish Embassy reported their survey of the health of residents to Lord Avebury and Andrew George MP in the aftermath of the eviction, the list was staggering. A young man living at Dale Farm had been left disabled after a car accident. A sixty-five-year-old woman suffered dementia, and her daughter, who had to care for her, had high blood pressure. An eighty-one-year old man with high blood pressure was on a breathing machine but without a formal carer to look after him or the equipment. Another woman had dementia as well as an over-active thyroid. After eviction day, the district nurse stopped visiting a seventy-six-year old woman with Parkinson's. There was also a youngster with Down's syndrome, hearing and breathing problems and an older woman with chronic obstructive pulmonary disease and osteoporosis. Since then the tally had only increased: a woman whose son had suffered brain damage and whose husband was ill; an older man with bowel cancer whose daughter had depression and two deaf children; a woman with a fractured spine, allegedly caused by a police attack during the eviction.[20] And of course Nora Sheriden's fall into the trench.

This litany of health complaints, all from people living on one site, were not out of line with data for the Gypsy and Traveller communities as a whole. 'There are striking inequalities in the health of Gypsies and Travellers, even when compared with people from other ethnic minorities or from socio-economically deprived white UK groups,' a 2004 paper on the health status of Gypsies and Travellers reported.[21] 'They are significantly more likely to have a long-term illness, health problem or disability that limits their daily activities or work, and a higher overall prevalence of reported chest pain, respiratory problems, arthritis, miscarriage and premature death of offspring.'[22] They also experienced 'high infant mortality and perinatal death rates, low birth weight, low immunisations uptake and high child accident rate'. The Confidential Enquiry into Maternal Deaths in the UK, in a report that looked across the entire population over the period from 1997 to 1999, found that Gypsies and Travellers have 'possibly the highest maternal death rate among all ethnic group[s]'.[23]

The government's latest report on the Gypsy and Traveller communities, dated April 2012, said: 'Studies consistently show differences in life expectancy of over ten per cent less than the general population, although a recent study stated that the general population was living up to fifty per cent longer than Gypsies and Travellers – so the disparity may be even more marked.[24,25] Further research indicated that the health of Gypsies and Travellers starts to deteriorate markedly when individuals reach age fifty.[26] Thirty-nine per cent of Gypsies and Travellers reported a long-term illness, compared with twenty-nine per cent of age- and sex-matched comparators, even after controlling for socioeconomic status and other marginalised groups. Travellers are three times more likely to have a chronic cough or bronchitis, even after smoking is taken into account. Twenty-two per cent of Gypsies and Travellers reported having asthma and thirty-four per cent reported chest pain, compared to five per cent and twenty-two per cent of the general population. They are far more likely to suffer miscarriages, neonatal deaths, stillbirths and maternal deaths during pregnancy and after childbirth. Studies show that Gypsy and Traveller women live twelve years fewer than women in the general population and men ten years fewer, although recent research suggests the life expectancy gap could be much higher.[27]

Being marginalised itself is a health risk, and Gypsies and Travellers' wariness about seeking help from authorities had many times extended to healthcare professionals. As a consequence, some treatable diseases were going undiagnosed, sometimes until they had reached a chronic or even terminal condition. 'In addition, lack of prior knowledge about the body in general, about medical conditions, prevention of ill-health and related health matters influence the likelihood of attendance for healthcare. Illiteracy was frequently mentioned as a handicap in this respect ... where there is also a fatalistic belief that nothing can be achieved by attending screening or potential early diagnosis, this can result in more serious outcomes ... a self-reliant attitude to health problems, combined with mistrust can also result in late presentation and inappropriate self-treatment.'[28]

Among Gypsies and Travellers, owning up to ill health, especially mental health problems, was often seen as shameful. At Dale Farm, for instance, around two-thirds of the women were on anti-depressants before, during and after the eviction, but none would admit it openly. One woman claimed that the doctors were 'giving out the pills like sweeties, in big bags' because they did not know where the women would be in future. Such a practice would, of course, increase the risk of overdosing. Uncertainty about housing is a particularly strong risk factor for anxiety and depression, so it was unsurprising that so many reported mental health problems, especially given their insecurity over tenure in housing, whether at an unauthorised site or in bricks and mortar housing where a landlord might suddenly decide not to allow Gypsies and Travellers (or a caravan parked out front).

More disturbingly, suicide had reached almost epidemic proportions, with the EHRC reporting an 'abnormally high mortality rate through suicide'.[29] Suicides by hanging had increased sharply. 'Despite the overall decline in suicide rates in Britain, analysis of trends over the past three decades demonstrates that suicide in the 1990s accounted for approximately one-fifth of all deaths amongst [Gypsy and Traveller] men under the age of thirty-four, the largest cause of death in men of this age group.'[30] The report continued: 'Evidence from a number of studies shows that Gypsies and Travellers have greatly raised rates of depression and anxiety, the two factors most highly associated with suicide, with relative risks 20 and 8.5 times higher than in the general population.'[31] These underlying mental health problems might have been treated with access to appropriate healthcare, particularly as working-class men are known to 'have a greatly increased rate of suicide when compared with other socio-economic classes'.

Irish-born people living in the UK have a higher rate of suicide than any other ethnic minority group living in the country. This increased tendency may, to some extent, be a reaction to anti-Irish racism and discrimination and may be relevant when considering suicide rates among Irish Travellers in Britain, but the EHRC found similarly high rates of suicide among Irish Travellers in Ireland, which made up 'nine per cent of all Traveller deaths in a ten-year sample of burials undertaken by the Parish of the Travelling People in Dublin'.[32] More recent figures suggest that Traveller suicides are six times higher than the settled population, accounting for a staggering eleven per cent of all Traveller deaths.[33] That statistic could be translated in a vivid way: in her twenty or more years of working with Irish Travellers, Margaret Greenfields observed that nearly ninety per cent of the families had 'experienced either suicide or parasuicide'.

Depression and the inability to recover from one major loss after another compounds the likelihood of suicide. The organisation Nexus in 2006 investigated the experiences of the relatives of Traveller suicide victims. On average, the people interviewed said they had known four or five members of their extended family — a parent, partner, sibling or first cousin — who had committed suicide, usually after a series of struggles, 'For many suicide victims, death was the culmination of a number of other events, including a reaction to time spent in prison, bereavements or other family tragedies.'[34] Among the many tragic cases of suicide was Bridget Joyce, who killed herself after being forced to witness the murder of her partner, Michael Foy, by her ex-husband. It is highly likely, said one support worker for Irish Traveller women, that some end up committing suicide because they believe it to be the only way out of domestic violence. 'It's like the Mafia. Death is the only escape.'

In spring 2013, after a Freedom of Information request, the extent of the asbestos contamination at Dale Farm was revealed, fuelling concern that the health both of Travellers evicted from the plot and of nearby residents has been harmed. Just a few weeks earlier, two tonnes of waste, including thirteen kilograms of asbestos-cement sheeting from the remains of a building, were identified and removed from the site by environmental health officers wearing protective gear and working on behalf of Basildon Council. Though council officials had previously claimed that there was no 'firm evidence' of asbestos on the site, it was found that at least six locations were contaminated. The Traveller families alleged that the asbestos was released when buildings were destroyed after their eviction.

Of course, around thirty of the evicted families still lived about one hundred yards away from the site in April 2013, and

Travellers' groups say that up to one hundred local families could potentially be affected by any contamination at Dale Farm. Candy says the bunding and other actions taken by the council after the eviction may have also disturbed oil-based contaminants in the soil – residue from the site's former use as a car-breaker's yard – as well as the asbestos. Basildon Council initially denied such accusations, saying they were 'not substantiated'. The Environment Agency report that had been designed to settle the matter was promised in autumn 2012, but had not yet appeared more than six months after its original due-date.

The Dale Farm families are suspicious as to why the council decided to remove asbestos after denying its existence. In response to such questions, Tony Ball said, 'We were aware that the site had been used previously as a scrap yard and there might have been stuff buried illegally. Asbestos is a concern, even if there is no danger to health, so to alleviate fears we removed it.'[35]

The council later said that it had cleared 'minimal shards' – eighty-eight fragments of asbestos cement, and in doing so has not admitted liability for the presence of any contaminants on the site that could affect people's health. And the question of liability for the clean-up remains contentious, especially after the eighty families living on the site were billed £4.3 million for the cost of evicting them.

Ramsden Crays Parish Council member David McPherson-Davis said there was still considerable concern among local residents about the safety of the site. Among other things, he wanted to know why the EA report had been delayed for so long. 'There must be sizeable pollution there, and the EA and the government department it reports to is trying to decide who put it there and who is responsible for cleaning it up. Asbestos dust is potentially life threatening. How far does the dust travel?'[36]

Others were vocal too. 'We are very concerned and quite angry that we have not seen this report as promised,' said Nigel Smith, the Labour group leader of Basildon Council. 'Local settled people, Travellers and children who even play on or near the site are all entitled to know whether or not it is safe for the local community.'[37]

Candy, who has been carrying out a health audit of the Travellers living roadside, said that some already have lung conditions and many of the children have been reporting problems with breathing. 'Over ninety-eight per cent of the children living roadside are using inhalers. Many are on antibiotics for chest infections or have had upset stomachs. To my knowledge this is not matched anywhere else in the country for similarly aged children.'[38]

The physical marginalisation of Gypsies and Travellers had deep emotional consequences. Charles Smith, the former chair of the Gypsy Council and former mayor of Castle Point, was also a writer, and dedicated one of his poems, entitled 'Reservations', to the scars that he was sure would come once the Caravan Sites Act became law:

> All penned up on the reservations
> On a bit of waste land, next to the sewage works
> Behind earth mounds, fences and walls
> Must not offend delicate eyes
> Out on the edge of town
> So we know they don't want us amongst them
> Keeping us at a distance on the reservation.

He ended with these lines:

> Kindly, you give us those reservations
> Look at why you have taken away.[39]

We in the settled community wring our hands over the reservations into which Aboriginal peoples have been herded over the past century and a half, and we try to understand the damage that has been wreaked upon their culture by those who were in power. Many people fought to end apartheid in South Africa, but we look away when it comes to our part in this piece of history.

For her part, Margaret Greenfields agrees. 'We have emerging evidence ... which suggests an over-representation of mental health issues and substance misuse among some members of the community. In my opinion this is a clear outcome of the cultural trauma experienced by members of the populations,' she said. 'One only needs to compare the literature on the outcomes and experiences of Australian aborigines and Gypsies and Travellers to see those broad similar experiences. For example, amongst Australian aborigines and First Nation peoples in Canada and America, we see well-documented evidence of family breakdowns, mental health issues, substance misuse and suicide. Thus it is greatly to the credit of Gypsies and Travellers that their communities remain so resilient and intact in the face of widespread marginalisation.'

One portion of our society has been abandoned, left to the injustice of self-policing, allowing the strong to lord it over the weak and men, far too often, to dominate women and children with virtual impunity. We have placed sites in contaminated places, where nobody else would want to live, almost certainly restricting the life expectancy of their residents. We have done little to nothing to bring Gypsies and Travellers in from the cold – to see them as fellow citizens, different from but equal to everyone else who makes a home within these borders. All of us need water, security, shelter, food and education, so that we can flourish, develop a strong sense of self and pass on our culture to our children. Is it too much to ask, said Candy Sheridan, quietly, one day after she had been signing forms for the Environment Agency at Dale Farm, confirming that some plots were polluted with asbestos, that Gypsies and Travellers should be granted these human rights too?

14
REVIVAL

Sitting over his campfire at the top gate of Appleby Fair in the second week of June 2012, just days after the Queen's Diamond Jubilee, Billy Welch was a contented man. His family was all around him, and the fair, which he organises, as his father did before him, was going off quietly, trading was good. Now, in a calm moment, he was taking stock, chatting with friends. One of the topics of conversation, of course, was the battle of Dale Farm, and the ongoing saga at Meriden.

Some people felt keenly the agony of the Dale Farm site clearance, and shook their heads in sympathy, asking in particular how the mothers were bearing up on the roadside. Others hazarded that the Travellers had brought it on themselves, by packing the site so full and bringing in outside activists, rather than doing for themselves. A few of the Dale Farm activists had been seen around the fair, handing out leaflets, something that Billy himself was not tremendously enthusiastic to see.

He was licking wounds, it was true, but Billy was a man looking to the future, or rather looking to find a better future by looking back into the past. Dale Farm had been demoralising; Meriden was shaping up to be a bad time too. Yet even in these barren times, he was sowing a kernel of hope. In the battle he had realised that Gypsies and Travellers were ready to speak for themselves. And he was trying to raise funding to make the first documentary of Gypsy folk to trace their travelling over the centuries back east across Europe, then onwards to Turkey, then on again into Iran, and finally all the way to India where, it's thought, they came from. 'We might go even further back,' he said. 'Some say we are the lost tribes of Abraham.' It might sound romantic, but at least today, unlike in Victorian times, the Gypsies were romanticising themselves. Billy continued: 'We aren't as shallow as people think. We managed to hang on to our culture for hundreds of years; the language we speak is ancient Sanskrit. We want to try and trace our history back, give our people a sense of pride.'

This was Billy's thirteenth year as spokesman for the fair, and he had grown into the task. Still, it was a big undertaking. Gypsies and Travellers from all over the world, numbering some ten thousand, come to Appleby each year. In the weeks beforehand, they retouch the paintwork on their bow-top wagons and spruce up their modern caravans. Then they set off. If they are travelling by horse (rather than putting the old wagons on trailers, an increasingly common practice), they stop every ten or fifteen miles, at traditional stopping places, where their families have rested and grazed their horses for generations. 'It's our Mecca,' said Billy, 'our pilgrimage. It's not just the fair that's important, it's the journey to the fair … Even when the fair is over, you'll still find hundreds of old Gypsies encamped in their wagons … The journey is as important as arriving,' he continued. 'It lets us reconnect with our roots.'

These old stopping places are opened up each year as 'temporary areas of acceptance' by the Multi-Agency Task Force, which manages matters such as licensing, policing, transport, animal welfare and human safety during Appleby. On the first day of the fair, officers from the police, fire, ambulance, even the RSPCA, squeezed into a room for a task force confab. Things were going well. Still, two villages en route to the fair reported having problems with the stopping-off points. Grasses not set aside for grazing had been eaten, and then trampled. The Gypsies involved said that grass in the area was already eaten down when they arrived.

One of the aims of the task force is to dispatch such problems and potential disputes quickly. The deputy mayor of Appleby, Andy Connell, said that local feeling had improved – the mood in the community was 'much happier than it used to be'. Many townsfolk, he added, made money out of it, although others resent the disruption. According to Connell, who is also a local historian, the fair in its current form developed in the eighteenth century, when it was primarily used as a market for selling livestock. After the railways came, and the cattle went to auction by freight train, horses – and their Gypsy owners – came to the fore.

The fairs offered a chance for people to let off steam and meet up with old friends, to 'network' with other families and organisations now that most of the community no longer work together in the fields. The last thing they wanted was to feel a threat over their heads. But Gypsies and Travellers have had to fight to retain the summer horse fairs. The major fairs – Appleby in Cumbria and Stow in the Cotswolds – had survived, but many local fairs had been opposed before disappearing. The Appleby Fair had faced two serious threats to its existence in the past century, once in 1947 and again in 1964. In both cases, the local council decided in the end not to push for closure, but other Gypsy fairs have not been so lucky. The fair at Horsmonden, in Kent, which evolved from a 'hopping fair' into a Gypsy horse fair, was closed down briefly in the 1990s; when it re-opened in 2006, it was saddled with restrictions from the council. And at Stow, where the traditional horse fair is held twice yearly, a local residents' group has been formed to oppose it, and many shops in the town close down, often suspiciously claiming a well-timed family holiday or the need for redecorating, during fair time. While it is illegal to bar entrance to shops and other venues on ethnic grounds, this is pretty much flouted in Stow. Even the church closes its doors during the duration of the fair.

In Appleby, however, most shops were open for business – and doing a brisk trade at that. More than 1,500 visitors were expected to arrive by chartered coaches on Saturday alone. Two hundred police had been mustered for duty during the fair, compared to the six who patrol the market town, population 2,500, on more usual days. The visitors and their watchers initially clustered along the swollen river bank, after a day and night of heavy rainfall, hoping to catch a glimpse of the horses being washed off before sale, but most were disappointed, because the river level was too high and the river had to be closed for most of the day

So instead, they made the walk up the hill to the fair ground itself, where gypsy cobs and lighter horses were being raced in the so-called flashing lane, to show off their qualities to interested buyers. Some were harnessed to traditional lightweight traps known as sulkies, others ridden bareback by the lads or the odd girl with hair streaming down her back. The cry 'Watch your backs!' would go up as the sulkies raced along. Horses that showed a straight line in the traces, and a high trotting step, raised appreciative cheers in the pouring rain.

The horses and ponies were not the only items up for sale. There were goats and donkeys as well as thick rugs and Crown Derby china for decorating a home, whether stopping for a few days or settling in to a pitch. There were also embroidered dresses and brightly-coloured leisurewear for the girls and women and beautifully cut shooting jackets and flat caps for the boys and men. 'Genuine Gypsy palmists' and fortune-tellers were out in force, awaiting the young women (and some men) looking to see what – or who – their future might hold.

Despite the conditions, many girls, hoping to be wooed at the fair, were dressed in tiny shorts, skirts and shirts that showed off their immaculate spray tans. Many tottered along the uneven grass verges to and from the town and on Fair Hill itself, trying to avoid the paths, which were inches deep in mud, in their high-heeled wedges. The ambulance service was standing ready to treat sprains and fractures due to 'inappropriate footwear'.

Most families had parked up in the same spot as last year, and the year before, and the one before that too. Among them were William and Janey Michaelson, who had visited Appleby since their childhood. In their caravan, chatting over a beef sandwich and a good mug of tea, William recalled his first visit to the fair seventy-three years previously, when he was just a babe in arms. Surveying the fair, he declared, 'You can travel all over the world and not see anything like this.'

Just a month earlier, in May, the Stow spring fair had been held. It was just as rainy at the time, and Vera Norwood, the former Tiller girl and former mayor of Stow-on-Wold, had been forced to buy wellingtons in order to venture down to the pub, where she was set to meet a few local councillors for a pre-fair walk-round. When they didn't turn up, she downed a rum with a companion and trudged down to the site, located on the outskirts of Stow, on the road leading out towards the village of Maugesbury. It's from Maugesbury that some of the staunchest opposition to the fair comes.

The gathering is held on land owned by the Smith families, headed by Isaac and Walter Smith. Though this was proving to be the rainiest fair for years, the families said they had not been allowed to put down any kind of path, even a removable one, with the council citing the fact that the field is located in the Cotswolds Area of Outstanding Natural Beauty, which is known for its limestone grassland. This was a frustrating development, all the more so since, as Vera pointed out, the local Tesco super-market had built paths and car parks in virtually the same area. With the rain and the mud, it was inevitable that the field would be destroyed, churned up by both many feet and bad weather, and some local residents would later seize the opportunity to ask how much the Gypsies were paying towards the clean-up.

For now, though, all of the worries about how the fair would go were only worries – though admittedly some of the worriers were ready to see trouble. Earlier in the day Vera had visited the local library, which was hosting an exhibition about the fair. The building was festooned with painted milk stools, churns and photographs from years past, a beautiful collection of history and tradition. At the centre of the exhibition was a display of the text of Edward IV's Royal Charter protecting the fair. While she was taking a spin around the library, she was accosted by Robin Jones, the current mayor of the market town. He was decidedly irked, asking her whether 'she had put them [the library] up to it' and suggesting that she was stirring up trouble by referring to Stow as a 'charter fair'. Vera, being someone who liked to build consensus, tried to calm him down, but this was not a good sign. After leaving the library, she walked down the high street. Many shops were shuttered, although it seemed a few less than the year before. In the local supermarket, the shop manager stood on guard when young Traveller children came in to buy milk, eyeing them suspiciously the whole time.

At Stow, as at Appleby, the Gypsies and Travellers were on show to the public, the stereotypes held by the settled community shadowing them. Mary Lovell, Isaac Smith's wife, was incensed, for example, by the way in which *My Big Fat Gypsy Wedding* had come to be seen as a fair representation of her community. 'Life is for the Gypsy people, not make-believe Gypsies. I'm not talking for all kinds; I'm talking for the *real* Gypsy people, who have lived in wagons, lived on the side of the road, have shared these things with other people for generations and [who] keep their old-fashioned ways with their children. And getting "grabbed" by boys, that's new,' she said, referring to the alleged practice, repeatedly depicted on the TV programme, of forcing girls to kiss boys. 'Grabbing a new girl and taking her name from them, that's wrong. Young Gypsy men would go to the parents. They would ask for the courting girls and then get married and we would sew the young girls' frocks, make them stand out a mile, but they didn't cost a billion to do that.'[1]

To people like Billy Welch and Mary Lovell, the fairs, if any-thing, were more important now than at any time in the history of England's Gypsies and Travellers. They were one of the few places that Gypsies and Travellers could come together to meet on uncontested ground and be themselves – not a subject of reality TV.

Many of the Gypsies and Travellers at Stow were talking about the draw of evangelical Christianity – and how it seemed a path for-ward, as families and as a larger community, though a challenging one. One well-respected woman had converted to the Light and Life ministry earlier in the year, and said that she was trying to bring together the old customs and the beliefs of the new church. 'I've read fortunes all my life and I goes out hawking still; I like to keep it going, the pegs, the favours, the tablecloths, it's lovely,' she recounted. 'I like to talk to people, tell them who I am, what I am, it's a way of life. I don't want to change it. We just want to be left in peace.' Unlike the McCarthy family members who had converted, she had found a middle ground, in her own mind, that allowed her to maintain some aspects of her travelling heritage – in particular her fortune-telling – and worship with Light and Life. 'We have a gift. If you can talk to a person and say things are going to be better, you are not doing anything bad. It's a gift from the Lord, [though] some of the Christians say it's from the enemy. If you gave them false hope then it's not from the enemy, it's what you believe ... There is only one God, and I love God. God will change their way of life ... either go to heaven or hell.'

Over the past several years, Light and Life had grown to be a crucial part of Romani Gypsy identity. Almost every Gypsy family (and a growing number of Irish Travellers) in the UK had at least one family member in the church, or had been affected by the church's work in some way. Around thirty churches had been opened. The church had become so dominant that on the evening before the Stow Horse Fair's traditional opening day, there was now a Light and Life prayer meeting, led by Siddy Biddle and his family, to bless the gathering. The rain was so heavy in May 2012 that the Stow vigil had to be cancelled.

But Pastor Davey Jones, Billy Welch's cousin and one of the leading figures in the church, made his way to Appleby the following month. A former altar boy turned quietly spoken pastor, Jones had found most organised religion in England to be 'cold and dead' and had yearned for something deeper. He soon realised that this wish was shared by many of his people – he was an English Gypsy himself, and today lived in a lovingly restored chrome caravan which he had bought from Billy's father. 'My people were in spiritual darkness,' said Jones, sitting in his immaculate caravan at Appleby. 'We had a form of religion but really, in our hearts, we weren't believers, because we held to the traditions of our people, like worshipping the dead. We lived a double life. Now many of them are experiencing a personal relationship with God for the first time.'[2]

The movement had started in Brittany, France, in the 1950s, Jones explained. There, an evangelical church, called *Vie et Lumière*, had been founded by a non-Romani father and son, Jean and Clément le Cossec.[3] The Cossecs converted Jones and many other English Gypsy elders over twenty years ago in a site in Darlington – known, only half-jokingly, as the 'Gypsy capital of England' – where Billy now lives with his extended family, as did his father before him. 'The church members from France visited my Dad, then he went back to France with Davey. My Dad brung them back here – he had a big marquee tent, just there, out the back, the very first one ever in this country,' Billy said. 'It all began here on Honeypot Lane caravan site.' Though Billy himself is not a member of Light and Life, his cousin Jackie Boyd is also a leading pastor in the church.

This wasn't the first time that England's Gypsies and Travellers had been evangelised. A century earlier, Anglican priests had tried to save them from their 'depraved' nomadic lifestyle. One famous preacher, 'Gipsy Smith', had emerged during the Victorian era – a member of the Salvation Army who travelled to and from America and attracted thousands of people to his services – but on the whole Christianity was something imposed on the travelling peoples by the settled majority.[4] Light and Life, in contrast, is a self-organised church.

It's thought that almost half of all Gypsies in France belong to the church. The number in the UK is lower – around a fifth – but with conversions coming at a high rate among both English Gypsies and traditionally Catholic Irish Travellers, that is changing year by year. Many newly arrived Roma from Central and Eastern Europe are also enthusiastically evangelical, with some choosing to join established English Gypsy churches, such as the London Gypsy Church, rather than starting their own satellite churches in areas with a growing Roma population, as in Luton. In the words of Angus Fraser, author of *The Gypsies*. 'There is ... something in the ecstatic aspect of evangelical faith – the witnessing for Christ – that is highly attractive to people whose traditional manner of life is in some way under threat' – and he adds, prophetically, that it is the first real example in Western Europe of a 'mass pan-Gypsy organisation, transcending tribal subdivisions'.[5]

All of the leading Light and Life identified themselves as Romani Gypsies. Jones stresses that none of the pastors in the church are paid, because, he said, if they were, some Gypsies and Travellers would suspect they were being converted to grab tithes or other donations. 'Some of our people were fortune-tellers and con-men. This makes it very difficult to con them. Either they are having a personal experience that is changing their lives – or they are not going to be deceived.' The Pentecostal religion was having a profound effect on some of these traditional aspects of Gypsy and Traveller culture. Fortune-telling is frowned upon. The church is sceptical of the appropriateness of teenage marriage, still common among Gypsies and Travellers. It also holds a very strict view on the use of illegal drugs and the overuse of alcohol. As a show of faith, believers practise speaking in tongues and divine healing.

One unforeseen result of the evangelical revival has been the growing number of new converts attending Bible school and the understanding of just how important education is. Most of these converts, including children, were being taught to read so that they could pore over Scripture. Gypsies and Travellers might not need to read and write for their chosen work, but they were going to literacy night school for their chosen faith. In turn, different professions were opening up to them and to the rising generation.

Not long after Appleby, Davey Jones had a revival meeting set to be held on the grounds of Carlton Towers estate, near Selby in Yorkshire. When he was talking up the meeting at Appleby, he said he was expecting around five thousand people to turn up. Instead, around twice that number descended on the estate, provoking an onslaught of anger among some of the local people, who felt that they had not been given proper notice of the gathering. The *Yorkshire Post* headline blared: 'Fury over village of Gypsies for festival'. The newspaper went on to say that 'residents have complained of gangs of youths marching through the village and disturbing houses'.[6] (The owners of Carlton Towers subsequently donated the fee they had received for hosting the meeting to the local village.)

Despite the splash and the claims, there was little evidence of such trouble. Youngsters were huddled in the middle of the village, but the village shopkeepers said that they had not had any problems – in fact, they had done well by the revival, selling extra soft drinks, milk, food and sweets. The police presence was relatively loose, though large in number.

The revival meeting itself displayed a remarkable integration of Gypsy culture into evangelical worship, a live-in, authentic religion, not a religion just for show. Around half of the women present donned headscarves as they entered the big circus tent, as a very literal reading of Scripture would suggest they should. The pastor who led the prayer meeting spoke to the congregation as only a fellow Romani could – chiding and praising his community in equal measure. He pulled the youngsters up on littering. He talked about how wives and mothers needed to raise 'good ingredients' to ensure a good life was led – a lesson that touched many of the women, who took great pride in their cooking and other home-making.

The atmosphere at the convention felt a little like Appleby – relaxed, cheery. Most of the men said they worked as tree surgeons, scrap dealers or small businessmen, mostly selling beds and the like, judging from their vans, and the women were caring for their children or cleaning and cooking, as well as praying. Several stalls had been set up to sell religious DVDs and books. But there was another element too, something that extended the sense of community beyond one family, one clan, or one caravan site. People called each other 'sister' or 'brother'. They were rebuilding their community, making it stronger, one convert at a time. Their 'silent revival' drew upon what was best about the travelling way of life – the strength of the family, the respect for elders, the strong impulse towards charity and the tolerance of people of all races.

Like many of the church elders, Walter Smith, who organises Stow Horse Fair, had seen a shift in the last few years, as the church was reaching more and more of his 'sisters and brothers', as he warmly called them. After an afternoon prayer meeting, he had retired to his caravan with his family. It was a peaceful scene – his grandchildren had been playing chess all morning and had just switched to a game of backgammon. Then Walter said grace before his wife served their homely meal of gammon, potatoes and cabbage.

Walter had been converted over twenty years before, around the same time as Davey Jones. He thought that there would be still more converts. 'We believe as Gypsy people that the end is coming very soon, and it's important to be saved. Our belief is in the Bible. In Luke 14:23, it says that to find new Christians you need to go out to the hedges and back roads, and we believe that Jesus was talking about us, the people of the hedges and the back roads,' he said. 'Gypsies are hard to get to; some of them will give you baloney and many have a lot of problems, and they have got to be set free from old ways like fortune-telling. There is only one way to get to heaven, and that's through Jesus.'

As Walter talked about the end being nigh, it was hard not to imagine that he was really talking about the end of a way of life being nigh – the life of travelling and trading on the road. The Light and Life church was a rock in hard times to him, and to many others. Many new members, in fact, were choosing to put down roots near a bricks and mortar church, a place where they may worship in the safety of their community. Travelling was something that they only did during holidays or horse fairs or, more and more, church conventions.

The church's tough line on the use of alcohol and drugs had also been a comfort to some in the community. There's a widespread fear of the growing menace of drugs, especially as a threat to younger Gypsies and Travellers. People could point to some young person who had fallen prey to unscrupulous drug dealers, and the church had helped a few of them to regain a foothold in the traditional, stricter way of life. The church offered a place for them to be proud of and rejoice in who they are, to throw off the sense of shame created by the constant stigma and stereo-types they felt were thrust on them by the settled community and the media.

Billy's cousin Jackie Boyd praised the church's ability to nurture the good in Gypsy and Traveller culture. 'In every culture there are things that are wrong. In our culture there are some good things, such as the family ties and the respect we have for them. But we used to have cultural jobs, like fortune-telling, that go against the word of God. It's only things that come against the word of God that need to change,' he said. 'It was never our intention to have Gypsy churches. We wanted to evangelise people, but we found so many difficulties with the church's understanding of Gypsies. They thought we had to become non-Gypsies if we were to become Christians. The people from the churches thought that if we were saved, we had to live in a house. But God is interested in the *spiritual* man. Chinese churches don't become white churches; they come to God as they are in their culture, and things that are wrong, He will change.'

He remembered one incident in particular that had shown him the light: 'When I first became a Christian, the pastor said he had to drive out the demons from the fortune-tellers. I told him they were not possessed by demons just because they told fortunes. The churches themselves had a lot to learn.'[7]

Now Life and Light was spreading the word throughout the world, building churches not just in the UK and France but in Eastern Europe too, and becoming a force for Gypsy and Traveller identity. 'If people want to deal with the Gypsies and get the truth, they need to deal with the evangelical Christians,' said Davey Jones. 'Our churches are cultural centres as well. Christianity isn't taking away from our culture. It's adding to it.'

Candy Sheridan said she was enthusiastic about the Gypsy church and its work in the UK, though she herself is a Catholic. 'I know of many broken Gypsy men whose lives have been revived and I have seen this success first hand,' she said. The academic Thomas Acton was also largely positive: 'Davey Jones and other Romani Pentecostal pastors are very creative theological thinkers. They are aware that they are not only leading a church movement, but an intellectual revival of their people.'[8]

Others have been more cautious. Professor of Romani Studies Ian Hancock, whose ancestors include British travelling Showmen and Hungarian Roma, was one of the doubters, despite seeing several strengths in the evangelical model of worship. 'They preach love in a powerful way, which is something Romanies don't hear. Roman Catholic and Orthodox churches are very impersonal, and some have refused to allow Romanies inside to worship. Secondly, the Born Again churches allow Romani individuals to have a say, and titles, and even become pastors with churches of their own.' But Hancock sees the prohibition of fortune-telling and of arranged and teenage marriages as 'gross cultural imposition'.[9]

He has not been alone in his doubts about the new church. One founder member of the Gypsy Council (who is also a celebrated writer about life on the road) named Dominic Reeve recalled some of the first converts turning up at Epsom Races when the races were still a favoured haunt of Gypsies and Travellers. 'A huge collection of wealthy-seeming French Romanies appeared one Race Week with new trailers, new Mercedes vans and a vast marquee,' he wrote of an encounter in the late 1970s. 'They were my first experience of Born Again Christians, later to prove a rather fanatical band of well-intentioned Bible fundamentalists, whose simple fire-and-brimstone message has presently been embraced by a large number of British Romanies and throughout Europe too, I believe. As a lifelong agnostic I was naturally a little depressed by this and can only hope it will pass, like other fashions.'[10] The 'fashion' had not passed – far from it.

At Appleby, Pastor Jones mused about what he meant when he said that 'if people want to deal with the Gypsies and get the truth, they will deal with the evangelical Christians'. 'We come to the fairs so people can see we are Christians, but not fanatics. We must draw our people to us.' He was looking ahead to an influential role in public life for his church members, though, he said, 'We are not interested in political power.'

Although it is the biggest, Light and Life is not the only church making inroads into the Gypsy and Traveller community. There is a movement to bring together all of the peoples of the Roma nation, whether they live in the UK, France or Spain or in Eastern Europe or Russia. Religion is one aspect of that, and as a result Roma and English Gypsies have begun to worship together. In addition, the growing numbers of Roma immigrants from Eastern Europe are establishing influential churches of their own.

In mainland Europe, where the overwhelming majority of the Roma population of around ten million live, living conditions had become nearly unbearable. Indeed, a May 2012 report published by the United Nations Development Programme, the World Bank and the European Union Agency for Fundamental Rights confirmed that the situation was grim beyond belief. In a survey of 84,000 households in eleven countries, only fifteen per cent of young Roma adults had finished upper-secondary general or vocational education, compared with more than seventy per cent of the majority population. Less than thirty per cent of Roma were in paid employment. About forty-five per cent lived in households lacking a kitchen, inside toilet, electricity or washing facilities. They were cordoned off in apartheid-like conditions, in separate communities pushed to the edges of towns and villages. They were frequently the target of hate crimes.[11]

No official figures exist, but the best estimate, from the advocacy group Equality, suggests that at least half a million Roma have come to the UK, with families settling in clusters around Glasgow, London, Manchester, Leeds, Kent and the East Midlands.[12] The influx has been huge – and may more than match the existing population of Gypsies and Travellers. 'Most people are intrigued by Gypsies and Travellers but the new Roma population is bigger than those two communities put together and still growing,' said scholar Robbie McVeigh.[13] One place where Roma have been settling fast is Luton, where the Church of England has appointed its first and only chaplain to the Roma people, Martin Burrell.

Martin, who previously worked with Kentish Romanies in his former parish, came to Luton in 2009, and started the Roma church there in the spring of 2011. 'Until recently you had to go abroad to do missions. The churches have not woken up to the fact that now there is a whole mission field on our doorsteps, a new world that is forming around us', he observed. I see it as a movement; God is moving us towards His future, where there are no divisions between different ethnic futures. We have to learn to live alongside each other. This patch is not ours, and what the Roma are saying to us is a challenge to all nations. The Roma are an ethnic group of some twelve million people who say that they don't want a patch [to] each, just somewhere to live.'

When Pastor Burrell started his work, a minister from the London Gypsy Church, Pastor Stevo, would come every fortnight to offer a service to those in the community who had adopted Pentecostal worship. That lapsed, however, due to differences between the two Roma communities: none of those at the London Gypsy Church were poor, while many in Luton were, explained Burrell. 'They were wonderful people, but a different social class. We are still trying to find the right model for our church. All the energies of my people are on surviving, but they are coming to church as well. The state has made it possible for them to come, but it has tied their hands behind their backs. They have to stretch the system just to survive. Somehow they will find a way to make this work – they are adventurous entrepreneurs after all.'

By the end of 2012 Burrell's Roma flock numbered around forty or fifty, many of whom are collected each week for a mid-week evening service by a church minibus. One of his congregation was Esmeralda, a fond grandmother with nimble fingers. This Wednesday evening in November 2012, she was sewing a duvet from fabric she had bought cheap on a market stall, with gold rings in her ears, a headscarf and a long, colourful skirt, awaiting Burrell's minibus to go to church in a small terrace in Luton, the one incongruous element. Her small sitting room was dominated by an enormous TV, tuned to Romanian television, and other women in the family would wander in and out, all wearing traditional headscarves. Esmeralda explained that her family had not always lived here. They had been forced to move several times due to problems with landlords.

Then it was time to make their way to the church. When she arrived, many members of the congregation were already assembled. The younger children darted about, translating from English for the older people – that is when they weren't delightedly cutting, sticking and colouring Christmas scenes that had been prepared by members of Christchurch, a church in Bushmead, for them.

The congregation that day included some Roma who had set up in Leicester, then arrived in Luton while they were travelling to find work and found the church by chance by coming across other ethnic Roma. Burrell, with characteristic generosity, invited them to minister to the Roma, taking a back seat himself. The newcomers explained that they had been trained as pastors back in Romania, by a pastor who had himself been trained by Jean le Cossec. During the service, which was conducted in Romanian, the women sat separately from the men. As part of their ministering, the Roma pastors took up a variety of instruments, including a keyboard, dulcimer and accordion, to share some traditional songs. The music was plaintive, almost Middle Eastern in feeling.

The Roma pastors were nearly destitute, but despite their lack of money, they were smartly turned out for worship, in gleaming shoes and pressed suits. They said that the only contact they usually had with English Gypsies and Irish Travellers was either working for them as labourers or competing with them for business at the local scrap yard – and sometimes coming to blows. One claimed he had escaped from near slavery conditions working for one Traveller family. Still, they remained remarkably cheerful in the face of their poverty, refusing an offer of petrol money from the congregation, even when they were told it was in thanks for their ministering. The men insisted that they did not deserve the money – whether or not it was considered a tithe – because they felt the congregation had not yet been saved.

Burrell's job, by his reckoning, was these days less preaching the Gospel and more advising on benefits. He would help his Roma congregation members to find work, fill out invoices, sign on at the job centre, apply to get National Insurance numbers. He said that recent changes in the employment law and budget had hit the community hard. 'Recently the job centre narrowed the goal posts so [the Roma] couldn't be self-employed any more, and they are really desperate. If they don't have anybody who speaks the language, it's pretty impossible for them.' If it doesn't work for them here, they will shift on, he said. 'They say if it doesn't work, they will go to Spain. One family came from Brazil. They will pitch up anywhere they can eke out an existence.'

Burrell, too, was stretched. He had expanded from one church to two – the church for the Roma people, plus Christchurch, which primarily serves the settled community. Some of the parishioners from Christchurch assist with his Wednesday evening service for the Roma. 'I am asked, "Is it appropriate for a minister to run a mission outreach programme in another part of the town? I move from a white English congregation to an Eastern European Roma group of people on the edge of everything, in what I call a holistic mission. We try and bring help to every part of their lives. We are stepping out onto the water here, and it is very risky. But God is there, on their lives, these people who live on the edge. God is found in the poor and marginalised, where we see another dimension of reality that doesn't get recognised.'

Religion is hugely important to many in the communities, but the struggles that Gypsies and Travellers are facing require not just spiritual answers, but political ones. For all its flaws, it seems as though the Pentecostal church will be the most likely source of political leadership in the coming years. 'There will still be a community in one hundred years' time, but they won't speak much Romani, and many of them will be living in houses, with a Romani Bible they can't read. The music and songs will go on,' Donald Kenrick, the scholar said. 'Many of them will be Pentecostals.'[14] Could a Martin Luther King arise out of this new church, and harness together the cords of political and religious strength? For other passions are stirring at the grass roots of the community, and though they have links to Light and Life, these passions are directed at a very different agenda.

Just a handful of English Gypsies and Irish Travellers have made it into political life in the UK over the past forty years. These include the late Charlie Smith, who was elected a Labour councillor in the 1990s and went on to become mayor of Castle Point in 2003; a year later, he was the only English Gypsy named to sit on the Equality and Human Rights Commission. Candy Sheridan too had twice been elected a councillor for the Liberal Democrats in North Norfolk, but stepped down just before the 2010 election. A number of organisations were becoming increasingly vocal, as well, with well-respected spokespeople, such as Candy and Joe Jones at the Gypsy Council, Siobhan Spencer at the Derbyshire Gypsy Liaison Group, Helen Jones at Leeds GATE and Yvonne McNamara at the Irish Traveller Movement. Some young people, including Blue Jones and Nadi Foy, were standing up to articulate the voice of the community.

They had allies, of course, including many of the activists from Camp Constant, who had since formed the Travellers Solidarity Network and launched the 'Fight for Sites' initiative. Some in the communities had welcomed this support, but just as many felt that this outside intervention would only worsen their situation. In October 2012, for the one-year anniversary of the Dale Farm clearance, the activists had staged a demonstration outside the Department of Communities and Local Government. Most of the Dale Farm residents were by now sick of the media coverage, and some said they were tired of the connection with the activists and felt it was not useful to their cause. In the end, although the Travellers Solidarity Network sent a minibus to Dale Farm to collect residents living roadside, only three women had come out – and all three turned pale and shocked when some of the activists allowed the demonstration to become physical, and police began arresting people. The network remains active, and many in it are genuinely committed to greater equality for the community. However, whether the network will ever be trusted by a critical mass in this very disparate grouping of peoples, bound by strong family and historical ties that are difficult to penetrate and understand, remains to be seen.

Billy Welch, for his part, wants to build on the enthusiasm from within the Gypsy and Traveller community – particularly in his hometown of Darlington. At least eleven per cent, and up to fifteen per cent, of Darlington's population self-declare as Gypsies or Travellers. The real figure may be higher, nearer to a third, as many have moved to houses in town and may not identify themselves for fear of harassment. Nearby Doncaster and York also have significant populations of Romani Gypsies and Travellers. This is where Billy said he intends to start his initiative, in the next round of local elections.

'We have gathered together influential people in the Gypsy and Traveller community, the *shera rom*, and the big men from the Irish Traveller community,' he explained. They had recruited, for instance, 'Big Dan' Rooney, a one-time bare-knuckle boxer who was now a prominent preacher with Light and Life, as well as the Irish Traveller Alexander J. Thompson. Billy's cousins, Davey Jones and Jackie Boyd from the Light and Life church were part of the conversation too. 'We are all talking to each other about what needs to change,' Billy said. 'We have all these Gypsy and Traveller organisations, around 120 all around the country, and yet they aren't run by people like us, the elders. The government loves a "yes man", so they have built up a white man's structure. We are going to change all that.' His big dream is that his people do it for themselves by being less secretive and engaging more with settled society. He wants to launch an Obama-style 'Yes, We Can' political campaign among his people, starting with getting people to the polls. 'We need a voice,' he says. 'So we need to vote.'

Billy estimated that close to a million people in the UK could claim some Gypsy or Traveller origin – a potential electorate that he said was all but ignored. Even if the figure were nearer to the official estimate of some 300,000, if the community voted together, this number could tip seats to preferred candidates in some areas. 'Eighty per cent of our people live in houses now, and they don't put that they are Gypsy on the census. We think the *gorgers* [settled people] can do what they want with their world; we live in our own world. My people aren't interested, but they will have to be, the world isn't the same place it was fifteen years ago. They are smothering us with laws and restrictions. We've got no voice in Parliament. When the authorities come down on us, I want my people to vote; I want the government to know how many of us there are. When there is a tight election, we could be the difference to someone getting kicked out. That is the only way we will get treated as equals, have some value in society. We need to register to vote. We are going to have to get involved in their world as well.'

He decided to launch his voter drive at the Appleby Fair in June 2013. Twenty people, some from the Light and Life church and others from clans from around the country, would distribute leaflets and talk to people as they wandered the fair grounds. 'I'm the *shera rom* of my tribe, and I'm talking to the heads of all the other families. Some of them cover big areas, some small, but they are all influential. The communities will listen to us. We will decide which party is the best for us and this will be a collective decision. In some areas, with around one million of us, we can swing a vote; round here we can definitely swing it.' He had heard from families in Scotland and Wales who supported his political campaigning as well.

Billy was motivated to become politically engaged by an experience some twenty years before. He was on his way home from a business trip to Germany, and was set upon by a National Front gang. He was beaten so badly that his family didn't recognise him when they visited him in hospital. Yet no action had been taken against the perpetrators of the attack. Then, in 2011, his outrage was renewed when he was barred from his local pub on the grounds that he was a Gypsy. Billy fought that case with the aid of the Equality and Human Rights Commission, but he was aware that, up and down the country, Gypsies and Travellers were being targeted for their ethnicity and routinely refused access to hotels, restaurants, pubs and clubs. He wanted to change that – make a stand, not just for himself, but for the community.

The attitude of Gypsies and Travellers needed to change, he explained. 'Our people have had a very coloured view of authority. The wider world has been out there and we have lived in our little world and thought, What they do doesn't concern us, that nothing that we would ever do would influence anything in the community, so we have just got on with our life. But things have changed. A lot has happened in the wider world. It's about time we started taking charge of our own destiny, started to influence. If we don't vote, we will never improve the situation,' he said.

'We live in a democracy and we don't use it. Because we don't vote, we don't have a value. Until we become worth something in electoral terms, to both local government and national government, they will continue to privilege the settled community over us. We are our own worst enemy, and that needs to change.' Other groups were also planning to help – Simon Woolley, Director of Operation Black Vote, fresh from working on the Obama re-election campaign, had offered advice. The Gypsy Council was helping to register the residents roadside at Dale Farm too – in an audacious plan to vote Len Gridley onto Basildon Council in 2014, to question the eviction and the money spent.

The voices of Gypsies and Travellers are being heard in other arenas as well. In October 2012, the East Anglian Museum of Rural Life in Stowmarket hosted an event celebrating Romani achievements in the arts.[15] Thomas Acton kicked off the event by charting the evolution of Romani art since the Second World War. 'Romani writers were trapped in a *gorger* world,' in the early years, he argued, with many works marked by a knowledge or direct experience of the Holocaust, the legacy of slavery in Eastern Europe, and sometimes both. For instance, Elena Lacková's

1956 play *The Burning Gypsy Camp* confronted the theme of the Holocaust. The great Romani novelist Matéo Maximoff wrote eleven books, some touching on his experience in a Gypsy camp during the war; twenty-seven of his relatives, he said, were killed in concentration camps in Poland. He became an evangelical pastor in 1961, translating the New Testament into Kalderaš Romani before his death.[16] 'What marks the early writers is their isolation', Acton said. 'They were paranoid; they lived in a world that didn't welcome them.'

Today, however, Romani art is another catalyst for change in the community – particularly the movement to build a Roma nation that transcends state boundaries. As the Roma art historian, curator and activist Timea Junghaus put it in the foreword to the book *Meet Your Neighbors*: 'We must recognise that constructing effective representations involves the artist as much as the scientist or the politician.'[17] Some of the most important members of that artistic movement – Damian and Delaine Le Bas, Daniel Baker and Ferdinand Koci among them – live in the UK, many of them British citizens.

Other talented artists with Romani/Traveller roots include Dan Allum, a Traveller who grew up in East Anglia and attended the exhibition opening. He recalled a childhood with little schooling, but much back-breaking agricultural labour. It seemed an unlikely way to begin a successful artistic career. But after landing work as a video producer, in 2002 he founded the Romani Theatre Company, for which he was the artistic director.

Allum was keen to extend the reach of his theatre projects to the settled community. He had created a series, *Atching Tan* ('Stopping Place' in Romani), for local BBC radio, as well as two spin-off plays, the first also called *Atching Tan,* which was shortlisted for two national radio awards, and *A Gypsy Wife*. Both plays were performed for Radio 4 by a cast of Roma, Gypsies and Travellers, including Damian Le Bas; Candis Nergaard; Sian Willett; Patricia Keegan; Maryanne, Dean and Sharon Loveridge; along with two non-Travellers, Brodie Ross and Danny Dalton. Reflecting on *Atching Tan,* Allum said: 'As a Traveller it was fascinating for me to write this script, because in many ways I faced the same dilemma when I was young. And although I did take a risk and step out of my community to work in the arts, I've always managed to keep close links with my community both personally and professionally … I've often heard or seen Travellers portrayed on radio, TV or film in such a clichéd way: it's either over-romanticised or just showing the bad side. I guess it shouldn't be surprising, as so few people know anything about the Gypsy community, it's so secretive and tight-knit.' He was impressed by the consideration of these new voices. 'BBC drama have been very sensitive and respectful to the Traveller community throughout and have always kept authenticity at the centre of the work. Even so I never thought in a million years I'd hear Traveller voices speaking the Romani language on Radio 4!' He was looking forward to seeing *Atching Tan* adapted for television, in a move that might be as ground-breaking for mapping Gypsy heritage in the UK as the book and TV series *Roots* was for a generation of black people in the United States.

The poet and ecologist David Morley was also there, to read from his work. Now a professor of creative writing at Warwick University, he had grown up in Blackpool with his mother, who, he said, was a 'half-blood Rom'. He had started writing at the age of twelve, when his father died and he had to earn money to support the family. 'I twigged that this writing work is indoors, and when you write you can disguise your gender and age with a typewriter – you can make it up. And it was easier than doing four paper rounds,' he remembered. 'For me there is always this connection between survival and writing – although in the cosy world of Ivy League universities, this is hard to get over to the great middle classes, that they can be co-equals, a very vital realisation that if you take one away, you take the other.' He then led the audience outside for a reading of some of his sonnets, conceived as a conversation between the nineteenth-century poet John Clare and his friend Wisdom Smith, a local Gypsy. It was a crisp autumn day, which gave the event a feeling of electricity.

He had been drawn to these figures from a time when the travelling lifestyle was more prominent – and the land was already under siege. 'In the New Year, I returned to my writing shed and found Wisdom Smith waiting there like an impatient Daemon,' Morley explained before starting. 'I sat down to work, as did he; and he wrote two sonnets. The next day he wrote three. Since then he has kept me busy on every writing day. The truth is, he is good at sonnets, and strong at dialogue; and his work is crisp, fresh and funny. After letting him take me over for two weeks, I looked at his work, then I looked at my own book – the book I had thought was working. The truth: Wisdom Smith was a better poet than me. His work was more alive than the poems I had spent the previous year writing. It was not "literature" as such – it was life. This was no "sideways and up" movement in voice, but a forward advance. And he was leading me by the nose. And so I gave in and let him. After all, he is writing my book, not me.' He then read some of the sonnets, old *vardos* and chrome caravans surrounding the audience:

The Act
A chorredo has burreder peeas than a Romany Chal.[18]

Wisdom swings to his feet as if pulled by an
    invisible hand.
'I shall show how this world wags without making
    one sound.'
And the Gypsy transforms himself first into a
    lawyer. He bends
a burning eye on invisible jurors. He simpers. He
    stands on his head
as the Judge and thunders silent sentence. Then
    Wisdom levitates
to tip-toe in pity and pride as a Reverend bent
    over his Bible
while an invisible scaffold gasps and bounces from
    a rope's recoil.

> The Gypsy hangs kicking until hacked down by
>   invisible blades.
> The world grinds to a stop on invisible springs,
>   bearings and axis.
> 'Do you ever tell lies, Wisdom?' 'All the long day
>   through, brother,'
> laughs the Gypsy. He lights his long pipe beneath
>   his hat's brim.
> 'But the brassiest of lies' – the Gypsy plucks – 'are
>   like this heather:
> a charm against visible harm and' – he crushes it –
>   'invisible harm.'
> And the friends look at each other across the
>   invisible stage of grass.

Next, Damian Le Bas, editor of *Travellers' Times* but also an accomplished poet, actor and budding playwright, took the stage, sharing a powerful poem about bigotry. It was drawn from a mosaic of real and fictionalised incidents, and described an imagined 'cousin' who had decided that he could not stand by while racist language was hurled at the family. A Gypsy relative of Damian's had driven by a local pub in his wagon, and one of the people at the pub had said: 'The dirty, inbred Pikey cunts – if you ask me the cunts are better off dead.' Damian's cousin had hit the racist with a snooker cue and then left. The poem recounted his cousin's supposed sense of closure:

> And the peace of the dead who took no stick
> Was bought ... so you went and said no word,
> And the breeze was light and cool.

Later in the day, after the readings and lectures were completed, the artists talked together about why such creative enterprises were so important to Gypsy identity in the twenty-first century. For David Morley, the issue was one of straddling two worlds, the one inhabited by the settled community and the other by Gypsies and Travellers, and the perception that everyone is trapped by the restrictions attached to each. Artists are able to move between those worlds, he believed, adding, 'I don't feel trapped in two worlds, I feel free in two worlds. I want to free people. We have got to spring that trap, the language trap, the identity trap.'

Then Dan Allum considered how he related to Morley's two worlds. 'Within the travelling community, you are sort of something different if you are an artist ... so I didn't take negative comments from my community to heart when I started doing stuff. And if people from outside didn't like what I was doing, I don't take notice either. I answer to myself; I work in both worlds, but ultimately it's my world,' he said.

Damian Le Bas had been brought up in a different way. His parents, Delaine and Damian Le Bas Snr, were (and are) both respected visual artists, whose work was selected for the Roma Pavilion at the Venice Biennale in 2007, among many other international art shows. To them, art is crucial in deepening the sense of self-representation within the community – challenging how mainstream culture views and depicts Gypsies and Travellers. Delaine's artwork was often made using brightly coloured textiles, which she sews, embroiders and paints herself, to create vibrant and appealing mixed-media installations that somehow subvert the horror of their subject – usually anti-Gypsyism, gender and nationhood. A recent work, *Witch Hunt*, for example, explores how Gypsies are treated in the UK. She described her goal thus: 'I'm drawing people in by the prettiness of the work, only for them to see that nothing is quite as it seems.' She freely identified herself as part of the Outsider Art community – those who produce from outside the establishment, such as people from minority groups, or those with mental health issues, who are often self-taught.

Her husband, an Irish Traveller with French Manouche Roma and Huguenot roots, started as an artist by sketching football crowds when he was a young child, then went on to study textiles at the Royal College of Art. His work has branched out to involve painting as well as drawing in oil pastel and pencil, and in recent years he has been re-envisioning maps and merging them with portraiture, visually questioning the boundaries of the new Europe, as the Roma nation spills exuberantly across borders. 'The maps I am doing are subversive – the way I am not respecting these borders or, indeed, the inter-bickering within the community,' he said.

The Le Bas family's artwork is in many ways a protest against the lives they have had to live – but they are also committed to gaining ever more exposure and recognition, both for the pieces and for the Gypsy and Traveller experience. Delaine had been campaigning, along with other artists, for several months to support the building of a memorial to the Roma Holocaust in Berlin – a commission that was unveiled in December 2012.[19] As Delaine said, 'You can bring attention to things in a different way through art; it is a powerful medium.' Curiously, though, the pair felt more accepted in the art world beyond Britain – perhaps because their outsider status was less of a threat in Europe and elsewhere. Regardless, their work served as a reminder to their community, that it is possible to do something new, outside of traditional trades – and yet remain true to your identity.

Identity was also in the mind of the Scottish singer-songwriter Ewan MacColl, whose ballad 'The Travelling People' has become almost an anthem. Without Gypsies and Travellers, MacColl argued, the traditional folk music of Britain and Ireland could have died out. These communities passed the old lyrics and music down, generation after generation, for centuries. In his day, MacColl had patiently collected field recordings of both songs and speech in Gypsy and Traveller encampments. Other singers, including June Tabor, soon followed his lead, as well as people from the communities themselves, such as Sheila Stewart, Thomas McCarthy and the Orchard family. Now, some twenty-five years after MacColl's death, such cultural preservation work is being honoured and valued. The young musician Sam Lee was nominated for the Mercury Prize in 2012 for his debut album, *A Ground of its Own,* featuring songs collected from Gypsies and Travellers. Though not a Gypsy or Traveller himself, Lee had trained for four years under the legendary ballad singer Stanley Robertson, a Scottish Traveller.

The resurgence of interest in so-called folk music is not a peculiarly English phenomenon. New bands with Roma roots have formed across Europe, including the Romanian Gypsy bands Taraf de Haidouks and Fanfare Ciocarlia and the Macedonian brass band Kocani Orkestar. The annual Guca Brass Band Festival in Serbia hosts many up-and-coming Roma bands who perform in the traditional style, but there are also new fusion groups combining Gypsy and Traveller sounds with rap, punk and jazz, including Jewish klezmer. Night clubs play records by the Shukar Collective, Besh o droM and Balkan Beat Box – including a special *Nuit Tsigane* ('Gypsy Night') in hot spots such as Le Divan du Monde in Paris. Often, at Appleby and Stow, the young Gypsy men driving cars rather than ponies are listening to this rap or punk-inflected music out of Eastern Europe.

Sam Lee, however, has been more focused on the traditional string music beloved by the older members of the travelling community – songs like 'On Yonder Hill' and 'Goodbye, My Darling' – that he had collected from all over England, Scotland and Ireland. Many of the songs touch on matters of love and separation – but also tell of a steely will to survive. As a young Jewish man from North London, he had been inspired to collect these songs in large part because of learning about the treatment of Gypsies and Travellers in Britain. 'Many are the indigenous people of this country – although Gypsies are not originally from here, the Irish and Scotch Travellers are pre-Celtic, as old a community as you will ever get in Britain. But the treatment they have had was very [similar to] what happened to Native peoples in other places. For instance, in 1968, when sites were opened up here, that was the same year that the Canadian government forcibly settled the Canadian peoples, such as the Inuit ... So there is that amazing time contiguity. There is also the nature of the lifestyle of the older Gypsies. Many were born in tents, and so many have lived outdoors, and because of that, they have this amazing affinity with the outside. To have that regularly enforced on such a deeply ancestral level, is quite a … nature–man relationship that many tribal peoples have.'[20]

Lee had begun by patiently knocking on doors on sites where he didn't know anybody. Mostly he had been welcomed, albeit with some caution, and as families got to know him, he experienced great warmth and hospitality. The fact that he was Jewish – 'another wandering tribe', as he termed it – seemed to help. During his apprenticeship under Robertson, his role was 'keeper of songs'. Most folk singers raid the archives of field recordings gathered by other musicians, most notably those housed in Camden's Cecil Sharp House, considered the home of English folk music. But Sam wanted to hear it from the Romani people themselves – they were not dead, just because their songs had been collected. He said that simple fact came as a surprise to some in the folk scene. 'None of them believed there were any singers out there; they thought it was dead. They didn't know about Gypsy culture; they thought that the precious oral tradition was dead, but actually it's still there. I have recorded songs from fell-pack huntsman, farmers, not just Gypsies – music is alive everywhere. The folk music world just wants its safe world on Radio 2 … It likes soft, fluffy, comfortable stuff. I have brought loads of Gypsy families down to Cecil Sharp House and it's terrifying for them. They sit down in the library and sing these ballads that they have no idea are hundreds of years old. And some people say, "Wow, it's lovely," but they have no idea what to do. It's like bringing the dinosaur into the Natural History Museum and saying, "Hey, watch it dance," and they say they only know about bones.'

He went on: 'Mahler said, "Tradition is tending the flame, not worshipping the ashes," and I think there is a huge amount of ash-worshipping in the folk world … Nobody is putting much effort into keeping the flame alight, and we mustn't let it die.'

Damian Le Bas Jnr said that his culture will survive, despite the oppression that so many continue to suffer in the UK. 'The living culture takes place far away from this analysis, when people are together at a horse fair, having a laugh and a joke. At some point you will get tired of the sad stuff. At home we have a laugh, we talk the Romani language, we reminisce, tell stories, jump on our horses and do nice things that are part of our culture – get some rabbits, cook mutton round a fire. Those nice things don't come across.' This sense of always being able to make it through, no matter the hardships, also rang true to Jake Bowers, the Romani journalist. 'We are shape-shifters. We have an innate defiance in us. I am optimistic about our survival here – after all, things are far worse abroad,' he said. Jake's own life story exemplifies this adaptability. He has just trained as a blacksmith as well as working as a journalist.

The default position is still one of pride in their separate culture and identity. As Robbie McVeigh had noted in 1997: 'Despite their marginalisation and subordination and the internalisation of anti-Traveller racist stereotypes, many Gypsies and Travellers still believe in their superiority. The use of the words "country people" and *gaujos* (which means bumpkin or clod-hopper) to describe all settled people, rural or urban, illustrates the nomad's sense of his or her privilege.'[21] Damian (senior) is aware of this too: 'We are a culture that likes to be separate, that's the elephant in the room – that Travellers don't like to be like anybody else. They might complain about racism, but they would never want to be anybody else, we are proud of our life.'

Jim, Noah Burton's brother, pulled on to the field in Meriden around the same time as Noah, and also lived and worked there until the families were forced to leave in March 2013. As his young family played around him in his spacious caravan, he considered his strong sense of ethnic identity, comparing it with that found among South Asian families: 'We stick together as a community, just as they do, we have similar morals. I feel safe with my family around me. Girls and boys aren't forced to leave home at eighteen. This is the way we have lived, we want to continue the way we live. It's a modern world and we have to make some changes, but to take me and put me in a house? No. I am a wild bird in a hedge, I am a wild bird, don't put me in a cage.'

Noah remained proud of his culture, though he thought some aspects of it were coming to a close. 'It's not that we think being a *gorger* is bad, but we just want to *hang on* to our culture. I know it's a changing culture but it's still pretty good, it's not dying. Look, you're talking to me in one of my friend's trailers, we live in a close-knit social setting, we like to keep near to nature. Here in the UK it's hard for us to up roots and go somewhere else for a few weeks. We have been put off the road really, but we have to adapt and do it differently.'

He paused for a moment, then added: 'We'll blend in, as we are forced off the road, but I was born to this, from my granny and granddad, and from generations back, from my living memory, we have travelled up and down, pulled on fairs, that's who we are. I can't say I'm somebody else, I can't pretend. I can stay in one spot for the rest of my life but it won't change who I am.' He can see the advantages of that – at least in economic terms. Like his brother, he could see the resemblance in the South Asian immigrant experience in the UK. 'You will see us forced off the road and we will be forced into jobs too. And then you'll see us take off – we will earn and do really well, once we adjust to the nine and five, just like Asians. Whites are lazy buggers; they won't work. Indians are very close to us, you know. Language is very similar, and the work ethic, and the family. Once we are more educated, our time will come.'

For Damian and Delaine le Bas, witnessing a rising generation of artists – such as the writer Louise Doughty and the artist Tracey Emin – discover their Gypsy and Traveller roots had proved poignant. 'For these other people who were already professionals, our life hasn't been their life, like going to weddings, funerals and so on,' Damian said. 'We live that life still and they are learning it. There will be a lot more of that to come. When we were in the wilderness, you would never have dreamed of this. But now there are "made" guys coming out as Gypsies, and it's quite interesting: Are we still vagabond beings or are we acceptable now?' But they look further afield as well.

Still, Damian insisted he was 'transnational' – not primarily

British in his mindset. Delaine added: 'The diversity is the thing to concentrate on, rather than the isolationism, that's what is important, being European in a different way and that actually that has lots of possibilities for everyone … We now have an international perspective. This is an important time; things are changing quite quickly; the old way of life is disappearing in front of us. But it's a case of thinking, "What are the possibilities with this, what has enabled us to survive?" And for me it's our adaptability … We are not seeing this as an end, but as a beginning.'

She mentioned one of her projects, entitled *Safe European Home*, which explored the community's feelings of rootlessness. The whole point of the artwork, she said, was to have people think, 'This could be you. That person in that shanty town is not somebody else, it could be you. Greece being a prime example. Suddenly other people are in our position, and how does that feel, how do you deal with that?' The current recession will drive new people into nomadism – and some will find it a positive choice, despite all the hazards and discrimination they will face, just as Damian and Delaine have.

That freedom of movement, the obvious adaptability and resilience of the Roma who had joined Martin Burrell's growing congregation in Luton, coming from homelands as dispersed as Romania and Brazil, was the same spirit that motivated Noah Burton as he travelled from Scotland and Wales to his field in Meriden, then off to 'either Sweden or Switzerland, not sure where really', following the work. What lessons could Noah share about the outmoded notion of an Englishman's home being his castle (defended, of course, tenaciously from having Gypsies as neighbours) in a time when owning property is no longer affordable for so many in the settled community? And what of the traditions that have been lost? As Sam Lee put it, 'So much of what was good has been outmoded by capitalism. We have been sucked into comfort but we have lost a wealth of knowledge and ideas along the way.'

What is a home, and what should it be? In a bold essay published posthumously in the book *The Anatomy of Restlessness*,

Bruce Chatwin wrote: 'Evolution intended us to be travellers. Settlement for any length of time, in cave or castle, has at best been a sporadic condition in the history of man. Prolonged settlement has a vertical axis of some ten thousand years, a drop in the ocean of evolutionary times. We are travellers from birth.'[22] We settled people, Chatwin concluded, take a 'hard line towards nomads', and had no right to the 'rationalised hatred and self-assumed moral superiority' that was used to restrict the Gypsy and Traveller way of life.[23]

After all, the number of migrants – economic nomads of all nationalities – is growing all the time. According to Guy Standing, Professor of Development Studies at the School of Oriental and African Studies, 'the mobility of people around the world has soared with globalisation. One billion people cross national borders every year, and the number is rising'.[24] Some three per cent of the world's population are estimated to be migrants from somewhere other than where they're now living. The world is on the move – we are going to have to get used to this, to find some way of coping with it. We should welcome the richness it can bring to our shores, if managed well, rather than being afraid and mean-spirited. We can learn from Gypsies and Travellers how to be more fleet of foot and adaptable to the changes that the world brings to the very shape of our doorstep.

This is a small island, it is true, but it also remains a wealthy island in the face of the ongoing financial storm. Surely it is big enough to make room for all its citizens. Surely after fifty or a hundred or a thousand years on these shores, as the case may be, Irish and Scotch Travellers and English Gypsies have the same right to be here as any other citizen. But surely we can also afford to be generous to the newly arrived Roma, as well, who are fleeing poverty, persecution and institutionalised discrimination, and who have come here seeking a better life, one for which they are all too keen to work. They have as much right to be here as any other citizens of the EU. It is time to stop living apart in this informal and invisible apartheid and try to start living together, more comfortably, side by side. These nomads, when all is said and done, are our neighbours – and we have much to learn from them. As Delaine Le Bas says, we need to create structures that allow all of us to be part of the world, in an equal but interesting way. 'There is a space is for everyone … Not just for the chosen few.'

On 1 December 2012, a grey winter's day, I drove back to Essex, to the parish of Wickford, near Dale Farm. The Sheridan family had invited me to join them at their local church, Our Lady of Good Counsel, in Wickford, to celebrate the confirmation of Nora's youngest son, Jimmy Tom, and Michelle's middle son, Patrick. Twenty-seven other children from Dale Farm would be celebrating their first communion or their confirmation with them that day.

I'd lost count of the times I'd driven up to Dale Farm with a cold feeling clutching at my stomach. I knew I was going to see families I had come to know so well and to like, experiencing yet more troubles. But this time was different. This time I was driving to see the Dale Farm families and to be part of a happier moment in their lives.

I got there just before eleven, and was greeted by Candy, who had stayed overnight to sort out drivers' licences for several of the men. Soon the stretch limos started to arrive – cream, pink, gleaming black. A procession of beautifully coiffured girls, their hair curled and studded with stars and glitter, fell out of them. Their white dresses, some even made by Thelma Madine, the so-called 'Gypsy dressmaker' up in Liverpool, were pure meringue. The boys were also turned out smartly, in blue shirts and beige suits. The proud mothers were resplendent, with glitter on their hair, tiny fascinators, and diamanté shoes. Nora and Michelle both had their hair up, and in blue and purple lace respectively, looked absolutely stunning. The men had all got back from working away in order to attend the celebration, and were got up in natty suits.

I recalled how many of them had no access to running water or electricity, and were struggling to make ends meet on the roadside. They had saved up for months so that their children would have a beautiful confirmation that they would remember for the rest of their lives. There was a lot of love in that church – and a lot of photographers, too, so many that the new priest, Father John, forced the snappers out into the hallway because he was finding it so disruptive. 'This is the House of God. Respect it,' he said as he ushered them out.

During the service, Jimmy Tom and one of Michelle's boys, John, read out prayers in their clear, bright trebles. The liturgy was read and then the priest said a few words about the lesson of the five loaves and two fishes that miraculously divided so that a congregation of five thousand could eat. The feeding of the multitude: a fitting act of faith, given the wing and prayer with which the residents at Dale Farm were somehow still surviving in spite of everything. Then the children were asked to come up to take their first communion, the girls struggling to contain their enormous skirts. The younger children were next handed their confirmation certificates. At this point, Father John allowed the photographers to come to the altar. There was a bit of a scrum, but something very real and vibrant could be felt in the church, as this community came all together, perhaps for the last time. Sean Risdale from the Irish Traveller Movement was sitting next to Candy and me. Quietly, he said, 'They are undefeated, somehow, despite everything.' This was true. Looking on and holding back tears, Candy reflected: 'There they all were, helping each other with each other's children, as they had done for so long, all dressed up for that special moment for children brought up in the Catholic faith. I knew they'd come from the roadside and they'd go back there that night. But they had this glimmer, this moment's glory and they were enjoying it.' And they were.

Later, as I stood with Nora and Michelle watching the family get themselves ready for yet more photographs for the album, Nora said proudly, 'We're still here. Together.' And then she put her arms around her boys, as the cameras clicked away.

ACKNOWLEDGEMENTS

I couldn't have written this book without the help of so many Romani Gypsies, Scotch and Irish Travellers, as well as Roma newly arrived in the UK. I thank them all for their help. I'm also very grateful to the many academics, politicians, police officers, artists and campaigners (on both sides of the fence) who have given up their time so generously, for a number of years, to talk with me.

In particular, I'd like to thank those who took the time to discuss, read or comment on sections of the book: Thomas Acton, Alice Bloch, Jake Bowers, Stuart Carruthers, Dan Allum, Damian Le Bas (Junior and Senior), Delaine Le Bas, Margaret Greenfields, Tom Green, Ian Hancock, Sebastian Hesse, Johnny Howorth, Zoe James, Donald Kenrick, Ann Kobayashi, Robbie McVeigh, John Pring, Grattan Puxon, Sean Risdale, Candy Sheridan, Jess Smith and Tony Thomson.

I'd like to thank the following families for their help and patience: the Burton family, the McCarthy family, the Sheridan family and the Townsley family, as well as the Gammells, the Egans, the Flynns, the Welch family, the Le Bas family and the Smith family. I'd also like to thank the many members of the Light and Life church who have been kind enough to talk to me, particularly Walter Smith, Davey Jones, Jackie Boyd and others, as well as Martin Burrell and the Roma families in his Luton congregation, and the other church people from different Christian traditions, in particular Father Dan Mason and the Reverend Robert Norwood. Thanks also to Vera Norwood for introducing me to the people of Stow Fair and for her generosity, time and trouble.

Particular thanks go to the family of Johnny Delaney, who were generous to give up their time to talk about Johnny's life and his death, at just fifteen.

Thank you to so many organisations who have helped me with background research, contacts and advice: the Gypsy Council; the Irish Traveller Movement in Britain; Leeds GATE; Families, Friends and Travellers; Liverpool Services for Gypsy and Traveller Families; Romani Arts; the University of Huddersfield and the Traveller Solidarity Network. I'd like to pay tribute to the Irish Traveller organisations in the Republic, whose work I have drawn on in this book, most notably Pavee Point, Donegal Irish Traveller Project and Nexus.

I would like to express thanks to my wonderful agent, Andrew Lownie, who has supported my career as a writer for many years. I'd also like to thank all at my publisher, Oneworld, in particular my editor, Robin, and the marketing and publicity team of Henry Jeffreys, Lamorna Elmer and Alan Bridger. Thank you to the Society of Authors, for providing me with a much-needed grant. Thanks also to my editors at *The Economist*, Merril Stevenson and Joel Budd, who have allowed me to write so much on the communities over the past six years, my friend and editor Tim Minogue (and others) at *Private Eye*, Mark Townsend at the *Guardian/Observer*, as well as Nick Pyke at the *Mail on Sunday* and Laura Davis at the *Independent*.

A special thanks to Sebastian Hesse and Tom Green, whose photographs appear in this book and enrich it on every level. Thanks also to the family of Dennis Sheridan, who allowed us to put his picture on the cover of *No Place to Call Home* — and thanks to Mary Turner, who photographed him.

The deepest thanks, as always, go to my family – Mary, Michael, Tom, Josie, Raffy, Paul, Margaret, John, Tiffany, Chris, Jane and children – and friends. I am always in your debt.

FURTHER READING

Thomas Acton, *Gypsy Politics and Social Change* (London: Routledge and Kegan Paul, 1974)

Thomas Acton (ed.), *Gypsy Politics and Traveller Identity* (Hatfield: University of Hertfordshire Press, 1997)

Thomas Acton (ed.), *Scholarship and the Gypsy Struggle* (Hatfield: University of Hertfordshire Press, 2000)

Zygmunt Baumann, *Modernity and the Holocaust* (Cambridge: Polity Press, 1989)

Howard Becker, *The Outsiders* (New York: The Free Press, 1963)

George Borrow, *Lavengro* (London: Nelson, 1851)

Martin Burrell, *The Pure in Heart, An Epistle from the Romanies* (Milton Keynes: Author House, 2009)

Bruce Chatwin, *Anatomy of Restlessness* (London: Jonathan Cape, 1996)

John Clare, *By Himself* (Manchester: Carcanet Press, 2002)

Colin Clark and Margaret Greenfields, *Here to Stay: The Gypsies and Travellers of Britain* (Hatfield: University of Hertfordshire Press, 2006)

William Cobbett, *Rural Rides* (London: Penguin, 2001)

Stanley Cohen, *Folk Devils and Moral Panics* (Oxford: Routledge Classics, 2011)

Robert Dawson, *Empty Lands* (Alfreton: Robert Dawson, 2007)

Robert Dawson, *Times Gone* (Alfreton: Robert Dawson, 2007)

Eammon Dillon, *The Outsiders* (Dublin: Merlin Publishing, 2006)

Fiona Earle, Alan Dearling, et al., *A Time to Travel: An Introduction to Britain's Newer Travellers* (Lyme Regis: Enabler Publications, 1994)

Isobel Fonseca, *Bury Me Standing, The Gypsies and Their Journey* (London: Chatto and Windus, 1995)

Angus Fraser, *The Gypsies* (Oxford: Blackwells, 1992)

Roxy Freeman, *Little Gypsy* (London: Simon and Schuster, 2011)

George Gmelch, *The Irish Tinkers: The Urbanization of an Itinerant People* (Prospect Heights: Waveland Press, 1985)

Erving Goffman, *Stigma* (London: Pelican, 1968)

Ian Hancock, *The Pariah Syndrome: An Account of Gypsy Slavery and Persecution* (Ann Arbor, Michigan: Karoma Publishers, 1987)

Ian Hancock, *We are the Romani People* (Hatfield: University of Hertfordshie Press, 2002)

D. Hawes and B. Perez, *The Gypsy and the State: The Ethnic Cleansing of British Society* (Bristol: Policy Press, 1996)

Jane Helleiner, *Irish Travellers: Racism and the Politics of Culture* (Toronto: University of Toronto Press, 2000)

Kevin Hetherington, *New Age Travellers: Vanloads of Uproarious Humanity* (London: Cassell, 2000)

Nan Joyce (and Anna Farmar), *My Life on the Road* (Dublin: A. and A. Farmar, 2000)

Donald Kenrick and Colin Clark, *Moving On: The Gypsies and Travellers of Britain* (Hatfield: University of Hertfordshire Press, 1999)

Donald Kenrick and Grattan Puxon, *The Destiny of Europe's Gypsies* (London: Heinemann, 1972)

Donald Kenrick and Grattan Puxon, *Gypsies under the Swastika* (Hatfield: University of Hertfordshire Press, 2009)

Charles Leland, *The English Gypsies and their Language* (London, 1873)

J.P. Liegeois and N. Gheorghe, *Roma/Gypsies: A European Minority* (London: Minority Rights Group, 1995)

Richard Lowe and William Shaw *Travellers, Voices of the New Age Nomads*, (London: Fourth Estate, 1993)

Robert Macfarlane, *The Old Ways* (London: Hamish Hamilton, 2012)

George McKay, *Senseless Acts of Beauty* (London: Verso, 1996)

Jim MacLaughlin, *Travellers and Ireland* (Cork: Cork University Press, 1995)

Alen MacWeeney, *Irish Travellers: Tinkers No More*, (Henniker, NH: New England College Press, 2007)

David Mayall, *Gypsy-Travellers in Nineteenth Century Society* (Cambridge: Cambridge University Press, 1988)

Henry Mayhew, *Mayhew's London* (London: Hamyln, 1969)

David Morley, *The Invisible Kings*, (Manchester: Carcanet, 2007)

Rachel Morris and Luke Clements (eds), *Gaining Ground: Law Reform for Gypsies and Travellers* (Hatfield: University of Hertfordshire Press, 1999)

Rachel Morris and Luke Clements, *At What Cost? The Economics of Gypsy and Traveller Encampments* (Bristol: Policy Press, 2002)

Judith Oakley, *The Traveller-Gypsies* (Cambridge: Cambridge University Press, 1983)

Colm Power, *Room to Roam: England's Irish Travellers* (London: Action Group for Irish Youth, 2004)

Grattan Puxon, *Freeborn Traveller* (Dublin: Small World Media, 2007)

Farnham Rehfisch (ed.), *Gypsies, Tinkers and other Travellers* (London: Academic Press, 1975)

Dominic Reeve, *Smoke in the Lanes* (London: Constable and Co, 1958)

Sandy Reid, *Never to Return* (Edinburgh: Black and White Publishing, 2008)

Ramona Constantin and Ciara Leeming, *Elvira and Me* (The Big Issue in the North Trust, 2012)

Jeremy Sandford, *Gypsies* (London: Secker and Warburg, 1973)

David Sibley, *Outsiders in an Urban Society* (Oxford: Basil Blackwell, 1981)

Charles Smith, *Not all Wagons and Lanes* (Essex: Essex County Council, 1995)

Jess Smith, *Jessie's Journey* (Edinburgh: Mercat Press, 2002)

Jess Smith, *Sookin' Berries* (Edinburgh: Birlinn Limited, 2009)

Maggie Smith-Bendell, *Rabbit Stew and a Penny or Two* (London: Abacus, 2010)

Southwark Women's Traveller Group, *Moving Stories, Traveller Women Write* (London: Traveller Education Team, Southwark, 1992)

Guy Standing, *The Precariat* (London: Bloomsbury Academic, 2011)

C.J. Stone, *Fierce Dancing* (London: Faber & Faber, 1996)

C.J. Stone, *The Last of the Hippies* (London: Faber & Faber, 1999)

Mikey Walsh, *Gypsy Boy* (London: Hodder and Stoughton, 2009)

Andy Worthington, *The Battle of the Beanfield*, (Lyme Regis: Enabler, 2005)

NOTES

INTRODUCTION

1   The research has been conducted by Turi King and Matt Sears in the Jobling Lab at the University of Leicester. The results are expected to be released in 2013. www2.le.ac.uk/projects/impact-of-diasporas/the-Romani-in-britain-projecth

1. 'CHANCE OF A LIFETIME'

1   Author interviews with Mary Ann McCarthy, 30 March 2006, 6 August 2010, 28 August 2011, 30 August 2011, April 2013, and phone interviews in 2006, 2007, summer 2009, 29 July 2010, 2012

2   Author interviews with Grattan Puxon, 30 March 2006, 19 September 2011, 18 October 2011, 6 and 11 January 2012, 6 February 2012, 19 June 2012, 19 October 2012, and subsequent email correspondence

3   Author interviews with Len Gridley, 19 September 2011, 24 May 2012, and subsequent phone interviews and local meetings, including church rooms, Wickford, 10 January 2013

4   Austin, Jon, 'How did Dale Farm get so big?', 9 December 2006, www.echo-news.co.uk/echofeatures/1065414.How_did_Dale_Farm_get_so_big_/

5   Austin, Jon, 'Trustee quits from Gypsy Council following *Echo* exposé', 21 April 2009, www.echo-news.co.uk/news/local_news/basildon/4305149.Trustee_quits_from_Gypsy_Council_following_Echo_expose/

6   Advocacy Net, 2005, 'Report: Evictions report of Roma and Irish Travellers', www.advocacynet.org/resource/466

7   Author interview with John Prescott, 17 December 2012. Subsequent quotes in this book are also from this interview.

8   BBC News, 'Timeline: Dale Farm Evictions', 19 October 2011, www.bbc.co.uk/news/uk-england-15367736

9   Author interviews with Sean Risdale, 19 September 2011, 19 October

2011, 26 September 2012, 13 October 2012, 30 November 2012, and subsequent email correspondence

10 Quarmby, Katharine, 'The siege of Dale Farm', *The Economist*, 6 April 2006, www.economist.com/node/6775075

11 Hansard, House of Commons Adjournment Debate, 14 July 2005, www.publications.parliament.uk/pa/cm200506/cmhansrd/vo050714/debtext/50714-31.htm

12 Author interview with Bryan LeCoche, Constant and Company, 4 April 2006; this interview was conducted for the article 'The siege of Dale Farm', *The Economist*, 6 April 2006

2. NEIGHBOURS AND NOMADS

1 Author interviews in 2006 and later, as well as other recollections recorded by the Irish Traveller Movement in Britain for a DVD, *Irish Travellers Talk about Their History* (2009)

2 Hancock, Ian, *The Pariah Syndrome* (Ann Arbor, Michigan: Karoma Publishers, 1986), www.reocities.com/~patrin/pariah-ch11.htm

3 Ibid.

4 Ibid., p. 113

5 Fraser, Angus, *The Gypsies* (Oxford: Blackwells, 2007), p. 112

6 Vesey-FitzGerald, Brian Seymour, *Gypsies of Britain* (Newton Abbot: David & Charles Ltd, 1973)

7 Weber, Leanne, and Benjamin Bowling, 'Valiant beggars and global vagabonds', *Theoretical Criminology* 12, 2008, p. 355; Beier, A.L., *Masterless Men* (London: Routledge, 1985)

8 Hancock, Ian, *We are the Romani People* (Hatfield: University of Hertfordshire Press, 2002), p. 21

9 Ibid., p. 26

10 McVeigh, Robbie, 'Therorising sedentarism: the roots of anti-nomadism' in Thomas Acton (ed.), *Gypsy Politics and Traveller Identity* (Hatfield: University of Hertfordshire Press, 1985), p. 19

11 Fraser, *The Gypsies*, pp. 113–14

12 Beier, *Masterless Men*, p. 64

13 Ibid.

14 Cohen, Stanley, *Folk Devils and Moral Panics* (Oxford: Routledge Classics, 2011)

15 Fraser, *The Gypsies*, pp. 123–6

16 Ibid., p. 130

17 Roberts, Samuel, *The Gypsies: Their Origin, Continuance, and Destination* (London: Longman, 1836), cited in Fraser, *The Gypsies*, p. 134.

18 Fraser, *The Gypsies*, p. 140.

19 Mayall, David, *Gypsy-Travellers in Nineteenth Century Society* (Cambridge: Cambridge University Press, 1988), p. 42

20 Kenrick, Donald and Grattan Puxon, *Gypsies under the Swastika*, (Hatfield: University of Hertfordshire Press, 2009), p. 9

21 Cobbett, William, *Rural Rides* (London: Penguin, 2001), pp. 44–5

22 Mayall, *Gypsy-Travellers*, p. 151

23 Ibid., p. 153

24 Ibid., p. 20

25 Ibid., pp. 153–4

26 Ibid., p. 156

27 Weber and Bowling, 'Valiant beggars and global vagabonds', p. 355

28 McMullan, John L., 'The arresting eye: Discourse, surveillance and disciplinary administration in early English police thinking', *Social and Legal Studies* 7, 1998, p. 97

29 Ibid.

30 Colquhoun, Patrick, quoted in McMullan, 'The arresting eye', p. 97

31 Chadwick, Edwin, 1839, quoted in McMullan, ibid.

32 Turner, Royce, 'Gypsies and parliamentary language: An analysis', *Romani Studies*, Series 5, 12:1, 2002, p. 5

33 Grellman, Heinrich M., *Dissertation on the Gipseys: Representing their Manner of Life, Family Economy. With an Historical Enquiry Concerning their Origin and First Appearance in Europe*, trans. Matthew Raper (London: Ballantine, 1807)

34 Hancock, Ian, 'George Borrow's Romani', in Pater Bakker (ed.), *The Typology and Dialectology of Romani* (Amsterdam and Philadelphia: John Benjamins, 1998), pp. 65–89

35 Ibid.

36 Ibid.

37 Behlmer, George K., 'The Gypsy problem in Victorian England', *Victorian Studies* 28:2, 1985, p. 243

38 Mayhew, Henry, *London Labour and London Poor* (London: Griffin, Bohn, and Company, 1861, vol. 1)

39 Himmelfarb, Gertrude, 'The culture of poverty', in H.J. Dyos and Michael Wolff (eds), *The Victorian City: Images and Reality* (London and Boston: Routledge and Kegan Paul, 1973, vol. 2), p. 715

40 Samuel, Raphael, 'Comers and goers', in Dyos and Wolff, *The Victorian City*, p. 153

41 Wilkinson, T.W., quoted in ibid., p. 130

42 Hancock, Ian, 'Marko', in *Special Issue: Gypsies, Index on Censorship*, 27:4, 1998, www.radoc.net/radoc.php?doc=art_a_intro_marko&lang=en

43 Raphael Samuel, 'Comers and goers', in Dyos and Wolff, *The Victorian City*, p. 153

44 Mayhew, Henry, quoted in ibid., p. 138

45 Ibid.

46 MacLaughlin, Jim, 1999, 'Nation-building, social closure and anti-Traveller racism in Ireland', *Sociology* 33, 1999, p. 129

47 Mayall, David, *English Gypsies and State Policies* (Hatfield: University of Hertfordshire Press, 1985), p. 34

48 Smith, George, *Gipsy Life* (London: Haughton and Co, 1880, vol. 4), www.gutenberg.org/files/28548/28548-h/28548-h.htm

49 Acton, Thomas, *Gypsy Politics and Social Change* (London and Boston, MA: Routledge and Kegan Paul, 1974), p. 120

50 Kenrick, Donald, and Colin Clark, *Moving On: The Gypsies and Travellers of Britain* (Hatfield: University of Hertfordshire Press, 1995), p. 52

51 Dawson, Robert, *Empty Lands* (Alfreton: Robert Dawson, 2007), p. 17

52 Kenrick and Clark, *Moving On*, pp. 53–4

53 'Report from the Departmental Committee On Habitual Offenders, Vagrants, Beggars, Inebriates, And Juvenile Delinquents' (Edinburgh: Neill and Co, 1895), summary at gdl.cdlr.strath.ac.uk/haynin/haynin0205.htm

54 Dawson, *Empty Lands*, p. 93

55 Ibid., p. 95

56 Ibid., pp. 103–4

57 Ibid., pp. 126–7

58 Reid, Sandy, *Never to Return* (Edinburgh: Black and White Publishing, 2008)

59 Burton, Basil, et al., 2008, 'Remembering our families', www.newforestRomanigypsytraveller.co.uk/stories11.html

60 Ivey, Joe, 'Our New Forest: A living register of languages and traditions', www.newforestcentre.org.uk/uploads/publications/65.pdf

61 Smith, Charles, *Not all Wagons and Lanes* (Essex: Essex County Council, 1995), p. 21

62 Although I use the term 'Roma' throughout the discussion of European nomadic peoples, the Roma are merely the largest nomadic group on the continent. The second largest group, the Sinti, were also persecuted during the Holocaust, and the estimated numbers of those who were deported or killed, or who died, include both Roma and Sinti.

63 Kenrick and Puxon, *Gypsies Under the Swastika*, p. 153

64 The deportation involved all Roma and some Sinti peoples.

65 'Transcript of the official shorthand notes of the trial of Joseph Kramer and 44 others', www.bergenbelsen.co.uk/pages/TrialTranscript/Trial_Day_013.html; 'Strangers in a strange land', www.humanityinaction.org/knowledgebase/278-strangers-in-a-strange-land-roma-and-sinti-in-the-netherlands-the-world-war-two-experience-and-after; Lifton, Robert Jay, 'What made this man?', *New York Times*, 21 July 1985, www.wellesley.edu/Polisci/wj/100/mengle.htm,

66 Kenrick and Puxon, *Gypsies under the Swastika*, pp. 146–8

67 Ibid., p. 156

68 Hancock, *We are the Romani People*, p. 48

69 Kenrick, Donald, and Gillian Taylor, *Historical Dictionary of the Gypsies (Romanies)* (Lanham, MD: Scarecrow Press, 1998), p. 4

70 grthm.natt.org.uk/timeline.php

71 Smith, Charles, *Not all Wagons and Lanes*, p. 22

3. NEVER AGAIN

1 Among their many collaborations, Donald Kenrick and Grattan Puxon wrote the first, much-acclaimed history of the extermination of European Roma. Thomas Acton, now Emeritus Professor of Romani Studies at the University of Greenwich, has charted the social, artistic and political changes in the Romani communities of Britain and the rise of Roma activism in Europe. He has spent the past few decades publishing most of the seminal books on the subject published in the UK.

2 Acton, Thomas, *Gypsy Politics and Social Change*, (London and Boston, MA: Routledge and Kegan Paul, 1974), p. 206

3 MacLaughlin, Jim, 'Nation-building, social closure and anti-Traveller racism in Ireland', *Sociology* 33, 1999, p. 129

4 Ni Shuinear, Sinead, 'Why do Gaujos hate Gypsies so much, anyway? A case study' in Acton, *Gypsy Politics and Traveller Identity*, p. 39

5 Helleiner, Jane, *Irish Travellers: Racism and the Politics of Culture* (Toronto: University of Toronto Press, 2000), p. 65

6 Author interviews with Nora Sheridan, 30 March 2006; 6 August 2010; 2 August 2011; 19 September 2011; 19 October 2011; 11 November 2011; 6 and 11 January 2012; 23 February 2012; 2, 12 and 24 May 2012; 20 June 2012; 19 August 2012; 6 and 28 September 2012; 15 October 2012; 1 and 10 December 2012; 10 January 2013; 28 February 2013

7 Author interviews with Candy Sheridan, 12 May 2011, 2 August 2011, 30 August 2011, 19 September 2011, 12 October 2011, 19

October 2011, 28 December 2011, 9 May 2012, 15 and 30 October 2012, 1 December 2012, and subsequent phone interviews and email correspondence

8   First Government Commission on Itinerancy (CI), 1963, p. 111
9   Helleiner, *Irish Travellers*, p. 61
10 Ibid., p. 71
11 First Government Commission on Itinerancy, p. 37
12 Ni Shuinear, Sinead, 'Why do Gaujos hate Gypsies so much, anyway?', pp. 40–1
13 MacLaughlin, 'Nation-building', p. 129
14 Ibid.
15 Ibid.
16 Gmelch, George, *The Irish Tinkers* (Prospect Heights: Waveland Press, 1985), p. 45
17 Ibid., p. 48
18 Puxon, Grattan, *Freeborn Traveller* (Dublin: Small World Media, 2007), p. 19
19 Acton, *Gypsy Politics and Traveller Identity*, p. 156
20 Burke, Mary, *Travellers* (Oxford: Oxford University Press, 2009), p. 206
21 www.youtube.com/watch?v=jR3mNrQ4lr0&feature=plcp
22 MacWeeney, Alen, *Irish Travellers: Tinkers No More* (Henniker, NH: New England College Press, 2007), p. 3
23 Joyce, Nan, and Anna Farmar, *My Life on the Road: A Traveller's Autobiography* (Dublin: A. and A. Farmar, 2000), p. 68
24 Grattan Puxon discussed these events with me in an interview in January 2012 while he was supervising a digger at Dale Farm.
25 Bhreathnach, Aoife, 2006, quoted in McVeigh, Robbie, *Travellers and the Troubles* (Donegal: Donegal Travellers Project, 2006), p. 30
26 Acton, *Gypsy Politics and Traveller Identity*, p. 156
27 Joyce, *My Life on the Road*, pp. 72–4
28 McVeigh, *Travellers and the Troubles*, p. 4
29 Ibid., p. 10
30 Ibid., p. 15
31 Morris, quoted in McVeigh, ibid.
32 McVeigh, ibid.
33 McVeigh, Robbie, 'Irish Travellers and the logic of genocide', in Michel Peillon and Tony Fahy (eds), *Encounters with Modern Ireland* (Dublin: IPA, 1997)
34 BBC News, 'Home targeted in petrol bombing', 21 February 2005, news.bbc.co.uk/1/hi/northern_ireland/4283005.stm

35 McVeigh, *Travellers and the Troubles*, p. 33
36 Ibid., p. 34
37 Ibid.
38 Burke, *Travellers*, pp. 206–7
39 Quoted in Acton, *Gypsy Politics and Social Change*, p. 163
40 Ibid., p. 173
41 'Gauje' is the term commonly used by Gypsies to refer to non-Gypsies. There is no widely accepted spelling of the word and it sometimes appears as 'gorger' (which closest reflects its pronunciation), 'gorgio', 'gorgia', 'gorgie', 'gaje' or 'gaujo'.
42 Quoted in Acton, *Gypsy Politics and Social Change*, p. 207
43 'Migration and settlement in late 20th-century Birmingham', www.connectinghistories.org.uk/Learning%20Packages/Migration/migration_settlement_20c_lp_04a.asp
44 Ibid.
45 *Guardian*, 3 July 1963
46 *Birmingham Mail*, 9 July 1963
47 Quoted in Acton, *Gypsy Politics and Social Change*, p. 175
48 Author interviews with Joseph Jones, 10 May 2012, 25 October 2012, 10 January 2013
49 'Tinkers', ATV Today, 16 September 1968, www.macearchive.org/Archive/Title/atv-today-16091968-tinkers/MediaEntry/12.html
50 MacColl, Ewan, and Peggy Seeger, 'Terror Time', 1966, lyrics at mysongbook.de/msb/songs/t/terrorti.html. All rights reserved.
51 Joyce and Farmar, *My Life on the Road*, p. 74
52 Okely, Judith, *The Traveller Gypsies* (Cambridge: Cambridge University Press, 1983), p. 19
53 Ibid.
54 Author interview with Eric Lubbock, 30 March 2012, and subsequently on a visit to Dale Farm. He became 4th Baron Avebury in 1971, so he is referred to as Lord Avebury.
55 Acton, *Gypsy Politics and Social Change*, p. 212
56 West Midlands Gypsy Liaison Group Report, 1973, www.connectinghistories.org.uk/Learning%20Packages/Migration/migration_settlement_20c_lp_04a.asp [MS 4000/1/8/19 reports file]
57 'Vox pop on Irish Travellers in Walsall', ATV Today, 23 September 1970, www.macearchive.org/Archive/Title/atv-today-23091970-vox-pop-on-tinkers-in-walsall/MediaEntry/15071.html
58 Kenrick, Donald, and Sian Bakewell, *On the Verge* (Hatfield: University of Hertfordshire Press, 1990), p. 26
59 Crowley, Una, 'Outside in Dublin: Travellers, society and the state

1963–1985', *Canadian Journal of Irish Studies* 35, 2009, pp. 17–24, eprints.nuim.ie/3025/1/UC_Backup_of_JCH_final.pdf

60 Joyce, *My Life on the Road*, p. 101

61 Ibid., p. 26

62 Ibid., p. 115

63 Helleiner, Jane, 'Traveller settlement in Galway city: Politics, class, and culture', in Chris Curtin, Hastings Donnan and Tom Wilson (eds), *Irish Urban Cultures* (Belfast: Institute of Irish Studies, 1993), p. 191

64 Garner, Steve, *Racism in the Irish Experience* (London: Pluto, 2004), p. 60

65 Cripps, John, *Accommodation for Gypsies: A Report on the Working of the Caravan Sites Act 1968* (Cardiff: Department of Environment Welsh Office, 1977)

66 Smith-Bendell, Maggie, *Rabbit Stew or a Penny or Two* (London: Abacus, 2010), pp. 256–7

67 Hansard, Parliamentary debate about Gypsies, 29 June 1977, hansard. millbanksystems.com/commons/1977/jun/29/gipsies

68 The papers were only released to the public in 2004. Casciani, Dominic, '"Prejudice" defeated Gypsy reform', BBC News, 14 May 2004, news.bbc.co.uk/1/hi/uk/3704167.stm

69 Marilyn Fletcher responded to emailed questions on 30 June 2012

4. NEW TRAVELLERS AND THE EYE OF SAURON

1 Dearling, Alan, 'Not only but also … some ramblings about the English festivals scene', 2001, www.enablerpublications.co.uk/pdfs/notonly1.pdf

2 Clark, Colin, 'New Age Travellers: Identity, sedentarism and social security', in Acton, *Gypsy Politics and Traveller Identity*, pp. 125–41

3 Mackay, George, *Senseless Acts of Beauty* (London: Verso, 1996), p. 11

4 Ibid., pp. 46–7

5 Ibid., pp. 36–9

6 Davis, J., R. Grant and A. Locke, *Out of Site, Out of Mind: New Age Travellers and the Criminal Justice and Public Order Bill* (London: The Children's Society, 1994), p. 6

7 Martin, Greg, 'New Age Travellers: Uproarious or uprooted?', *Sociology* 36:3, 2002, pp. 723–35

8 Author interview with Tony Thomson, 12 March 2012

9 Freeman, Roxy, *Little Gypsy* (London: Simon and Schuster, 2011), p. 36

10 Mackay, *Senseless Acts of Beauty*, p. 33

11 Reilly, Gill, '"The enemy within": Thatcher's secret war on CND revealed', *Daily Mail*, 7 January 2012, www.dailymail.co.uk/news/article-2083489/Margaret-Thatchers-secret-war-CND-revealed.html

12 Clark, 'New Age Travellers: Identity, sedentarism and social security', in Acton, *Gypsy Politics and Traveller Identity*, p. 129

13 Lowe, Richard, and William Shaw, *Travellers: Voices of the New Age Nomads* (London: Fourth Estate, 1993), p. 68

14 Ibid., pp. 91–2

15 Freeman, *Little Gypsy*, p. 74

16 Clark, 'New Age Travellers', in Acton, *Gypsy Politics and Traveller Identity*, p. 129

17 Hansard, 'Hippy convoy (New Forest) debate', 3 June 1986, hansard.millbanksystems.com/commons/1986/jun/03/hippy-convoy-new-forest

18 Clark, Colin, and Donald Kenrick, *Moving On: The Gypsies and Travellers of Britain* (Hatfield: University of Hertfordshire Press, 1995), p. 105

19 Turner, 'Gypsies and Parliamentary language', pp. 1–34

20 Hansard, 'Itinerants Debate', 15 June 1989, hansard.millbanksystems.com/commons/1989/jun/15/itinerants

21 Ibid.

22 Conservative Party press release, 1992, quoted in Luke Clements and Sue Campbell, 'The Criminal Justice and Public Order Act and its implications for Travellers' in Acton, *Gypsy Politics and Traveller Identity*, p. 61

23 McVeigh, 'Therorising sedentarism' in Acton, *Gypsy Politics and Traveller Identity*, p. 6

24 Ibid., p. 7. Later, of course, Central and Eastern Roma were in newspaper sightlines too. Shortly before the accession of Eastern Europe countries into the EU in 2004, the *Daily Express* warned off the Roma in a series of front-page stories featuring headlines such as 'Gypsies: You can't come in'.

25 Hansard, Criminal Justice and Public Order Bill, Second Reading, 11 January 1994, hansard.millbanksystems.com/commons/1994/jan/11/criminal-justice-and-public-order-bill

26 Clements and Campbell, 'The Criminal Justice and Public Order Act' in Acton, *Gypsy Politics and Traveller Identity*, p. 61

27 Mackay, *Senseless Acts of Beauty*, p. 49

28 Howard, Michael, 1994, quoted in Mackay, ibid., p. 161

29 Hansard, 'Gipsies, Essex debate', 19 June 1995, hansard. millbanksystems.com/commons/1995/jun/19/gipsies-essex

5. THINGS CAN ONLY GET BETTER

1 Andrew Mackay from a debate on 'Law of Trespass', *Hansard*, 15 January 2002.

2 Power, Colm, *Room to Roam: England's Irish Travellers* (London: Action Group for Irish Youth, 2004)

3 BBC News, 'Boys guilty of killing "Gypsy"', 28 November 2003, news.bbc.co.uk/1/hi/england/merseyside/3246518.stm

4 Townsend, Mark, 'A burning issue in the village', *Observer*, 16 November 2003, www.guardian.co.uk/society/2003/nov/16/ raceintheuk.uknews

5 Ellinor, Rebecca, 'Gypsy caravan burnt in village bonfire', *Guardian*, 31 October 2003, www.guardian.co.uk/uk/2003/oct/31/race.world1

6 Payne, Stewart, 'Outrage as "gipsies" are set alight at village party', *Telegraph,* 20 November 2003, www.telegraph.co.uk/ education/3321895/Outrage-as-gipsies-are-set-alight-at-village-party. html

7 Hansard, 'Travellers' sites', 19 November 2003, www.publications. parliament.uk/pa/cm200203/cmhansrd/vo031119/halltext/31119h04. htm

8 Bowers, Jake, and A. Benjamin, 'Pitch battles', *Guardian*, 28 July 2004, www.guardian.co.uk/society/2004/jul/28/politics.localgovernment

9 www.planningportal.gov.uk/general/news/stories/2005/mar/2005-03-Week-4/gypsyplan

10 Author interview with Eric Pickles, 2010, conducted for *The Economist*. Since then, I have requested further interviews with Mr Pickles on several occasions, in both 2012 and 2013, but he has not been available.

11 'This is dangerous, vile nonsense', *Guardian*, 23 March 2005, www. guardian.co.uk/uk/2005/mar/23/race.budget2005

12 Hinsliff, Gaby, 'Howard: I'll clear illegal Gypsy sites', *Guardian*, 20 March 2005, www.guardian.co.uk/politics/2005/mar/20/ conservatives.localgovernment; Happold, Tom, 'Tories back *Sun*'s Gypsy campaign', *Guardian*, 18 March 2005, www.guardian.co.uk/ politics/2005/mar/18/media.media?INTCMP=ILCNETTXT3487

13 Barkham, Patrick, 'Gypsy groups report the *Sun* to the police', *Guardian*, 10 March 2005, www.guardian.co.uk/media/2005/mar/10/ pressandpublishing.localgovernment,

14 European Court of Human Rights, *Connors v The United Kingdom*, Application no. 66746/01, 27 May 2004

15 Smith-Bendell, *Rabbit Stew and a Penny or Two*, p. 262

16 Author interview with Steve McAllister, 15 March 2012

17 'Pursued by prejudice', *Scotsman*, 19 August 2007, www.scotsman. com/news/pursued-by-prejudice-1-1421903

18 Author interview with Alan McDonald, 15 March 2012

19 Author interview with Marcela Adamova, 3 February 2013

20 www.equalityhumanrights.com/key-projects/good-relations/gypsies-and-travellers-simple-solutions-for-living-together/

21 Author interview with Tony Ball, 11 April 2012, and numerous phone interviews including 22 March 2013, and at court 9 August 2010, 13 October 2011, 9 January 2012

22 Austin, Jon, 'New bid for Pitsea Traveller site', *Echo*, 4 October 2007, www.echo-news.co.uk/news/1734033.print/

23 Hansard, 'Gypsies and Travellers Debate', 22 May 2008, www. publications.parliament.uk/pa/cm200708/cmhansrd/cm080522/halltext/80522h0005.htm

24 Author interview by phone with Julie Morgan MP, 9 November 2012

25 Austin, Jon, 'BNP won't be able to remove Travellers', *Echo*, 1 September 2008, www.echo-news.co.uk/news/local_news/3632271. BNP_wont_be_able_to_remove_travellers/

26 I requested an interview with John Baron and was invited to the Commons to interview him on 19 November 2012. By the time I arrived at Westminster the interview had been cancelled due to urgent business. However, he did provide me with a detailed statement to several questions instead of a face-to-face interview.

27 Brown, Martyn, '7,500 sites for Gypsies on the way', *Daily Express*, 21 November 2008, www.dailyexpress.co.uk/posts/view/72245

6. PAYBACK

1 'Guidance on Managing Anti-social Behaviour related to Gypsies and Travellers', Department of Communities and Local Government (DCLG), March 2010, www.communities.gov.uk/publications/housing/anti-socialbehaviourguide

2 Quarmby, Katharine, 'Travellers' Travails', *The Economist*, 12 August 2010, www.economist.com/node/16793224

3 'Full text: Conservative-Lib Dem deal', BBC News, 12 May 2010, news.bbc.co.uk/1/hi/uk_politics/election_2010/8677933.stm

4 Grayson, John, 'Playing the Gypsy race card', Institute of Race

Relations, 4 June 2010, www.irr.org.uk/news/playing-the-gypsy-race-card/

5 'Eric Pickles calls on councils to crackdown on unauthorised bank holiday building', press release, Department of Communities and Local Government (DCLG), 28 May 2010, www.communities.gov.uk/newsstories/planningandbuilding/1602649

6 Buchanan, Kirsty, and Eugene Anderson, 'Eric Pickles helps end rural blight of gypsy sites', *Daily Express*, 29 August 2010, www.express.co.uk/posts/view/196236/Eric-Pickles-helps-end-rural-blight-of-gypsy-sites

7 Confidential author interview, unnamed EHRC official, 2 September 2011

8 Power, Colm, *Room to Roam: England's Irish Travellers* (London: Lottery Community Fund, 2004), p. 19

9 Quarmby, 'Travellers' travails'

10 'Tough guy Sarko', *The Economist*, 26 August 2010, www.economist.com/node/16889547

11 'Don't mention the war', *The Economist*, 16 September 2010, www.economist.com/blogs/charlemagne/2010/09/row_over_roma

12 Author interview with Father Dan Mason, 4 December 2012.

13 'Bailiffs move in for Basildon traveller site evictions', BBC News, 7 September 2010, www.bbc.co.uk/news/uk-england-essex-11211938

14 Author interviews with Jonathan Oppenheim, 20 May 2012, 18 October 2011, and email correspondence

15 Author interviews with Jacob Wills, 28 August 2011, 21 February 2012, 19 October 2012, and subsequent email correspondence

16 I obtained information on how Essex Police gauged the threat of the growing resistance to the clearance through a number of Freedom of Information requests made in June 2012 which were eventually responded to in some detail in October 2012. I was also allowed to conduct an extensive interview with Superintendent Iain Logan, a senior police officer for the force, who was the Silver Commander for the eviction, planning the tactics for the day. I was given audio of some stages of the eviction, from radio logs and the Air Support Unit.

17 Freedom of Information request to Essex Police, obtained 10 October 2012.

18 Freedom of Information request to the Home Office, obtained 12 October 2012, and reported upon in Quarmby, Katharine, et al., 'Rotten boroughs' column, *Private Eye*, 18 October 2011.

19 Ibid.

20 Ibid.
21 Quarmby, Katharine, 'All the fun of the fair', *The Economist*, 19 May 2011, www.economist.com/node/18712487
22 Freedom of Information request to Essex Police, obtained 10 October 2012
23 Ibid.
24 Author interview with Candy Sheridan, 28 August 2011, and notes from meeting.
25 Author interviews with Sebastian Hesse, 10 May 2012, 25 October 2012, plus subsequent phone interviews and email correspondence
26 Author interview with Jacob Wills, 29 August 2011
27 Author interview with Jacob Wills, 21 February 2012
28 Author interviews with Ann Kobayashi, 19 September 2011, 12 October 2011, 30 May 2012, 10 January 2013
29 Freedom of Information request to Essex Police, obtained 10 October 2012
30 Ibid.

7. 'WE WILL NOT LEAVE'

1   Quarmby, Katharine, 'Trouble ahead', *The Economist*, 20 September 2011, www.economist.com/blogs/blighty/2011/09/gypsies-and-travellers
2   Barkham, Patrick, 'Vanessa Redgrave gives support to Dale Farm Travellers', *Guardian*, 30 August 2011, www.guardian.co.uk/world/2011/aug/30/vanessa-redgrave-dale-farm-travellers
3   Harris, Paul, 'UN team accuses council of "violating international law" by evicting travellers on extraordinary visit to Dale Farm (and even compared it to China and Zimbabwe)', *Daily Mail*, 14 September 2010, www.dailymail.co.uk/news/article-2037358/Dale-Farm-eviction-UN-team-accuses-Basildon-Council-violating-international-law.html
4   Author interview with Cormac Smith and Tony Ball, 11 April 2012. Specific points discussed in the interview were later confirmed in several subsequent phone interviews and email correspondence.
5   The media coverage of Dale Farm was split just like the campaign within the site itself. On one side were (loosely) the *Basildon Echo*, the *Daily Express*, the *Daily Mail*, the *Telegraph* and the *London Evening Standard*, which took aim at the activists and were sometimes openly hostile to the residents at Dale Farm. On the other side were the *Guardian* and Left-leaning magazines such as the *New Statesman*,

which were more sympathetic. As a writer for *The Economist*, I tried to steer a middle ground, putting forward both sides of the argument – an approach that was also seen in the pages of *The Times* – but it was a tricky story to get right, in terms of giving all the parties their say. At the time, I was also writing the occasional story on Dale Farm for *Private Eye*, mostly focusing there on the money being spent on both sides to fund the campaign.

6   Freedom of Information request to Essex Police, obtained 10 October 2012.

7   Snell, Andrew and Emily Fairburn, 'The *Sun* goes undercover for Dale Farm diary', *Sun*, 7 September 2011, www.thesun.co.uk/sol/homepage/features/3887347/The-Sun-goes-undercover-for-Dale-Farm-diary.html

8   'Assurance given over Christian Gypsy Festival', BBC News, 26 July 2011, www.bbc.co.uk/news/uk-england-essex-14295891

9   Author interview with Father Dan Mason, 4 December 2012. Since the eviction, Father Dan has moved from Crays Hill to a parish in East London. He remains in close contact with the Dale Farm community, however, as the chaplain for Gypsies and Travellers in the diocese.

10 'Dale Farm: Labour leader Ed Miliband supports evictions', BBC News, 1 September 2011, www.bbc.co.uk/news/uk-england-14752048

11 'Travelling to a better future', Welsh Government, 28 September 2011, wales.gov.uk/topics/housingandcommunity/communitycohesion/publications/travellingtoabetterfuture/?lang=en

12 Frost, Vicky, 'Channel 4's big fat Gypsy ratings winner', *Guardian*, 7 February 2011, www.guardian.co.uk/media/2011/feb/07/big-fat-gypsy-weddings

13 Quarmby, 'Trouble ahead'

14 Ibid.

15 Author interview with Marina Pepper and others, 19 September 2011. The interviews were made in preparation for (but not used in) the article 'Trouble ahead', *The Economist*, 20 September 2011

16 'Dale Farm Evictions live', Guardian News Blog, *Guardian*, 19 September 2011, www.guardian.co.uk/uk/blog/2011/sep/19/dale-farm-evicitons-live

17 I reported on the day's events for *The Economist*. Quarmby, Katharine, 'Judgement day', 13 October 2011, *The Economist*, www.economist.com/blogs/blighty/2011/10/dale-farm

18 Author interview with Marc Willers, 19 December 2012

19 'Dale Farm eviction: Travellers refused appeal bid', BBC News, 17 October 2011, www.bbc.co.uk/news/uk-england-essex-15342282

8. EVICTION

20 Author interview with Superintendent Iain Logan, Specialist Operations, Essex Police, 23 October 2012, and subsequent email correspondence

21 Freedom of Information request to Essex Police, obtained 10 October 2012

22 Author interviews with Billy Welch, 9 June 2012, 10 November 2012, and phone interviews

23 I was among the reporters helped onto the site that day by the legal monitors, and quotes from Dale Farm residents and activists come from interviews conducted during 19 October, unless otherwise noted. Also see Quarmby, Katharine, 20 October 2011, *The Economist*, 'The fight moves on', www.economist.com/blogs/blighty/2011/10/evictions-dale-farm

24 Author interview with Joanna McCarthy, 22 December 2012

25 Author interviews with Michelle ('Mary') Sheridan, 30 March 2006, 28 August 2011, 19 October 2011, 29 November 2011, 11 January 2012, 24 May 2012, 1 and 10 December 2012, 10 January 2013, 28 February 2013

26 Craig-Green, Susan, 2011, advocacynet.org/wordpress-mu/scraiggreene/

27 Ensor, Josie, 'Dale Farm eviction: As it happened', *Telegraph*, 20 October 2011, www.telegraph.co.uk/news/uknews/law-and-order/8837820/Dale-Farm-eviction-as-it-happened-October-19.html

28 Ibid.

29 Author interviews with Kathleen ('Pearl') McCarthy, 12 October 2011, 19 October 2011, 15 October 2012, and by phone in December 2012 and January 2013

9. CLINGING TO THE WRECKAGE

1 As observed by the author on a visit on 10 January 2011

2 Quarmby, Katharine, 'Bleak midwinter', *The Economist*, 14 January 2011, www.economist.com/node/21542792

3 www.guardian.co.uk/uk/video/2012/apr/20/dale-farm-eviction-video

4 Ibid.

5 Ibid.

6 travellersolidarity.org

7 'Boys guilty of killing Gypsy', BBC News

8 Coxhead, John, *'Moving Forward': How the Gypsy and Traveller Communities Can Be More Engaged to Improve Policing Performance*

(London: Home Office, 2005); Coxhead, John, *The Last Bastion of Racism* (Stoke on Trent: Trentham Books, 2007)

9   www.cps.gov.uk/westmidlands/us_and_the_community/
10 Personal communication with Rosemary Thompson, October 2011.
11 Quarmby, 'Bleak midwinter'
12 British Red Cross, 'Dale Farm, December 2011–February 2012', unpublished report.

10. CAUGHT

1   www.bedfordshire.police.uk/about_us/news/news_2011/110912_-_operation_netwing.aspx
2   www.bedfordshire.police.uk/about_us/news/news_2011/110912_-_slavery_offences.aspx
3   'Workers held at Green Acres site "got veiled death threats"', BBC News, 19 April 2012, www.bbc.co.uk/news/uk-england-beds-bucks-herts-17773902
4   'Family exploited homeless on Greenacres site', BBC News, 18 April 2012, www.bbc.co.uk/news/uk-england-beds-bucks-herts-17755278. Other Connors family members were facing retrial in April 2013, during the writing of this book.
5   'Servitude trial: Four of Connors Traveller family guilty', BBC News, 11 July 2012, www.bbc.co.uk/news/uk-england-beds-bucks-herts-18644539
6   'Traveller family guilty of forced labour', BBC News, 14 December 2012, www.bbc.co.uk/news/uk-england-gloucestershire. In this case, the convicted individuals were William Connors (age fifty-two), Brida (Mary) Connors (forty-eight), their sons, John (twenty-nine) and James (twenty), and son-in-law Miles Connors (twenty-three).
7   'No link to slavery allegation arrests', *Nottingham Post*, 14 September 2011, www.thisisnottingham.co.uk/link-slavery-allegation-arrests/story-13326740-detail/story.html#axzz2MZIYbYss
8   Author interviews with Jake Bowers, 3 September 2012, 3 October 2012 and subsequent email correspondence
9   Okely, Judith, 'Gypsies travelling in southern England', in Farnham Rehfisch (ed.), *Gypsies, Tinkers and Other Travellers* (London: Academic Press, 1975), p. 60
10 Author interview with Janette McCormick, 5 September 2012
11 Stanton, A.K., 'An impressionistic account of the discrimination suffered by White ethnic minorities in Newark', unpublished paper, 1994, cited in Fletcher, H., et al., *The Irish Community:*

Discrimination and the Criminal Justice System, (London: National Association of Probation Officers, Federation of Irish Societies, Action Group for Irish Youth, Irish Commission for Prisoners Overseas, and The Bourne Trust, 1997), p. 16

12 Fletcher et al., *The Irish Community*, p. 18

13 Devereaux, D., 'Enforced invisibility: The Irish experience of the Criminal Justice System', unpublished MA thesis submitted to the School of Law, Manchester Metropolitan University, 1999, quoted in Power, Colm, 'Irish Travellers: Ethnicity, racism and pre-sentence reports', *Probation Journal* 50:3, 2003, pp. 252–66

14 Power, ibid., p. 261

15 Mac Gabhann, Conn, *Voices Unheard: A Study of Irish Travellers in Prison* (London: Irish Chaplaincy in Britain, 2011), www.iprt.ie/files/Voices_Unheard_June_20112.pdf

16 Cusack, Jim, *Irish Times*, 11 January 1996, quoted in 'The media and race reporting', Calypso Productions, homepage.tinet.ie/~calypso/racism/media.html

17 Myers, Kevin, *Irish Times*, 19 January 1996, quoted in 'The media and race reporting', ibid.

18 Moore, Kevin, *Sunday Independent*, 4 February 1996, quoted in 'The media and race reporting', ibid.

19 Synon, Mary Ellen, 'Time to get tough on Tinker terror culture', *Sunday Independent*, 28 January 1996, www.indymedia.ie/article/63540?author_name=CC&comment_order=asc&condense_comments=true&userlanguage=ga&save_prefs=true

20 Synon's misstep came when she wrote a similarly offensive article about athletes competing in the Special Olympics in 2000: 'It is time to suggest that these so-called Paralympics … are – well, one hesitates to say "grotesque". One will only say "perverse" … surely physical competition is about finding the best – the fastest, strongest, highest, all that. It is not about finding someone who can wobble his way around a track in a wheelchair, or who can swim from one end of a pool to the other by Braille.' Her editor was forced to apologise.

21 Lentin, Ronit, and Robbie McVeigh, *Racism and Anti-Racism in Ireland* (Belfast: Beyond the Pale, 2002), p. 6

22 'Deasy suggests birth control to limit traveller numbers', *Irish Times*, 14 June 1996, www.nccri.ie/travellr.html

23 County councillor interviewed by the *Cork Examiner*, 18 July 1989, and quoted in 'Travellers in Ireland: An examination of discrimination and racism', National Consultative Committee on Racism and Interculturalism, www.nccri.ie/travellr.html

24 MacGréil, Micheál, *Prejudice in Ireland Revisited: Based on a National Survey of Intergroup Attitudes in the Republic of Ireland* (Maynooth: National University of Ireland, 1996), quoted in Lentin, and McVeigh, *Racism and Anti-Racism in Ireland*, pp. 62–3

25 Ibid.

26 Lentin and McVeigh, ibid., introduction

27 Connolly and Keenan, 2000, Brown, 2004, quoted in Drummond, Anthony, 'The construction of Irish Travellers (and Gypsies) as a "Problem"', in Mícheál Ó hAodha (ed.), *Migrants and Memory: The Forgotten Postcolonials* (Newcastle-upon-Tyne: Cambridge Scholars Publishing, 2007)

28 Haughey, Nuala, 'Two in five Travellers would like to live in a house or flat', *Irish Times*, 20 October 2001

29 Okely, 'Gypsies travelling in Southern England', in Rehfisch, *Gypsies, Tinkers and Other Travellers*, p. 60

30 Berger, A. A., *Essentials of Mass Communications Theory* (London: Sage Publications, 1995). The role of the media in reporting on particular communities has been well analysed. I have also carried out content analyses of reporting of disability hate crime and also of welfare benefits for my book *Scapegoat: Why We Are Failing Disabled People* (London: Portobello Books, 2011) and for a chapter in the book *Disability Hate Crime and Violence*, edited by Alan Roulstoune and Hanna Mason-Bish (Oxford: Routledge, 2012).

31 Lazarsfeld, Paul F., Bernard Berelson and Hazel Gaudet, *The People's Choice: How the Voter Makes Up His Mind in a Presidential Campaign* (New York: Duell, Sloan and Pearce, 1944)

32 www.mediawise.org.uk/wp-content/uploads/2011/03/Portrayal-and-participation-of-minorities-in-the-media.pdf

33 www.levesoninquiry.org.uk/wp-content/uploads/2012/03/Submission-by-Media-Wise-Trust.pdf

34 http://www.levesoninquiry.org.uk/wp-content/uploads/2012/07/Submission-from-The-Irish-Traveller-Movement-April-20121.pdf

35 'ECRI report on the United Kingdom', European Commission on Racism and Intolerance, March 2010 (fourth monitoring cycle), www.coe.int/t/dghl/monitoring/ecri/country-by-country/united_kingdom/GBR-CbC-IV-2010-004-ENG.pdf (p. 39)

36 Morris, Rachel, *Gypsies and Travellers: Press Regulation and Racism* (Cardiff: Cardiff Law School, 2000), p. 213

37 I wrote about the TV programme in a comment piece for the *Independent* in July 2012. Of the 108 comments on the piece (the third most viewed that week in the newspaper), over half were hostile to the

communities; a smaller number were explicitly racist. Quarmby, Katharine, 'Gypsy culture is much more than dresses and make-up', *Independent*, 23 July 2012), blogs.independent.co.uk/2012/07/23/ gypsy-culture-is-much-more-than-dresses-and-make-up/

38 www.asa.org.uk/Rulings/Adjudications/2012/10/Channel-Four-Television-Corporation/SHP_ADJ_197451.aspx

39 'Seminar report on Gypsies, Roma and Travellers in the media', Irish Traveller Movement in Britain, 20 June 2012, irishtraveller.org.uk/ wp-content/uploads/2012/07/Seminar-report-on-Gypsies-Roma-and-Travellers-in-the-Media.pdf

40 Swinford, Stephen, 'Leveson's regulator could be hijacked by "sinister" pressure groups, *Telegraph*, 2 December 2012, www.telegraph.co.uk/ news/uknews/leveson-inquiry/9717664/Levesons-regulator-could-be-hijacked-by-sinister-pressure-groups.html

41 Maher, Sean, *The Road to God Knows Where* (Dublin: Veritas, 1998), p. 151

42 Baumann, Zygmunt, *Legislators and Interpreters* (London: Polity Press, 1995), p. 94

43 MacLaughlin, Jim, 'Nation-building, social closure and racism in Ireland', *Sociology* 33, 1999, p. 147

44 Thomson, Tony, *Traveller* (Brighton: Friends, Families and Travellers Support Group, 1997), p. 5

45 Drummond, 'The construction of Irish Travellers (and Gypsies) as a "problem"'

11. GYPSY WAR IN MERIDEN

1 gypsytrailercaravans.webeden.co.uk/#/big-just/4533622715

2 Acton, Thomas, 1998, 'Authenticity, expertise, scholarship and politics: Conflicting goals in Romani studies', Inaugural Lecture Series, University of Greenwich, www.gypsy-traveller.org/pdfs/ acton_article.pdf

3 Author interviews with Noah Burton, 1 December 2011; 1 February, 22 February and 25 April 2012; and 13 February 2013; plus short telephone interviews to clarify particular points.

4 www.meridenraid.org.uk

5 www.meridenraid.org.uk/?p=247

6 Author transcript, Solihull Metropolitan Borough Council planning meeting, 1 February 2012.

7 Author interview with Deborah Martin-Williams, Head of Communications, Solihull Metropolitan Borough Council, 1 February

2012

8   Author interviews with confidential source, carried out in person, by telephone and by email in November and December 2011 and January 2012

9   Garland, Jon, and Neil Chakraborti, 'Recognising and responding to victims of rural racism', *International Review of Victimology*, 13:1, 2006, pp. 49–69; see also Chakraborti and Garland, 'Protean times? Exploring the relationships between policing, community and "race" in rural England', *Criminology and Criminal Justice*, 7: 347, 2007

10 Garland and Chakraborti, 'Recognising and responding to victims of rural racism', pp. 49–69

11 Author interviews with Barbara Cookes, December 2011, 4 February 2013, plus phone interviews in 2012 and 2013

12 Freedom of Information request to Solihull Metropolitan Borough Council, responded to 27 January 2012

13 Personal communication from David McGrath, received 6 March 2012

14 Author interview with Susan and Senga Townsley, 25 April 2012

15 Wilkes, David, 'Why we won't give ground to the Bin Laden of Meriden: Villagers step up fight to halt new gipsy camp', *Daily Mail*, 4 May 2010, www.dailymail.co.uk/news/article-1271529/Why-wont-ground-Bin-Laden-Meriden-Villagers-step-fight-halt-new-gipsy-camp.html

16 Author interview with Senga Townsley and Noah Burton, 1 December 2011

17 www.meridenraid.org.uk/?p=376

18 *EU Reporter*, 'Protest in Strasbourg', 23 September 2010, www.eureporter.co/story/protest-strasbourg/

19 Dale, Paul, 'Government steps in over Meriden Gypsy site row', *Birmingham Post*, 29 September 2010, www.birminghampost.net/news/west-midlands-news/2010/09/29/government-steps-in-over-meriden-gypsy-site-row-65233-27360053/

20 JoePublic Blog, *Guardian*, 26 October 2010, www.guardian.co.uk/society/joepublic/2010/oct/26/travellers-residents-battle-green-belt-site

21 Baldwyn, Kat, 'Residents celebrate as Gypsies lose appeal to stay at Meriden camp', 26 October 2011, *Birmingham Post*, www.birminghampost.net/news/west-midlands-news/2011/10/26/residents-celebrate-as-gypsies-lose-appeal-to-stay-at-meriden-camp

22 Author interviews for a short film for the *Guardian* website about the Meriden situation, and for research on this book, were postponed

on at least three occasions: once over half term, 20/21 February 2012, and then again on 24 February 2012, after train tickets had already been booked. The interviews were then rescheduled at Meriden RAID's convenience for Monday, 27 February 2012, and were abruptly cancelled that day. An interview for the same day with a local councillor, Jim Ryan, was also cancelled, with the same reason given as that given by Meriden RAID. In the end, after so many cancellations and lost filming days, the film was not transmitted.

On 6 March 2012, David McGrath provided a written statement in response to questions provided to him, with the request that his statement be reprinted in full, without editing of his responses. The statement is reprinted in the appendix on pages 321–9. Notes referencing this statement are noted in the book as the 'Personal communication' received from David McGrath on 6 March 2012.

David McGrath and Doug Bacon were also contacted on 20 June 2012, when I was writing a short article about parish council payments made to residents' groups opposing Gypsy and Traveller sites for *Private Eye*, to ask them about whether they had carried out paid consultancy work for a parish council. McGrath promised to respond one day later but did not do so.

David McGrath was contacted again on 30 January 2013, as this book was nearing completion, to make further comment. He did not reply to the interview request.

23 Author interview with David McGrath, 1 February 2012
24 Personal communication from David McGrath, received 6 March 2012
25 Author interview with Barbara Cohen, 8 March 2012, and subsequent email correspondence
26 Personal communications from Hockley Heath Parish Council, commencing with email received on 2 February, 14 February, 20 February, 21 February, with legal decision received 6 March 2012; Quarmby, Katharine, et al., 'Rotten boroughs' column, *Private Eye*, 15–28 June 2012; Quarmby, Katharine, et al., 'Rotten boroughs' column, *Private Eye*, 29 June–12 July 2012
27 I contacted Neil Whitelam and the group on 5 and 6 March 2012, through Facebook and their site, asking for a statement on his involvement with the RAID group and the British National Party. None was forthcoming before this book went to press.
28 Personal communication from David McGrath, received 6 March 2012
29 Erfani-Ghettani, Ryan, 'Localism, populism and the fight against

sites', Institute of Race Relations, 8 November 2012, www.irr.org. uk/news/localism-populism-and-the-fight-against-sites/
30 I emailed David McGrath and asked for a last interview on 30 January 2013, but he did not reply to the interview request.
31 Author interview with John Prescott, 17 December 2012

12. TARGETED

1 Cohen, *Folk Devils and Moral Panics*
2 Powell, Ryan, 'Civilising offensives and ambivalence: The case of British Gypsies', *People, Place & Policy Online* 1:3, 2007, pp. 112–23, extra.shu.ac.uk/ppp-online/issue_3_281107/documents/ civilising_offensives_british_gypsies.pdf
3 Richardson, Joanna, *Can Discourse Control?* (Exeter: Imprint Academic, 2006)
4 Richardson, Joanna, 'Policing Gypsies and Travellers', Plenary Paper to the Housing Studies Association Conference (HSA), (Lincoln: September 2005)
5 Cemlyn, Sarah, Margaret Greenfields, Sally Burnett, Zoe Matthews and Chris Whitwell, 'Inequalities experienced by Gypsy and Traveller communities: A review' (London: Equality and Human Rights Commission, 2009), p. 150, www.equalityhumanrights.com/ uploaded_files/research/12inequalities_experienced_by_gypsy_and_ traveller_communities_a_review.pdf
6 Ibid., p. 151
7 James, Zoe, 'Eliminating communities? Exploring the implications of policing methods used to manage New Travellers"', *International Journal of the Sociology of Law* 33, 2005, p. 163
8 Cemlyn, Greenfields, et al., 'Inequalities experienced by Gypsy and Traveller communities', p. 151
9 Lombroso, Cesare, *Criminal Man* (Durham: Duke University, 2006), p. 119
10 Cemlyn, Greenfields, et al., 'Inequalities experienced by Gypsy and Traveller communities', p. 151
11 Dawson, Robert, *Crime and Prejudice: Traditional Travellers* (Derbyshire: Dawson and Rackley, 2000)
12 Author interview by phone with Janette McCormick, 19 September 2012
13 I visited the supermarket with the town's former mayor, Vera Norwood, on 9 and 10 May 2012 and visited the fair again on 24 and 25 October 2012

14 James, Zoe, 'Policing marginal spaces: Controlling Gypsies and Travellers', *Criminology and Criminal Justice* 7, 2007, pp. 367–89

15 Ibid.

16 Greenfields, M., et al, *Gypsy Traveller Accommodation (and Other Needs) Assessment 2006–2016* (High Wycombe: Buckinghamshire Chilterns University College, 2006), www.southglos.gov.uk/NR/rdonlyres/92A18DC8-DE24-4A66-991F-0ECF1E3CF0C3/0/PTE070602.pdf; Greenfields, M., and R. Home, 'Assessing Gypsies' and Travellers' needs: partnership working and "The Cambridge Project"', *Romani Studies* 16:2, 2006, pp. 105–31; Greenfields, M., and R. Home, 'Women Travellers and the paradox of the settled nomad', in Lim, H., and A. Bottomley (eds), *Feminist Perspectives on Land Law*, (London: Routledge-Cavendish, 2007), pp. 135–54; author interview with Margaret Greenfields, 26 October 2012

17 'Councillor suggested minefield should be built around Travellers site', *Cambridge News*, 26 September 2012, www.cambridge-news.co.uk/News/Councillor-suggested-minefield-should-be-built-round-travellers-site-26092012.htm

18 Quarmby, Katharine, et al., 'Howell of rage', *Private Eye*, 13 December 2012

19 Mayall, David, *Gypsy Identities, 1500–2000: From Egyptians and Moonmen to Ethnic Romani* (London: Routledge, 2004), p. 174

20 'Travellers refused entry to north London pub', BBC News, 25 November 2011, www.bbc.co.uk/news/uk-england-london-15899248

21 Acton, Thomas, 'International Romani politics: More successful than commonly realised?', paper given at the National Gypsy, Roma and Traveller Symposium, City Hall, Cardiff, 22 June 2012

22 Sometimes, the term *kris* is used to refer to Romani law in general, as in Big Just Burton's fines, mentioned in Chapter 11.

23 Acton, 'International Romani politics'

24 Author interview with Damian Le Bas Jnr, 20 August 2012, 13 October 2012, plus subsequent email correspondence

25 refuge.org.uk/files/1001-Forced-Marriage-Middle-East-North-East-Africa.pdf. The FMU has been attempting to carry out research on forced marriage in the travelling community, and I have been asked by a number of experts in the field whether I would be interested in contributing to a bid on this, which I refused, as there doesn't seem to be evidence of a widespread problem.

26 Brown, Jonathan, 'We tackled grooming gangs. Now we have to confront forced marriage among Travellers', *Independent*, 21 May 2012, www.independent.co.uk/news/people/profiles/nazir-afzal-we-

tackled-grooming-gangs-now-we-have-to-confront-forced-marriage-among-travellers-7769697.html

27 I contacted Nazir Afzal by email on 21 May 2012 but he was unavailable for further comment.

28 www.gypsy-traveller.org/your-family/health/domestic-violence/

29 gypsymessageboard.wordpress.com/2012/05/29/the-question-of-forced-marriage-in-the-traveller-community/

30 The site for Gypsy and Traveller women is provided by Solace Women's Aid, www.solacewomensaid.org/about-us/refuges

31 Cemlyn, Greenfields, et al., 'Inequalities experienced by Gypsy and Traveller communities'

32 Author interviews with Janie Codona, 10 October 2012, 15 November 2012

33 Author interviews with Bernie O'Roarke, 8 October 2012, 15 November 2012

34 'Murder victim's 12-hour torture', *Manchester Evening News*, 8 June 2006, menmedia.co.uk/manchestereveningnews/news/s/215227_murder_victims_12hour_torture

13. LIFE ON THE MARGINS

1 'New scrap-metal regime becomes law', *Material Recycling World*, 28 February 2013, www.mrw.co.uk/news/new-scrap-metal-regime-becomes-law/8643580.article

2 'Witness statement of Raymond Bocking', submitted to the High Court of Justice, Queens Bench Division, *Patrick Egan vs. Basildon Borough Council,* Claim no. CO/11/666, 25 September 2011. The statement included documents regarding Ray Bocking's appeals regarding enforcement notices that were sent by the Planning Inspectorate of the Department of the Environment and dated 26 May 1994.

3 *Private Eye* interview with Ray Bocking, 4 July 2012; 'Private Eye interview with Ray Bocking', *Private Eye*, 27 July–9 August 2012

4 Cripps, *Accommodation for Gypsies*

5 Cemlyn, Greenfields, et al., 'Inequalities experienced by Gypsy and Traveller communities'

6 Johnson, Chris, and Mark Willers, *Gypsy and Traveller Law* (London: Legal Action Group, 2007), p. 79

7 'Designing Gypsy and Traveller sites: A good practice guide', Department for Communities and Local Government (2008), www.gov.uk/government/uploads/system/uploads/attachment_data/file/11439/designinggypsysites.pdf

8 'Gypsy, Roma and Traveller achievement', Department for Education, 14 November 2012, www.education.gov.uk/schools/pupilsupport/inclusionandlearnersupport/mea/improvingachievement/a0012528/gypsy-roma-and-traveller-achievement

9 Author interviews with Delaine and Damian le Bas Snr, 13 October 2012, 9 November 2012, 16 March 2013 and subsequent email correspondence

10 Smith, David, and Margaret Greenfields, 'Housed Gypsies and Travellers in the UK: Work, exclusion and adaptation', *Race and Class*, 55:3 2012, pp. 48–64

11 Ibid.

12 www.travellersaidtrust.org.uk

13 Author interview with Margaret Greenfields, 26 October 2012, and subsequent email correspondence

14 www.clearwatergypsies.com/parallel-lives.html

15 Author interview with Ian Hancock, 22 June 2012, and email correspondence

16 Pati, Anita, 'After Dale Farm: Managing Gypsy and Traveller sites', *Guardian*, 14 October 2012

17 Ibid.

18 Smith and Greenfields, 'Housed Gypsies and Travellers in the UK', pp. 48–64

19 Ibid.

20 Quarmby, Katharine, and Mark Townsend, 'Mental illness now blights many Dale Farm families', *Observer*, 20 October 2012, www.guardian.co.uk/uk/2012/oct/20/dale-farm-families-in-squalor

21 Van Cleemput, P., et al., 'Health-related beliefs and experiences of Gypsies and Travellers: A qualitative study', *Journal of Epidemiology and Community Health* 61, 2008, pp. 205–10

22 Parry, G., et al., *The Health Status of Gypsies and Travellers in England* (Sheffield: University of Sheffield, 2004)

23 Van Cleemput, P., 'Social exclusion of Gypsies and Travellers: Health impact', *Journal of Research in Nursing*, 1 March 2010

24 Barry, J., B. Herity, J. Solan, *The Travellers' Health Status Study: Vital Statistics of Travelling People* (Dublin: Health Research Board, 1987); Maureen Baker, *Gypsies and Travellers: Leeds Baseline Census 2004–2005* (Leeds: Leeds Racial Equality Council, 2005)

25 'Progress report by the ministerial working group on tackling inequalities experienced by Gypsies and Travellers', Department for Communities and Local Government, 2012, pp. 8–18, media.education.gov.uk/assets/files/pdf/m/ministerial%20working%20

group%20report%2012%20april%202012.pdf

26 Richardson, J., J. Bloxsom and M. Greenfields, *East Kent Sub-Regional Gypsy and Traveller Accommodation Assessment Report (2007–2012)* (Leicester: De Montfort University, 2007), www.doverdc.co.uk/pdf/EastKentGTAAreport17July07.pdf

27 'Progress report by the ministerial working group on tackling inequalities experienced by Gypsies and Travellers', pp. 13–14

28 Van Cleemput, 'Social exclusion of Gypsies and Travellers: health impact'

29 Cemlyn, Greenfields, et al., 'Inequalities experienced by Gypsy and Traveller communities', p. 22

30 Ibid.

31 Ibid., p. 77

32 Ibid., p. 78

33 Stack, Sarah, 'Traveller suicide rates soar at six times the settled community', *Irish Independent*, 4 October 2011, www.independent.ie/national-news/traveller-suicide-rates-soar-at-sixtimes-the-settled-community-numbers-2895924.html

34 Nexus, *Moving Beyond Coping: An Insight into the Experiences and Needs of Travellers in Tallaght in Coping with Suicide* (Tallaght: Tallaght Travellers Youth Services, 2006), iol.ie/nexus/suicide%20and%20the%20young%20traveller.pdf

35 Author interview with Tony Ball, 22 March 2013

36 Author interview with David McPherson-Davis, 23 March 2013

37 Author interview with Nigel Smith, 29 March 2013

38 Author interview with Candy Sheridan, 23 March 2013; the interviews in this section were originally conducted for Quarmby, Katharine, and Mark Townsend, 'Dale Farm asbestos find fuels concerns for health of evicted Travellers', *Observer*, 31 March 2013, www.guardian.co.uk/uk/2013/mar/31/asbestos-dale-farm-travellers

39 Smith, Charles, *Not All Wagons and Lanes* (Essex: Essex County Council, 1995), p. 26

14. REVIVAL

1 Quarmby, Katharine, 'Big dreams at Appleby Fair', *Huffington Post*, 13 June 2012, www.huffingtonpost.co.uk/katharine-quarmby/big-dreams-at-appleby-fair_b_1587339.html

2 Quarmby, Katharine, 'A silent revival', *The Economist*, 30 June 2012

3 The movement in Britain is known interchangeably as 'Light and Life' and 'Life and Light', but I've used the former throughout the

book to match the church's website, www.lightandlifegypsychurch.
com.

4   www.biblebelievers.com/gypsy_smith/index.html

5   Fraser, *The Gypsies*, p. 315

6   As quoted at travellerspace-gypsyroads.blogspot.co.uk/2012/07/
fury-over-village-invasion-of-gypsies.html

7   Author notes from Life and Light convention, 1 August 2012

8   Author interviews with Thomas Acton, 22 June 2012, 13 October
2012, plus a subsequent phone interview for *The Economist* and
email correspondence

9   Author interview with Ian Hancock, 22 June 2012, and email
correspondence

10 Reeve, Dominic, *Beneath the Blue Sky* (London: Abacus, 2007), pp.
8–9

11 'The plight of Europe's Roma', *The Economist*, 25 May 2012,
www.economist.com/blogs/easternapproaches/2012/05/
europe%E2%80%99s-biggest-societal-problem; 'Widespread Roma
exclusion persists, find new surveys', United Nations Development
Programme (2012), europeandcis.undp.org/news/show/C15701B7-
F203-1EE9-B1F8B88C17029CA1 (24 May)

12 equality.uk.com/Roma.html

13 Author interview with Robbie McVeigh, 9 September 2012; this
section also includes quotes from author visit to the Luton Roma
church, 28 November 2012, and an author interview with Martin
Burrell, 15 June 2012

14 Author interview with Donald Kenrick, 19 July 2012

15 Author interview with Sam Lee, 24 November 2012; the interview
followed a private concert at the Dog and Gun that had been organised
by promoter, artist and mutual friend Pete Lawrence

16 Rombase, Matéo Maximoff, romani.uni-graz.at/rombase/cgi-bin/
artframe.pl?src=data/pers/maximoff.en.xml

17 Junghaus, Timea, *Meet Your Neighbours* (New York City: Open Society
Institute, 2006), p.7

18 This Romani text is a quote from 'Lil of Romano Jinnypen' ('Book
of the Wisdom of the Egyptians') collected by George Borrow and
published in *Romano Lavo-Lil: Word-Book of the Romany* (John
Murray, 1905). Borrow translated the phrase as 'A tramp has more
fun than a Gypsy.'

19 'Merkel opens Roma Holocaust Memorial in Berlin', BBC News, 24
October 2012, www.bbc.co.uk/news/world-europe-20050780

20 Words of the Wheel Arts event at the East Anglian Museum of

Rural Life, 13 October 2012. I attended the event at the invitation of Damian Le Bas Jr, who organised it along with Thomas Acton; I also recorded some of the proceedings.

21 McVeigh 'Theorising sedentarism: the roots of anti-nomadism', in Acton, *Gypsy Politics and Traveller Identity*, p. 12

22 Chatwin, Bruce, *The Anatomy of Restlessness* (London: Jonathan Cape, 1996), p. 102

23 Ibid., p. 80

24 Standing, Guy, *The Precariat* (London: Bloomsbury Academic, 2011), p. 90

APPENDIX

Full text of statement submitted by David McGrath, chairman of Meriden RAID, on 6 March 2012. Reprinted in full, as requested.

Dear Katharine

Thank you for your questions. I would be grateful if you could reprint the statement below – which includes my answers – in full without editing my response to your questions.

Kind regards

David McGrath

Dear Ms Quarmby

I note that you are wish [sic] to broadcast a programme regarding the dispute in Eaves Green Lane without giving Meriden RAID the clear opportunity to participate in the making of this programme at an appropriate time. You will be aware that we are keen to participate in the making of your film – and your new book – and we have indicated that a time in early April would be the best time to do this. This timing is based on advice that we have received suggesting that we should not give detailed interviews on the specifics of the legal dispute in Eaves Green Lane as there are two Court cases pending.

We are anxious that the court appearances of the Travellers should not be prejudiced in any way and will be happy to discuss all points with you – on camera – after the dispute has been resolved – hopefully the end of the this month (March 2012).

Nevertheless you have exercised your right to broadcast (which I respect) and I am happy to answer the written questions that you have tabled (below) as I feel that this is only way in which any level of balance can be incorporated into your work. I think that your questions are fair and I hope you agree that my answers are fair too. I do not see this as an opportunity to enter into correspondence – merely a holding position until you are able to schedule appropriate interviews – giving all sides a fair opportunity to participate.

I am pleased to answer your questions as follows:

1. Solihull Council has informed the Guardian that you trained two of the members of the planning committee who subsequently went on to reject the planning application for the Gypsy site at Eaves Green Lane. Do you consider that your involvement in training councillors, who were then closely involved with taking a decision on a planning application to which you were opposed, is a conflict of interest?

I provide training for Councillors from many Local Authorities. This training is not on Planning matters as I am not qualified to do so. Contact with Local Authorities is through Training Managers not the Councillors. I provided two x 2-hour training sessions for Solihull Council for two groups of Councillors on Chairing Public Meetings and Overview and Scrutiny. This training was completed well before the dispute in Meriden arose.

I would have had no contact with Councillors before or after the seminar and had no control over which Councillors would be attending nor any interest as to which committee they might sit on. I did not attend or speak at the Planning Meeting of 7 July 2010 which made a decision consistent with the recommendations of its officers. Any informed or fair minded person would not be able to construe anything or [sic] than absolute probity in my actions.

2. If not, why not?

This is explained above.

3. A partner of a member of RAID was arrested for urinating in front of a Gypsy woman in 2010. Do you consider that this was inappropriate and did you take any action to prevent such incidents from happening again in the future?

I understand that – some two years ago – an individual relieved himself in some bushes behind one of the camps on private land and an allegation was made, that this was seen by one of the occupants of the site resulting in the arrest of that individual. I also understand that no criminal charges were brought, indicating that there was insufficient evidence of any crime having been committed. RAID have and will continue to remind members to have regard to their actions so that we conduct our protest in a peaceful lawful and dignified manner.

4. An email from a senior police officer, Keith Portman, written in 2010, suggested that he felt that bricks near the entrance to Eaves Green Lane had been fly-tipped in an attempt to implicate the Gypsies in fly-tipping or were there so that RAID members could blockade the site. (I can send you the email if you would like to see it.) Was this incident connected to RAID members and if so, did you take any action against it?

In the e-mail to which you refer, Inspector Portman states he is 'unsure as to who dumped the bricks' and then gives a view as to who may have done so. Meriden, like many rural areas is subject to fly-tipping and had the Insp had evidence to support his personal view, I have no doubt he would have acted upon it. I am unaware of any party being responsible for the dumping of bricks but I did ask the Council to remove debris as it was inappropriately located. I also from time to time voluntarily pick litter from the Lane and value greatly our countryside.

RAID welcomes and encourages robust and thorough investigation of all allegations of any anti-social behaviour regardless of the origin of the allegation (settled or Travelling community) and have communicated such to the police.

RAID have requested and continue to request a CCTV camera be installed following threats and intimidation by the occupants of (and visitors to) the site in order that all allegations can be properly investigated. Surprisingly we understand the occupants of the Travellers site have objected to such installation.

5. Doug Bacon, the vice-chair of RAID, served as a police officer alongside some of the officers now policing the situation at Meriden that has arisen out of the conflict between Meriden RAID and the Gypsies (according to information obtained from West Midlands Police). Do you consider this a conflict of roles and do you intend to do anything about it? If you do not wish to answer this question, please send to Mr Bacon so he can answer for himself.

Mr Bacon ceased being a serving member of West Midlands Police nearly 8 years ago, and is a private resident of Meriden. He has not served alongside those officers involved in policing Meriden for at least 11 years in some cases longer and in the case of the senior officer Sector Inspector Portman never.

The role of the Police in this matter is one of keeping the peace and the prevention and detection of crime and one in RAID's view in which the Police have maintained strict professional neutrality as one would expect of such a public body.

Mr Bacon's role is simply providing information to the police on RAID activities, a central point for the reporting of incidents (not solely confined to those connected with Eaves Green Lane) and managing the expectations of the local residents with regard to police powers and procedures.

The Police have no part to play in the planning process, therefore to construe a conflict of roles is not only inaccurate it is nonsensical. On a personal point I would add that Mr Bacon has played an invaluable role as a level headed leader who – along with our wider RAID membership – has always insisted that RAID opposes the unlawful development in Eaves Green Lane in a way which focuses on the material legal and planning issues – nothing else.

6. *Holderness RAID, which states on its website that it is in almost daily contact with Meriden RAID, has as its chair a former British National Party candidate for the area. It also cites, in its press area, the news that 'Andrew Brons, British National Party MEP for Yorkshire and the Humber has shown his support for our case'. Does it concern you that a far-Right party is supporting the activities of a RAID group? Do you feel that it taints the brand of what you call 'ethical localism' and lays RAID groups generally open to the accusation of closet racism?*

We do not seek nor do we welcome the interest or involvement of any person or group within Meriden RAID who holds extreme views. Our campaign is non political and focused on green belt and planning issues (including opposing a local housing scheme).

Anyone who uses the unlawful and unethical tactics that we have seen in Meriden (attempting to 'steal a march on the planning process' by Bank Holiday land grabs, denying residents the chance to comment on proposals before they are executed, destroying the green belt etc) would be opposed – whether they were Travellers, multi national corporations or individual developers.

It is also worth mentioning that we have had support and financial donations from members of the wider Travelling community who are repulsed by the way in which the reputation of their community overall is being sullied by a small number of irresponsible developers. In Meriden, we have lived peacefully with Gypsies and Travellers in Meriden for hundreds of years and are determined that this incident should not poison that relationship. But unlawful and inappropriate development is what it is – and should be opposed irrespective of the cultural, ethnic etc background of the developers.

In making reference to quotes on RAID web sites (your next question) you have omitted to make reference to our web site whereby a statement has been in place since October 2011. It states:

The Secretary of State has DISMISSED the appeal by
the Travellers for both permanent AND temporary
occupation of the site. Meriden RAID Chairman
David McGrath said 'We are relieved that Solihull
Council, The Government Planning Inspector and the
Secretary of State all agree with us that this unlawful
site is totally inappropriate and causing daily harm
to our Green Belt. Our protest camp will stay until
we see clear action from the Council and Courts to
enforce the decision. The focus should now be on
how we urgently ease people from an unlawful and
unsustainable site to one where their needs can be
met AND to re-instate the land. <u>We are determined
that this episode will not taint the good relations
between the settled community and the wider travelling population which has played a valued part in
our community life for generations.</u>

7. *Holderness Raid has on its website the following section:*

> *RAID would like to thank to the tireless work of dedi-
> cated villagers, the nationalists who set up RAID in
> the best interests of the villagers and members of the
> wider community who helped by writing to the plan-
> ning office and attending the RAID meeting to make
> their feelings known. The council said it was the largest
> response they have ever had to a planning application.
> Without the effort put in by upstanding members of
> our community we may well have had a fully fledged
> gypsy site down mill lane.*

*Does it concern you that RAID groups such as this, which you say
you are gathering together in a large alliance and for which you held
a national conference last year, talk about 'nationalists setting up
RAID' – which sounds like coded language for the BNP? Will you
disassociate the National RAID alliance from such language and*

make it clear that the national RAID Alliance does not support racism against Gypsies, Roma or Travellers?

Meriden RAID utterly rejects racism and we have consistently made our view on this matter clear. Meriden RAID was formed spontaneously from ordinary concerned residents, determined to oppose an unauthorised development causing massive harm to a Greenfield site in the Green Belt in the heart of the Meriden Gap.

The conference in January 2011 was organised to elicit the views of residents from across the country in similar situations and facilitate discussion on a response to the Governments proposal to change the ministerial guidance for Gypsy and Traveller sites. We believe that the only long term solution to unauthorised development is the provision of authorised sites through a plan led approach based on genuine verifiable need with full engagement by the Travelling Community with Local Authorities and the settled community, in appropriate locations, coupled with robust action against those who seek to develop by stealth.

8. As I told you in a previous email, we are also looking at proposed sites in the Solihull area, one of which was, until recently, Hockley Heath. On the Hockley Heath Residents website (www.hockleyheath. org.uk/hhra–gypsy–site.html), it states that you and Doug Bacon have been 'formally appointed to work on our behalf' and further states that they have raised £4,560 so far towards your bill, which is, the website says, 'just over half the amount required'. Is this money going to Meriden RAID, to your company, or to you personally?

This money will be paid to my company and from this will be deducted the services of a Planning consultant, researcher and ecologist. Residents in Hockley were concerned that they should have a professionally prepared response evaluate [sic] a proposal to locate a Traveller site in Hockley Heath. The reports identified clear planning reasons why the site would be inappropriate.

Solihull Council also carried out its own independent survey and also concluded that the site was inappropriate.

9. Do you consider it is legitimate business to look for paid work opposing proposals by local councils to find Gypsy/Traveller sites when Meriden Raid is a voluntary group?

Yes. Although my services would be to facilitate the evaluation of a site not necessarily oppose it. If there are clear reasons why a site IS suitable (e.g. in brownfield areas, sustainable locations) then I can see no reason why I should oppose this. You will be aware that I & RAID have not opposed all plans to expand Gypsy and Traveller provision in Solihull. We feel that it is essential that appropriate provision is made at suitable sites on a plan led basis to avoid the ugly spectre of unlawful developments such as we have seen in Meriden.

It should noted that the site referred to in Hockley Heath was put forward by a private individual and was never therefore a 'proposal by the Council'.

Meriden RAID raised and spent over £67,000+ engaging the services of planning consultant, highways consultant, ecologist etc. Meriden RAID cannot pay for other groups. Local groups must raise funds in the same way and pay for the expert analysis.

10. Do you see any conflict of interest between seeking paid work opposing proposals for proposed legal sites when at the same time you are seeking paid work as a trainer of councillors who may well have to decide whether such sites go ahead?

No – I have already explained that I neither provide training in planning matters neither do I form relationships with Councillors given that I am simply booked to provide training to groups on unrelated matters. I do not have contact with Councillors before or after my seminars. This answer is also expanded on in question 1.

11. Your own land, which we understand you purchased in 2007 and on which you live after having retrospectively applied for planning permission, is in the green belt. Why do you consider it is legitimate for you to live in the green belt after retrospectively applying for planning permission, and not the Gypsies at Eaves Green Lane?

I did not – and have never – applied for retrospective approval to build in the green belt in a personal or business capacity. I applied for change of use to keep filing cabinets in a bungalow and to use it for administrative purposes (without prompting from the Council). Permission was granted as there is no adverse impact on my neighbours, the building or the green belt. This is only the same level of use as a home/office scenario.

I trust that this answers your questions and look forward to further chats on camera after the Courts have made their decision in March.

Good luck with your film and your book.

Kind regards

David McGrath
Chairman Meriden RAID

INDEX

ABOUT THE AUTHOR

Katharine Quarmby's journalism has appeared in *The Economist*, *Private Eye*, *The Times,* the *Mail on Sunday* and the *Guardian*, among other publications. She has been a finalist for the prestigious Paul Foot Prize and has produced films for BBC *Newsnight* and *Panorama*. Her first book, *Scapegoat*, on hate crimes against disabled people, won the AMIA International Literature award. She lives in London.